COMMERCIALS ARE HOT—
BUT SO IS THE COMPETITION

Working in commercials is one of the most exciting careers in showbiz, and the hunt for performers with special magic never ends. The market for talent is huge, and so are the rewards—and now two of the top names in the business have written the most complete and practical guide to breaking into commercials and making the most of the many professional opportunities it provides. The wealth of expert advice answers questions like:

- What should you wear when you have a head shot taken— and how do you pick the best ones?
- How do you pursue a career in regional markets outside the major cosmopolitan areas?
- Who are the key players in the commercial industry—and what part do they play in your career?
- What seven qualities give you the winning edge in an audition?
- How does a parent both promote and protect a child in the fast commercial track?
- And how you can win in the high-stakes game of—

BREAKING INTO COMMERCIALS

TERRY BERLAND, formerly the head of casting for the third largest agency in the world, BBDO in New York, now heads her own casting company and teaches a workshop, "Acting in Television Commercials," around the nation. DEBORAH OUELLETTE is an award-winning photographer and writer in the industry who serves as a judge and guest speaker at regional and national modeling talent competitions.

BREAKING INTO COMMERCIALS

Terry Berland
AND
Deborah Ouellette

THE COMPLETE
GUIDE TO MARKETING
YOURSELF,
AUDITIONING TO
WIN, AND GETTING
THE JOB

A PLUME BOOK

PLUME
Published by the Penguin Group
Penguin Books USA Inc., 375 Hudson Street,
New York, New York 10014, U.S.A.
Penguin Books Ltd, 27 Wrights Lane,
London W8 5TZ, England
Penguin Books Australia Ltd, Ringwood,
Victoria, Australia
Penguin Books Canada Ltd, 10 Alcorn Avenue,
Toronto, Ontario, Canada M4V 3B2
Penguin Books (N.Z.) Ltd, 182–190 Wairau Road,
Auckland 10, New Zealand

Penguin Books Ltd, Registered Offices:
Harmondsworth, Middlesex, England

First published by Plume, an imprint of Dutton Signet,
a division of Penguin Books USA Inc.

REGISTERED TRADEMARK—MARCA REGISTRADA

ISBN 1-56865-426-X

Printed in the United States of America
Set in New Aster
Designed by Stanley S. Drate/Folio Graphics Co. Inc.

CONTENTS

ACKNOWLEDGMENTS   *ix*

FOREWORD BY JASON ALEXANDER   *xi*

INTRODUCTION   *1*

I

PUTTING TOGETHER A WINNING PROMOTIONAL PACKAGE

                                                        5

1 GETTING HEAD SHOTS   *7*

The Makings of a Good Commercial Head Shot • Differences
Between a Commercial Head Shot, a Theatrical Head Shot,
and a Commercial Composite • How to Get the Best Head
Shot • How Much Will It Cost and How Long Will It Take? •
Summary

2 RÉSUMÉS AND COVER LETTERS   *28*

What Is a Résumé and What Is Its Purpose? • What Goes on
a Résumé and in What Order? • Presenting the Information
on Your Résumé • Getting Your Résumé Printed • Updating
Résumés • What Is a Cover Letter and What Is Its Purpose •
Targeting Your Head Shot/Résumé Mailings to the Right
People • Following Up on Your Mailings • Summary

3 OTHER TOOLS YOU'LL WANT TO CONSIDER   *40*

Equipment for Keeping in Touch • Record-Keeping Supplies

4   TRAINING   *44*

How Classes in Commercial Technique, Improvisation,
Scene Study, and Cold-Reading Prepare You to Do
Commercials • Interview with John Fionte • Finding a Good
Coach • Cost of Training • How Often You Should Train •
Interview with Sandy Shurin

5   SCAMS   *49*

Why Scam Artists Are So Successful • How to See a Scam
Coming a Mile Away • Common Industry Scams • Reporting
and Investigating Scams • Interview with David Vando

6   NETWORKING AND GOAL SETTING   *58*

Networking • Goal Setting • Summary: Super Success
Strategies • Goal Planning Sheet

II

TAKING YOUR ACT ON THE ROAD

                                                           67

7   THE KEY PLAYERS IN THE INDUSTRY   *69*

Agents • Managers • Casting Directors • Producers •
Directors

**8   WHAT YOU NEED TO KNOW ABOUT AGENTS,
MANAGERS, AND UNIONS**   *72*

All About Agents • Do You Want a Manager? • Conducting a
Dynamite Interview • Keeping in Touch with Your Agent •
Handling Contracts and Agreements • Why Actors Might
Want to Drop Their Agent • Why an Agent Might Want to
Drop an Actor • The Unions and Their Jurisdictions •
Interviews with Carol Ingber and Al Onorato

9   THE AUDITIONING PROCESS   *88*

Getting Auditions • The Day of the Audition • The
Competitive Edge

10   THE TECHNIQUE   *102*

Getting Started • In the Audition Room • Analyzing the
Script • Leaving the Audition Room

11   THE SELECTION PROCESS   *121*

The Creative Team • How the Talent Are Selected •
Understanding the History of a Commercial

12   THE CALLBACK, THE BOOKING, THE SHOOT   *128*

The Callback • The Booking • The Shoot: Interview with
Barbara Mullins

13   HOW MUCH CAN I MAKE?   *138*

Television • Radio

14   WORKING IN REGIONAL AREAS   *146*

Advantages and Disadvantages of Working in Regional Areas
• Commuting • Moving to a Larger Market • Interview with
Tom Jourden

15   VOICE-OVERS   *154*

What Are Voice-overs and Who Does Them? • Voice-over
Markets • Types of Opportunities in Voice-over • What It
Takes to Succeed • How to Get Started Doing Voice-overs •
Marketing and Packaging Yourself as a Talent • Tapping the
Regional Markets • The Taping Session: Interview with
Barbara Goldman • Animation

16   MODELS CROSSING OVER INTO
COMMERCIALS   *171*

Why More and More Models Are Getting Into Commercials
• How Commercial Experience Can Be a Stepping-stone to
Television and Film • How Modeling and Talent Conventions
Offer Opportunities to Expand into Other Areas • The Role
of a Good Manager in Making the Transition • How Fashion
Print Work Differs from Making Television Commercials •
What It Takes to Cross Over • Training • Opportunities in
Foreign Markets • Compensation • Interviews with Elle
MacPherson, Carmen, Tim Saunders, and Patrick Johnson

17 **KIDS IN THE BUSINESS** *184*

What Types of Kids Do Well in Commercials? • Getting
Pictures • Résumés for Kids • Finding an Agent • Managers •
Training • Tips on Auditions • Commonsense Safeguards for
Showbiz Kids • When to Consider Commuting or Relocating
to a Larger Market • What Parents Can Expect •
Compensation • What It Takes for Kids to Make It in the
Business • Interviews with Max Casella, Robert Meegan, Pat
Meegan, Alan Simon, and Sue Schachter

III

WRAPPING IT ALL UP

223

18 **WHAT IT TAKES TO MAKE IT IN**
COMMERCIALS *225*

What Do Agents and Casting People Look For in an Actor? •
What Are Common Misconceptions Newcomers Have About
the Industry? • Pet Peeves

GLOSSARY *231*

APPENDIX *241*

INDEX *247*

ACKNOWLEDGMENTS

Our deepest appreciation goes to everyone who helped us bring this book to life. We couldn't have done it without you.

Jason Alexander, Max Casella, Robert Meegan, Pat Meegan, Elle MacPherson, Halle Berry, Carmen, Tim Saunders, Patrick Johnson, Judy Savage, Helen Rogers, Alan Simon, David Vando, Vincent Cirrincione, Tyrene Gibson, Suzettte Vazquez, Carol Ingber, Al Onorato, Barbara Mullins, Tom Jourden, Barbara Goldman, Charlie Adler, Maurice Tobias, Sue Schachter, Vincent Versace, Jinsey Dauk, Lori Wyman, Karmen Kruschke, Patty Kallis, Judith Jacobs, Sandy Shurin, Chris Farrell, Gregory Bouldin, Jo Doster, Laura Fogelman, Kathy Hartigree, Jane Schaffmaster, Traci Danielli, Suzanne Haley, Kay Tanner, Mark Bonney, Michael Powell, Fosi, Jaki Baskow, Katie Stoll, Heather Laird, Jack Stevens, Jenny Saks, Joan Clark, Shirley Hamilton, J. D. Fryer, Andy Garrison, Steve Roland, Steve Garrin, Nick Omana, Karen Apicella, Manya Nogg, Carla Lacey, Mary Corell, Al Smith, Marty Terry, Monika Simmons, Claudia Speicher, Rosemary Savage, Florette Morgan-Broadwater, Bonnie Metcalf, Abigail Eaton, Vickie Panek, Lynn Blumenthal, Annette Amato Outlan, Tom Fluke, Debra Docherty, Karen Fields, Anna Fishburn, Chris Taylor, Tish Lopez, Rick Wigginton, Joan Tiabbi, Lisa Fincannon, Sheila Boy, Joan Gringer, Bonnie Singer, Nancy Mancuso, Ray Seide, Donna Fazzari, Carol Fass, Lucy Heim, Michael Terry, Paul Brown, Bruce Ready, Tom Capps, Todd Mason, Alan Krinsky, Terri Hanauer, Nathan Schwan, Sara LaDee, Amy Taksen, Liz Lewis, Ellen Brodie, Nancy Vines, Jeff Danis, Linda Ferrara, Jerre Hookey, Daisey Sinclair, Bobbi Gelman, Carol Carlson, Jan Brethauer, Barbara Hedges, Chris Taylor, Lauri Gapp, John and Linda Fionte, Laurie Katapski, Kirk Evans, Linda Fidelman, Charlene Bramble, Suzanne Clark, Janice Reichard, Susan Hamilton, Eric Hoppel, Mora Tighe, and Deena Levy.

Special appreciation to Alan Nevins, Cindy Cassell, and Julia Serebrinsky.

FOREWORD

by Jason Alexander

When asked how I got started as an actor, I tell people I "fell" into the business. . . .

I can't remember a time when I wasn't performing. I don't know where my interest came from, but it was entrenched by the time I was six. When I was twelve or thirteen, I was taking it seriously enough to do everything I could do locally—in New Jersey, where I grew up.

I was doing school plays, community theater, and children's theater. One of the children's shows we were doing was seen by a television producer who thought it would be a neat idea to film it as a children's special for television.

In order to do it, we all had to join the union. The show aired in New York, New Jersey, and Connecticut. The day after it aired, a manager (Neiderlitz & Steele) called me up and asked if I would like to be a client. I stayed with them for the next nine years and they guided me into the business.

Throughout college, all I did was commercial work, which was great. I always thought of commercials as thirty-second movies. I was working with people who really knew what they were doing. It had all the excitement of doing film work with none of the tedium because it moved so fast.

Fortunately, my career was always progressive. The work I did always begat other work, and I was lucky that it stayed of a certain quality. Even though some things flopped, the people I got to work with were spectacular.

There was my Broadway debut, *Merrily We Roll Along,* written by Stephen Sondheim and George Furth and directed by Hal Prince. The show was not a success for them but it sure was for me.

My next show, *The Rink*, was only a moderate success, but with stars like Chita Rivera and Liza Minnelli, the composer John Kander and lyricist Fred Ebb, and the playwright Terrence McNally, I was surrounded by brilliant people.

Then I worked with Neil Simon, which was a tremendous opportunity. Some years later, I won a Tony for *Jerome Robbins' Broadway*, which, ironically, was a show I never wanted to do. I thought it was going to be a humongous dance review, and I could move but not dance . . . certainly not like that. I finally got dragged into that show, which turned out to be a great experience.

I also started doing little teeny roles in film, and every now and then, I'd be out in L.A. doing a series.

I was never one to sit back and let things happen. It's very important for actors to take charge of their careers and always work at fine-tuning their craft.

When asked what advice I would give to actors who have taken one weekend workshop and feel they have mastered some technique, I always say that in my experience, the craft of acting is something that comes with age, maturity, and insight. People without training think that all you have to do is learn your lines and show up; professionals know that it takes a long time to learn the tools, techniques, and skills that are as important to an actor as color is to a visual artist or theory is to musicians.

Some of these tools are very technical. Others are instinctual. The technical skills came very easily to me, which is not ncessarily the norm for most people. Most people struggle with the technical skills.

What I had trouble with was what we call the emotional life of the character. For some actors it comes naturally, and in fact, that's all they can do. They're emotional as hell, but they don't know how to craft it or shape it.

So, no matter which end of the fence you come down on, I think it takes a lifetime of work to bring the other half up to snuff.

There are very successful, well-known actors who have never taken a class in their lives. They don't believe in it. They don't do any homework. They just show up on the set and do what comes naturally. And they do it very, very well. But my feeling is that without a technique or craft, there's no way to prepare. You can only cross your fingers and hope for the best.

I don't think you can study enough. The trick is to find someone who speaks your language and techniques you understand. It's a very delicate situation, being in class, because you're using your own ego and your own imagination as tools. And your tools are often criticized.

How do you find a good coach? Word of mouth. By observing. The best way is to talk to someone whose work you admire. Find out if they're studying and where. Go check them out. It's really trial and error. You'll know if someone is speaking your language and if it's an atmosphere you think you'd like to work in.

If you don't know any actors, call a local university that has an acting program and see if any of the teachers or professors teach outside the school, or call the local unions to see if they have any recommendations.

Anyone who reads my story is going to think that this is the easiest business in the world and unfortunately, nothing can be further from the truth. *The first thing you're going to find when you get into the business is the biggest catch-22 in the world.* Do you want to work as a professional or as an amateur? If you want to work as a professional, you have to get into the unions and you can't get into the unions without a professional job. One way to get into the union is to audition for a union job and to get booked.

Challenge number two is, how do you market yourself? Nobody knows how to market him/herself. Actors have a very unrealistic idea of what they are about. Homely people think they are leading men and leading ladies. I've seen very funny people try to be dramatic actors. I've seen people who have no sense of humor try to do comedy. Old people try to play young, young people try to play old.

Certainly you have to believe that you can do anything. You should believe that, but on a realistic, commercial level you have to know what it is that you present.

Are you going to New York, L.A., or Chicago? Are you going to London? Are you going to go to good regional theater? Are you going to focus on theater? On television? On commercials?

Challenge number three is learning to control your career. Actors have to try and do career planning. Many actors tend not to do this and nobody seems to tell them that they have to.

Actors have to go and read and when they find material that's right for them that can be developed, they should develop it. Buy it. Get into improvisational theater groups and get up on stage with people. If you sing, develop a sort of cabaret act. Form theater groups within your community. See what kind of theater thrives in your area and have something special ready that will get you noticed. This way, you're not always going to them and begging for a job. They will come to you at work and say they like what you do.

You have to own your career. It's the hardest thing to do but if you don't do it, you are just waiting . . . and waiting *kills* talent. Waiting kills careers.

What it takes to make it in this business is a certain level of *desperation*. I always tell people, particularly young acting students, "If there's anything else you could do and be happy—not even exquisitely happy but just happy, pursue it, because, in my observation, this business is only for people who have no other option." If it is not your end-all, be-all, something you really must have or you'll jump off a bridge, then don't get on the bridge. It's not for you.

However, if you decide it *is* for you, you need a sense of bravura. You need a thick hide that's only thick on the outside. It has to be very thin on the inside or your vulnerability, your compassion, will die. And no actor can survive without them.

I don't know how to tell you to develop that hide. I don't think anyone does, but it is an absolute job requirement. You're going to hear "No!" a hell of a lot more than you'll hear "Yes!"

What's the best way to deal with the inevitable frustration and rejection that goes along with a career in this business? Have a life beyond the business.

Find other things you love to do. Have people outside the profession in your life. Don't get stuck with acting as your only realm.

Stay involved with your community. Stay involved with current events. Learn other things. Learn a skill. I once spent months learning to roller-skate, then got a job because I knew how to roller-skate.

Learn a language. Learn a new business. Go someplace you've never been before, even if it's only ten miles away. Observe people. Talk to people in other professions so if you ever play a stockbroker, for instance, you've done your research already. Just don't get stuck. You have to stay in motion.

It's a real didactic profession because it comes down to "I got it" or "I didn't get it." It's that hot and cold.

Actors always crack me up because they'll do an audition and they'll ask the agent to call and get feedback. What good is the feedback? It's only one person's opinion. "Did I get the job?" "Yes or no." If I did, then I did good. If I didn't get it, for whatever reason, it didn't happen.

The only reason you need feedback is if somebody says, "He comes in with a real chip on his shoulder," or "He comes in and his hygiene is not good." This is the only kind of feedback you want to get. Other than that, you took your shot and it did or didn't happen.

I think, in the business, there's an illusion that everything has to happen very quickly. There are a lot of young stars. The movies in particular right now are youth oriented and there's a feeling that if you haven't participated in this business by the time you are twenty-five or thirty, it's too late.

My feeling is that anyone who is supposed to be doing this and who has real ability, real commitment, will find success. And success is defined very individually.

There are some people who will feel successful playing the classics at the Seattle Repertory. There are other people who will feel extraordinarily successful making six figures a year doing commercials, even if they've never performed elsewhere. Others will not be happy unless they are a box office star.

Success comes in many forms and you have to decide as an actor, "What do I want?" "Where will I be happy?"

Success is not always about making money. It's not always about being in a big theater. It's not about being in front of a camera. And it doesn't have to happen fast.

You may not get a particular job. You may not do well at an audition, but you are working on a craft. The craft gets better. You perform the craft and you do it over and over and over again . . . and you *love* it.

You enjoy doing it. You love studying it. You like displaying it.

Actors get better every year they're living. It's a craft about maturity. So live. And grow. And stop knocking your brains out trying to succeed on somebody else's terms.

Succeed on your own terms and in your own time.

Good luck!

INTRODUCTION

Our goal in creating this book is to help you break into commercials with a clear, concise sense of how the industry works. People all around the country from every walk of life are exposed to commercials. Many people who watch commercials, hear them on radio, and see them in print aspire to do commercials as a full- or part-time career.

Commercials seem more accessible than parts in film or TV shows—and they *are*. More people have been able to break into the business and join the Screen Actors Guild (SAG)* though commercial work than through any other medium in the industry. Roles in commercials are cast for performers of all ages, types, and ethnicities. According to union figures, SAG members earned more than $501 million from commercial work in 1995. All over the country, advertising agencies, producers, directors, and casting people wade through hundreds of head shots and résumés daily, searching for new faces to use in the next ad campaign.

Commercials have changed lives. With the earnings from commercial work, actors have financed college educations, underwritten family businesses, and supported themselves while making the transition into film and television.

Commercial work is big business, but it is not easy. Everyone can think about being in a commercial but not everyone knows how to go about entering the field. Competition is fierce. To make it in this industry, you have to be better prepared than the person sitting next to you at the audition. Tal-

*SAG is the union governing actors in film. This includes motion pictures (whether shown on television or in movie theaters) and television commercials. (See Chapter 8: What You Need to Know About Agents, Managers, and Unions.)

ent alone won't do it. It takes a combination of talent, business savvy, training, the ability to audition effectively, and a lot of hard work. To get to the point where you have the competitive edge, you must invest the time and energy necessary to fine-tune your skills to razor-sharp precision.

Our travels around the country and involvement in the educational development of talent have given us firsthand information on the wants, needs, dreams, aspirations, and misconceptions of today's performers. Our combined professional experience of thirty-six years (Terry has been a casting director and industry coach for over twenty years, and Deborah has been an industry photographer and writer for over sixteen years) gives us an everyday, hands-on perspective on what it takes to make it in the business.

This is the first book of its kind to acknowledge that most actors who make it to the "ivory tower" (major markets) start out in secondary, regional areas. We have interviewed professionals in every state who either represent, cast, or book talent—individuals who enjoy developing actors, care about their talent, and are interested in maintaining a high level of professionalism. This book brings you their insights. We hope it will provide clear guidance to those who are just breaking into the business, as well as to seasoned professionals. We want you to find the highest degree of professionalism in your own market.

You must be aware that there will be trials and tribulations, frustration and rejection. And then there are the scams—rip-offs by unsavory individuals or groups who make their living preying on unsuspecting people who desperately want to break into the business. A virtual gauntlet of obstacles and disappointments awaits you if you tread unknowingly into a world where both magical and tragic events can occur. The more you know and understand about the business beforehand, the more likely you are to avoid the pitfalls, *and* the better your chances of launching a successful career.

Your commitment to reading *Breaking Into Commercials* and applying its concepts is a major step toward developing a career in commercials. You'll learn to create a winning promotional package, write a strong résumé and cover letter, set goals, and network effectively. You'll discover how to meet the right people in the industry. You'll develop the competitive edge needed to become the next "new face," and you'll learn how to give a winning audition so that you will be considered for the job regularly.

By collaborating with some of the most respected names in the industry, we have been able to create a complete framework for making a serious move into commercial work. *Breaking Into Commercials* takes you step-by-step through the entire process of becoming a commercial actor. We'll take you into the audition room, teach you how to read a commercial script, and show you what to expect on the set after you book a job. Special summary pages and commercial exercises will help keep you on track and focused on your goals.

By the time you get to the final chapter of *Breaking Into Commercials,* you will have a strong base from which to expand your career. To reinforce some of the most important concepts necessary to create a successful commercial career, we conclude the book with invaluable advice from industry professionals from markets across the country. You'll learn the common misconceptions fledgling actors have about the business, industry "pet peeves," and what it takes to really make it as a performer. You'll close the book feeling prepared, well-informed about the industry and how it works, and confident that you know enough to get out there and go for it.

To get the most from this book, read each chapter thoroughly (and keep the book handy as a quick reference), then act on any exercises or activities suggested. Doing so will help keep you on track and ready for the next step. This book is meant to be an "active" reference. By doing each exercise and reviewing the special summary pages at the end of chapters, you'll be well on your way to getting your commercial act together.

Our best wishes go with you as you make your way through what we hope will be an exciting, fulfilling, lucrative career.

I

PUTTING
TOGETHER
A WINNING
PROMOTIONAL
PACKAGE

1

GETTING HEAD SHOTS

❏ THE MAKINGS OF A GOOD COMMERCIAL HEAD SHOT

In this business, to really go out and sell yourself, you need a calling card, and that calling card is your commercial head shot.

The commercial head shot is your most important marketing tool. Getting the right shot is essential to finding work in the industry and represents an initial opportunity to *(a)* introduce yourself, *(b)* provide a hint of your personality, *(c)* arouse the interest of the viewers, and *(d)* make them want to meet you. A great head shot can literally make or break your chances of getting called for work.

It helps to know something about commercial technique *before* having a commercial photo session. Take a workshop from a professional to explore commercial technique and discover who you are. Also, watch commercials on TV. This will begin to give you a point of reference—a point of view as to attitude and an understanding of the energy required for commercial shoots.

You should have a realistic idea of what type you are commercially (age range, physical look, and personality traits). Examples of physical "looks" are:

1. *Character.* This is someone with extreme features (large nose, bushy eyebrows, puffy cheeks, heavy, etc.), likable, or even funny looking. If you fit into the character

category, a chipped tooth or a space between the teeth could add to or be natural for the character.

2. *P&G* (Procter & Gamble look). A generic, middle-American look with well-proportioned, middle-of-the-road, attractive features. Extremely beautiful people or character types do not fit this category. P&G types are healthy looking, bright, and happy.

3. *Pretty or handsome* (but not a model, not glamorous). This is someone who is natural and approachable.

4. *Model type.* Someone with above average looks, extremely good looking or striking. Model types generally have high cheekbones, strong jawline, perfect teeth, excellent skin, and a well-proportioned, toned body. The camera seems to enhance their exceptional beauty.

5. *Slightly off-beat/slightly quirky.* Individuals who are specifically different from the average, middle-American look. Prototype: Barbra Streisand (pretty with a nose that is not perfect), Tom Hanks (good-looking with nose and mouth slightly off center).

6. *Quirky/pretty and funny.* Prototypes: Rosanna Arquette, Goldie Hawn, Cher, Meg Ryan.

7. *Urban/city type.* Someone with a stylish edge, with an intense, trendy look. Not outdoorsy looking.

8. *Suburban type.* Plainer, casual, relaxed, sporty, rugged, outdoorsy looking.

9. *Ethnic.* Caucasian, Afro-American, Asian, Latin/Hispanic, Indian, Native American, Jewish, European, etc.

When viewing commercials, study the actors. Make note of the types of people and which products they are used for. What are their energies? What are they wearing? What hairstyles do they have? Which products use humor? Where might you fit in? Could you be the "mom" or "dad"? A seasoned executive? A student? A construction worker? Don't box yourself into one type. Notice all the opportunities available to you. The more you know about commercials, the more comfortable you will be at your photo shoot.

Commercials are generally energetic and upbeat. People in commercials are friendly and approachable. No one is evil-looking, scary, or really angry. Instead, they are frustrated in a manner that invokes humor and is approachable. A good head shot is generally taken straight-on (so the camera can capture all your features). Your commercial head shot should reflect a happy, energetic, open personality. Your expression should be very *alive,* very animated and smiling. A smile shows your clean white teeth.*

L.A. photographer/actor Vincent Versace has experienced this vital part of the commercial process from both sides of the camera. "Your headshot exists in a casting director's hands for about five seconds. It's either going to be dropped in the circular file [wastebasket] or it's going to be placed in the 'call' file. Every casting director says, 'The eyes *have* to talk to me. They really have to speak to me and the picture has to *look* like the actor.' "

Jinsey Dauk, a New York–based head-shot photographer, adds: "A great head shot isn't just about having perfect makeup or hair; it's about warmth, communication, and a certain openness that invites the viewer right into the photograph."

❏ DIFFERENCES BETWEEN A COMMERCIAL HEAD SHOT, A THEATRICAL HEAD SHOT, AND A COMMERCIAL COMPOSITE

An actor might have three different photographs with three different looks that he or she uses to get work.

Your *commercial head shot* (fig. 1) is used to get work in commercials. Commercial head shots are well-illuminated and have an overall bright appearance, letting the happy, upbeat side of your personality shine through; you look very warm and approachable—very "pleased to be here."

Simple, clean-looking makeup and hairstyling as well as careful attention to wardrobe selection are important for these photos. Open-necked collars and medium tones set the right ambiance for a successful commercial photograph. Clothing and jewelry should not distract the viewer's eye from moving directly to the face and eyes of the photo.

---

*Advertising clients are looking for good teeth, not discolored, stained, or chipped ones. If you are about to have your teeth fixed (or lose weight or have your hair styled), do so *before* your photo shoot. Your photo must be the best possible representation of what you currently look like.

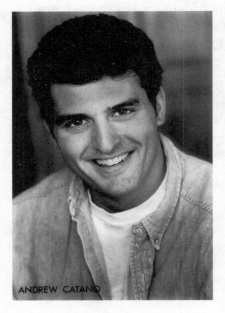

ANDREW CATANO

FIGURE 1. Commercial head shot. Male head and shoulders type. (JINSEY DAUK)

FIGURE 2. Two shots illustrating the difference between (female) commercial and theatrical shots. (MICHAEL LAMONT)

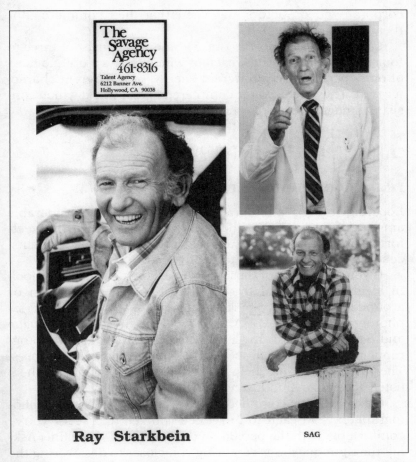

FIGURE 3. **Commercial print composite.** (COURTESY OF THE SAVAGE AGENCY, LOS ANGELES)

Theatrical head shots (fig. 2) are more serious, showing strong eye contact and dramatic attitudes. Hair, makeup, and wardrobe choices may be more dramatic. Deeper-toned backdrops may be used along with subtle to rich variations in lighting. Actors use these shots to get parts in theater, television, film, and soap operas. For work in industrial films* or

---

*Industrials are promotional films used either to educate employees or to promote companies. They can be produced strictly for in-house use or to be shown at promotional events such as trade shows.

corporate videos, actors may use either their commercial or theatrical head shot.

Commercial composites (fig. 3) generally consist of three to four photographic prints, each of which shows a unique facet of one's personality, a different energy, or a different character type. They are used for commercial print work, which consists of magazine ads, brochures, and catalogs.

❑ HOW TO GET THE BEST HEAD SHOT

FIND A GOOD PHOTOGRAPHER

Locating a good photographer can involve a considerable amount of research, but the results will be well worth the effort. Word of mouth is always the best referral. Talk to agents, coaches, and other actors to secure leads.

If you have none of these resources, the next step is to look in local and regional trade publications. If you live in or around New York City, pick up a copy of *Back Stage*. It carries photography ads. In Los Angeles, you might try *Drama-Logue* and *Back Stage West*. In Chicago, see *Audition News*. Photographers also post ads at local drama clubs and in bookstores. The *Yellow Pages* may help, but make sure the photographers listed specialize in industry head shots.

Once you have compiled a list of at least three or four photographers, call each to introduce yourself and see if you're comfortable with the person on the other end of the line. Asking the right questions can bring you closer to discovering the best person for the job.

QUESTIONS TO ASK

1. Does the photographer prefer to shoot in the studio or "on location" (somewhere other than the studio)?

2. Does the photographer prefer to shoot standard head-and-shoulder shots or three-quarter body shots* (fig. 4). Is he comfortable doing both?

---

*The trend is to include three quarters of the body in the photograph, with or without borders around the print. Standard head-and-shoulder shots are still the most widely accepted in smaller, regional areas.

FIGURE 4. **Female commercial three-quarter body shot.** (VINCENT VERSACE)

3. How far in advance is the photographer booked?

4. Is a deposit required to hold the booking?

5. What happens if you have to cancel? How much notice is required to cancel, and is there a cancellation fee?

6. How much will the photo session cost?

7. How many rolls of film are included in the shooting fee?

8. Are any enlargements (prints) included?

9. Who owns the negatives?

10. Is a hairstylist and/or makeup person available? If so, is there an extra charge for this service?

11. How many changes of clothing are allowed?

12. How much time should you put aside for the shoot?

13. How long after the shoot will it take to get your proof sheets?

14. How long does it take to get enlargements made?

15. How much does it cost for extra prints?

16. Is retouching* included in the print fees? If not, how much will it cost and does the photographer provide for or arrange for this service?

17. Can the photographer recommend a printer to make larger quantities of your photographs?

18. What happens if you're not happy with the results of your shoot (or the enlargements)?

VIEW THE PHOTOGRAPHER'S WORK BEFORE YOU MAKE A CHOICE

After hearing what each photographer has to say concerning these issues, decide which ones you still want to pursue and make an appointment to see their work. Look carefully at each professional's portfolio (sample photographs), then ask yourself:

1. *Do the head shots all look the same, or can you see each actor's individual personality shining through?* According to Vincent Versace, "You should not be able to identify the photographer by any one specific image. The photograph needs to be about the subject, not about the photographer."

2. *Are the photographs well lit and printed correctly?* A good commercial headshot should display all the characteristics of a well-developed black-and-white print. This means that you should see a rich black tone (check the iris of the eye) and a clean white tone (see the "catch lights"† in the eyes) somewhere in the print, as well as a nice range of gray tones throughout the image. The image should be sharp, crisp, and in focus. The lighting should clearly separate the subject from the background and, if the setting is outside, the background

---

*On commercial prints, a photo artist (retoucher) tries to minimize minor flaws in the image, touching up temporary blemishes, stray hairs, and scratches or dust spots (white spots caused by dust on the negative).

†Catch lights are the reflections in the eyes caused by the photographer's light(s).

should be out of focus. Nothing in the picture should distract from the subject. There should be no obvious, unflattering shadows. The photographs should not show excessive grain* and should be printed on high-quality, matte-finished photographic paper.

After viewing each photographer's work, take time to go over your notes (you should have a lot to work with by now), decide which photographer you're most comfortable with, and call to make an appointment.

Note: Although it's important to take price into consideration, don't let that be the key factor in selecting a photographer. Your commercial head shot can open (or shut) doors for you, so it pays (literally) to work with the best photographer within your budget.

Florida casting director Lori Wyman says, "I notice that people try to skimp a little when they are first starting out. People who know nothing about this business end up spending a lot of money and time before they find the right place and the right people. Do it right the first time. Otherwise, if you choose someone just because he was cheap, you may end up having to do it over again."

PREPARE FOR THE SHOOT

Once you decide on a photographer, it's time to get together everything you will need at the shoot. Most photographers will discuss wardrobe, hair, and makeup dos and don'ts either at the initial consultation or when you call to book a shoot.

Photographer Jinsey Dauk explains, "Clothing should direct all attention to your face. V necks do that naturally and so are great choices for photo shoots. Solid colors work best— avoid busy patterns or polka dots. Textures are wonderful— sweaters and jackets work well. Bring lots of casual stuff. If you have a doubt about it, bring it; the photographer can help you decide which things to wear once she sees it."

Vincent Versace adds, "My preference is to have people bring in as many changes of clothes as possible. It's obvious

*Grain is generally caused by overexposure or overdevelopment of the film (high-speed films are naturally grainy). This exaggerates the tiny dots that make up the image, producing an unacceptable print.

we won't shoot them all, but it is much better for the person if we go through everything together and decide what we want to shoot.

"It's always important to photograph people in their favorite clothes. Texture can be interesting to the eye, perhaps a sweater—not with a pattern, but with nooks and crannies (and I don't mean Thomas' English Muffins). Things that work best are wool, cotton, silk (incredible because of the way it catches light), and denim (the official industry uniform). Soft clothes *work* in commercials."

WARDROBE CHECKLIST

1. Make sure your clothing is clean, fitted, in good condition, and well pressed.

2. Choose simple styles with open necklines.

3. If you want to wear glasses in the shoot, make sure they have "no-glare" lenses or purchase a set of frames in your favorite style without the glass. This will prevent glare from the photographer's lights and reflectors.

4. Leave your hat at home. Agents and casting people want to see your hair. If you are bald, they need to see that too.

5. Don't wear distracting ruffles, bows, patterns, or jewelry. No gold chains or earrings on men, please. Guys, if you do decide to wear your earring, know that it puts you in a very definite character category. Be sure this is what you want. If so, don't expect to get a call to audition for the wholesome dad, boyfriend, or guy-next-door based on this particular photo.

6. Do not turn up the collar on your jackets and shirts. Doing so may imply an attitude that is not consistent with the energy required in commercial work.

7. Avoid wearing white. When viewing a photograph, the eye naturally goes to the lightest area of the print first. Your goal is to have the viewer focus immediately on your face and, more specifically, your eyes (some photographers whiten the whites of the subject's eyes to draw the viewer's attention to them). If you wear white,

the viewer's eye will go to your clothing first, then travel to the face and eyes. Stay with medium-toned clothing (something that will produce a rich gray tone in black and white), which, with a medium-gray background, will wrap around the subject and draw the viewer's eye to the most important part of the print—*you!*

Your hair should be clean, healthy, and styled in a simple, attractive manner (no "big" hair). Stay away from overly trendy hairstyles. If your hair reflects a specific fad, you will limit your opportunities to audition. Some advertisers go with current styles. However, in smaller regional areas, advertisers tend to prefer a more generic look—a neutral, classic, all-American image. Make a choice as to how you want to market yourself.

Guys should look freshly shaved. If you grow a beard as fast as you can cut it, bring your razor with you (watch the new blades—opening an artery can create serious complications at the shoot). You might want to ask the photographer whether you should come in with a beard or partial growth, then shave part way through the shoot, giving you two different looks. There is less work for bearded fellows, but if you can grow a beard fairly quickly, it might turn out to be an asset.

You should not look made-up in your commercial head shot. The look for commercials is clean, fresh, and energetic. Women often have a tough time getting a good commercial shot because the photographer (or the women themselves) wants to capture their pretty side instead of bringing out the depths and layers of their personality. Commercial shots are not glamorous. Make sure you end up with a "personality" shot, *not* a beauty shot.

Los Angeles makeup artist Karmen Kruschke notes, "The stylist's goal is to make people look as they will look when they go into the audition, so I try to get some history on their experience in putting on their own makeup. If someone doesn't wear a lot of makeup, it's important not to put a lot on them—at least, the look is not very made-up. The skin should look nice and smooth. No heavy lip liner or eyeliner. This is not a fashion shoot. It's not about how beautiful you can be for a day. It's about looking and being who you are."

The makeup artist may do some corrective work to minimize heavy circles under the eyes. There may be a need to highlight or darken specific areas of the face to bring out cheekbones or play down other features. That's why you'll hear, "Oh God, I would *never* wear this (makeup) out in public." And you never would—except for a photo shoot.

Men generally require only a bit of powder to tone down overly shiny skin. They may also need a little corrective work. Trust the stylist to do whatever is necessary to make you look good in front of a camera.

Aside from the obvious benefits of having a hair/makeup person available at the shoot, having a stylist there also means you don't have to worry about anything (like whether your makeup is shiny or if your hair is out of place). This goes for the photographer, too, so both of you are free to do what you do best—you to act and the photographer to take pictures.

There are a few more suggestions for preparing for your photo shoot:

1. Get a good night's sleep before the shoot. It is important to arrive at the session well rested, in a positive frame of mind, and ready to give your very best.
2. Have everything you need for the shoot laid out the night before to avoid rushing to get it all done the next morning. This will save a *lot* of unnecessary stress.
3. Bring some of your favorite music to the shoot—something lively and upbeat to help set the mood for a pleasant, comfortable shoot.
4. Do not schedule anything important directly after the shoot. It will be hard to keep your mind on the task at hand if you are thinking about whatever you've scheduled next.
5. If for any reason you feel you cannot give one hundred percent to the shoot, call and try to reschedule. The camera doesn't lie. If you have a headache or are in a negative mood, you *will* see it in the pictures.

Giving careful consideration to the planning and preparation of your photo session will help guarantee successful results.

WHAT TO EXPECT THE DAY OF THE SHOOT

Plan to arrive at the photographer's studio approximately fifteen to twenty minutes prior to your scheduled appointment (allow yourself plenty of time to shower and dress). When you arrive you'll be told where to hang (and change) your clothes. The photographer will go through your wardrobe, helping you select the best pieces for the shoot.

At some point during the process, you'll be expected to pay the photographer. You may be asked to sign a release or agreement of some form, outlining the specific conditions of the shoot—price, services rendered, plus any specific considerations. *Be sure you read the document before signing it.* Pay special attention to any part of the agreement that deals with the photographer's claims concerning copyright. By law, it is illegal to make a copy of a photographer's work without explicit permission. This means you may not take your original photographs to a lab and have a duplicate negative made from it. This is a direct violation of copyright law for which both you and the lab can be sued. Unless your contract states otherwise, your photographer has the exclusive right to make copies of your photographs for you.

Some controversy arises here. Many people argue that when an actor pays the photographer to create a head shot, this becomes "work for hire" and therefore does not come under the same provisions of copyright law. But, if you sign an agreement giving the photographer total control over the use of the photographs, you may find yourself in a pickle when you try to get mass reproductions of your pictures without getting explicit permission from him or her.

When you take your original photographs to get reproductions from a printer, the printer will require a release from the photographer before expediting your order. Technically, mass production of head shots involves an entirely different photographic process. A photographer who offers this service generally sends the original pictures out to a printer who specializes in mass production of industry head shots, then marks the price up anywhere from 25 to 100 percent or more! To do this is neither illegal nor unethical; however, keep in mind that if you are able to take your head shots directly to the printer yourself you avoid paying the markup. If you sign an agreement without making a specific provision that allows you to use the printer of your choice, you may have no choice but to order all reproductions through the photographer.

The law clearly protects photographers against copyright infringement. One way to avoid misunderstandings later is to read carefully any agreement put before you and negotiate an arrangement that serves your best interests. Many actors refuse to sign any kind of agreement. Very few photographers are willing to turn down an attractive fee just to stand on principle. If you do decide to work with a photographer who insists that you sign an agreement, be aware that, as with any other contract, *both* parties have the right to negotiate the terms. This doesn't have to be complicated. Simply have the photographer cross out (and initial on all copies) the parts you don't agree with. There is usually space on any agreement for additions and amendments. That is where you'll put any special considerations the two of you have worked out.

When you negotiate your contract, keep in mind that you want to:

1. Deal with the printer of your choice, without going through the photographer.
2. Use your originals for publicity without paying an extra fee to the photographer. Most agreements give the photographer the right to use your likeness in their advertisements and other publicity—you paid for the shoot, it's only fair that you be free to do the same.

Note: Make sure you request that the photographer not stamp any part of the enlargements you purchase with a copyright notice. Photographers do this to give public notice of their claim to copyright. Without it, they are still protected by the law. With it, you will have one heck of a time getting a printer to make reproductions from your original prints.

Negotiating a fair agreement allows both you and the person who creates your commercial head shot to utilize the results in a manner that enhances both parties' career interests.

After you've paid the photographer and agreed to the terms of the shoot, it's time to let the hair/makeup person (if available) work his magic. Then you'll get into your first outfit and you're ready to shoot.

What happens during the actual shoot is as individual as each photographer's style. Some photographers suggest specific scenarios to help draw out the subject's personality. Others are naturally comedic and charming, using their own personality to entice you to reveal yours. Any successful shoot is a collaborative effort in which photographer and actor work together to create an image that will attract the eye of casting directors.

SELECTING THE RIGHT SHOT

After the shoot, photographers either send the film out to a professional lab to be developed or do the developing themselves. Next, the negatives are laid out on a single sheet of photographic paper and exposed to light in the darkroom, creating a contact sheet—a mini set of proofs exactly the same size as the negatives from which you will select the images to enlarge.

If you're not accustomed to looking at contact sheets, a magnifying glass (or photographer's loupe) can be very helpful. Generally photographers indicate which images they prefer. It's a good idea to take the contact sheets home, look them over carefully, and then put them aside for a while before making a final selection. If you have access to other industry professionals (agents, casting directors, acting coaches, other actors), you may want to ask which ones they think represent you best. Look for the one or two shots that best capture your personality. Many times, your agent will want to decide which shot they want you to use.

After you have decided which images to enlarge, decide on the retouching. Have your selections enlarged and take a last look to see that all the qualities you want for your final shot (which seemed to be there when you looked through the magnifying glass) are indeed there.

RETOUCHING

Before you run off to the printer with your eight-by-ten, discuss with your photographer any touch-up work that needs to be done. For example:

1. Are there any temporary blemishes or dark areas under the eyes?

2. Are there any distracting features in the photograph, such as stray hairs or unwanted reflections in the eyes (or glasses)?
3. Are there minor scratches or spots on the print?
4. Would the image be enhanced by lightening the white areas of the eye?

If the answer to any of these questions is yes, then the photo retoucher is your next stop before going to the printer. The retoucher is an artist who specializes in working with photographs (and/or negatives) and is responsible for enhancing the image by using special techniques and equipment to minimize flaws in the image. The key word here is *minimize*. The artist, like the photographer, is not a magician. Some problems may not be totally eliminated with retouching, but can be improved upon. With skillful retouching, only the trained eye can tell the work has been done.

Unless the photographer has indicated otherwise, the cost of retouching is generally not included in the price of the print. Ask for a referral to a good photo artist and, if possible, deal directly with the artist instead of going through the photographer (saving markup costs). In some cases, however, the photographer may be better qualified to explain to the artist exactly what needs to be done. It's your decision whether to handle this yourself or to ask for help from the photographer.

The cost of retouching varies, depending on the job being done and the caliber of the artist doing the work. Expect to pay less for anything that involves darkening a light area of the print and more for anything that requires lightening a dark area. Assuming you have a head shot you're happy with, the extra investment to fine-tune your presentation makes good business sense.

Retouching a print is a one-time investment. As long as you keep your originals in good condition, any enhancement done should last the lifetime of the print. Handle your originals by the edges only and keep them out of direct sunlight or they may start to fade or discolor.

One last thing about retouching—*don't overdo it!* The purpose of retouching is to enhance the print, not to change the way you look. Remember, when you walk through the door, the casting director expects you to look like your pictures. If, for instance, you have the artist straighten your teeth in the picture and then come to an audition with crooked teeth, you have misrepresented yourself. You do not look like your picture. What happens if the call is for a toothpaste commercial, which requires you to have perfect teeth? Do you think a casting director would ever call you again after you deliberately misrepresented yourself? Probably not.

Trust your photographer and the retoucher when it comes to deciding whether or not to touch up a print (and how much). Don't try to make everything look perfect. Just have the artist minimize anything that takes away from your personality.

WORKING WITH PRINTERS

Once you have a "finished" eight-by-ten (printed well and retouched, if necessary), it's time to take the original to a printer who specializes in mass producing photographs for actors. It pays to shop around. It is not unusual to use a printer from another state. Get referrals from other actors and agents. Printers across the country vary in price and in what you get for the money. Call and request a price list from several printers (if you're really on top of things, you took care of this while waiting for your enlargements to come back from the retoucher).

Again, while price is a consideration with most people, make your final decision based on quality of service. If two or more companies produce work of equal quality, but one gives significantly more reproductions for the money, it's easier to narrow your selections.

An order form is usually included with each printer's information packet. Be sure to indicate exactly how you want your copies produced. The preferred format is eight-by-ten reproductions on matte (nonglossy) double-weight stock. Have your name printed on the front (see fig. 1). Avoid fancy type styles and oversized or undersized letters. Also, expect to pay in full at the time you place your order.

PICTURE POSTCARDS AS A MARKETING TOOL

Picture postcards (see fig. 5) can be a great way to keep in touch with the industry. You can send postcards to announce something you're currently appearing in, just to say hello, or to remind casting directors that you're still out there. Some actors even use them for thank-you notes.

Some people have their postcards printed horizontally, placing two head shots side by side, showing two different aspects of their personality. Others take a humorous approach, creating a comedic photograph, appropriately captioned to amuse the recipient.

The same printer who mass-produced your headshots can create a mini version printed vertically on postcard-sized paper with your name on it. Picture postcards are a wonderful, cost-effective tool for marketing yourself as a commercial actor.

TOD MASON   **(212) 724-2800**

FIGURE 5. Head shot postcards are an excellent way to keep in touch with people in the industry and to show some individualism and personality. (COURTESY OF TODD MASON)

❑ HOW MUCH WILL IT COST AND HOW LONG WILL IT TAKE?

COSTS

Photographers: These vary in price depending on what part of the country they work in, their level of experience, and the amount of prestige they have built up in their market. Rates can range from $75 to $250 in regional areas and $200 to $450 (and up) in larger markets. As with anything else, higher price does not necessarily guarantee higher quality.

Stylists: Expect to spend approximately $50 to $100 for the hairstylist and another $50 to $100 for the makeup person. (If you're lucky, your photographer works with someone who does both and there's some break in the fees.)

Film/processing/contact sheets: These costs are generally included in the photographer's shooting fee.

Enlargements: If not included in the shooting fee, eight-by-ten enlargements can run on average $15 to $20 per photo.

Retouching: Budget approximately $10 to $25 for a general touch-up (more for complicated jobs).

Printers: These can run from $80 per five hundred eight-by-tens to as much as $250 or more. Add another $40 to $60 for picture postcards.

All things considered, expect to spend approximately $750 to $900 by the time you've gotten through the process of shooting, enlarging, retouching, and printing your photos.

TIME FRAME

There are many variables to consider here. The amount of time it takes to get through the process may change due to individual schedules or unforeseen problems (your print gets damaged or lost, for instance). Basically, these are the time frames you may reasonably expect:

	Approximate Time Frame
1. Researching photographers (including calls, interviews, portfolio review, and making appointment)	2 weeks
2. Getting proofs back from the shoot	1 week
3. Getting input on proofs, making your selections, and getting order to photographer	1 week
4. Getting enlargements back from lab	1 week
5. Retouching	1 week
6. Getting mass-produced headshots and postcards from printer	2 weeks
Total amount of time to get through the process:	**Approximately 8–9 weeks**

Eight to nine weeks! You can see why it is important to get moving right away. Use the tip sheets that follow to help yourself move smoothly through each step as you create the most important part of your marketing package. Your ability to get through the step of getting your pictures done could very well be the first indication of whether you have the wherewithal to continue in this business.

❏ SUMMARY

TO-DO LIST

☐ Research photographers

☐ Call for appointments to see samples of work

☐ Choose photographer

☐ Make appointment for photo session

☐ Prepare for shoot

☐ Order enlargements

☐ Arrange for retouching (if needed)

☐ Order mass reproductions from printer

Congratulations! You've just completed one of the most important tasks in compiling your presentation package. You have your commercial head shot. You're ready now to move on to the next step.

2 RÉSUMÉS AND COVER LETTERS

❏ WHAT IS A RÉSUMÉ AND WHAT IS ITS PURPOSE?

A résumé is a one-page summary of your vital statistics, experience, training, and special skills. Its purpose is to attract the interest of an agent or casting person by outlining the most attractive, marketable traits of the product it is advertising—*you!*

❏ WHAT GOES ON A RÉSUMÉ AND IN WHAT ORDER?

Do include:

1. Your name (centered at the top of the page).
2. Union affiliation (if applicable), or note that you're "SAG eligible" if that's the case.
3. Agency representation (if applicable). In regional areas, your agent generally will provide you with stickers or labels to put on your résumé to show that they represent you.
4. Statistics.*
5. A phone number (other than a personal number) where you can be reached.
6. Experience (credits in theater, film/TV, commercials, etc.).
7. Training (classes, workshops, college degrees, etc.).

*Statistics (stats) include your name, union affiliation and agent (if applicable), height, weight, eye and hair color, and a contact number (service, machine, or pager) where you can be reached.

8. Special skills (dialects, American Sign Language, sky-diving, horseback riding—anything you do *well*).

Don't include:

1. Your social security number, your address, or your personal phone number (for security reasons).
2. Your age or an "age range." Let casting directors look at your photo and decide for themselves if you are what they are looking for.

❏ PRESENTING THE INFORMATION ON YOUR RÉSUMÉ

How you list industry-related *experience* on your résumé depends on which market you come from. In Los Angeles, film and television credits are usually listed first (fig. 6). In New York, theater credits are mentioned first. If you live in a smaller, regional area, start with your strongest credits. When in doubt, list theater credits first. Theater provides a strong foundation for actors and is the purest form of acting experience.

If you're just starting out, you'll probably be relying primarily on your look, training credits, and special skills to open doors for you. After you have a well-developed résumé, your experience (credits) will be your best PR tool. Don't worry if, at first, you don't seem to have much to put on your résumé; there are ways to present your humble beginnings (without lying) that will give your presentation a professional appearance while you're building your credits.

In a beginner's résumé, for instance, present community theater experience. Mention the name of the production, the role you played, and the theater or theater group. Figure 7 demonstrates how a regional beginner's résumé can be cleaned up to look more professional without exaggerating or fabricating credits.

When listing *commercial* experience on a résumé geared toward the Los Angeles, New York, or Chicago market, it's best to simply put "List Upon Request" next to that category. Listing a commercial could imply that you have a conflict, which would eliminate you from any related casting opportu-

FRANK MULLER
AEA AFTRA SAG

OFF AND OFF-OFF BROADWAY

THE CRUCIBLE	Cheever	Roundabout Theater Co.
		Dir. Gerald Freedman
CYRANO DE BERGERAC	Cyrano	Riverside Shakespeare Co.
		1989 NYC Parks Tour
HENRY V	Henry	Riverside Shakespeare Co.
KING LEAR	Edmund	Riverside Shakespeare Co.
UNDER MILK WOOD	First Voice	Irish Arts Center
THE TAMING OF THE SHREW	Tranio	Colonnades Theater
DREAMING ON TIPTOE	Web	East Coast Arts (New Rochelle)
SALT LAKE CITY SKYLINE	The Guard	Public Theater (NYSF)
	U/S Joe (John Lithgow)	Dir. Robert Allen Ackerman

REGIONAL

LONG WHARF (NEW HAVEN CT)

A FLEA IN HER EAR	Tournel	John Tillinger

CAPITAL REP (ALBANY NY)

THE BIG KNIFE	Charlie Castle	Bruce Bouchard

ARENA STAGE (WASH. D.C.)

HAMLET	Fortinbras, U/S Hamlet	Liviu Ciulei
A STREETCAR NAMED DESIRE	Sailor	Marshall Mason
THE CAUCASIAN CHALK CIRCLE	The Tradesman, Ironshirt	Martin Fried
DON JUAN	Ramee/Violette	Liviu Ciulei
IDIOT'S DELIGHT	Don Navadel	Ted Cornell
CURSE OF THE STARVING CLASS	Slater, U/S Wesley	Douglas Wager
AH, WILDERNESS	Arthur	Ted Cornell
TALES FROM THE VIENNA WOODS	The Boyfriend	David Chambers
DESERT DWELLERS	Road Chief	Steven Robman
ANGEL CITY	Lanx	Douglas Wager

TRAPIER THEATER (WASH. D.C.)

ROSENCRANTZ AND GUILDENSTERN ARE DEAD	Guildenstern	Hugh Lester
THE IMPORTANCE OF BEING EARNEST	John Worthing	Edward Crowe
THE FANTASTICKS	El Gallo	Ted Walch

TELEVISION

AROUND THE BEND	WLAC (NASHVILLE)	2 Educ. Series Plots
FREELANCE	ITV (LONDON)	Principal
ONE LIFE TO LIVE	ABC	
ALL MY CHILDREN	ABC	

COMMERCIALS (O/C & V/O)
Conflicts Available On Request

NARRATION
Approximately 60 novels for Recorded Books Inc. and others

SP. SKILLS
Numerous Accents/Dialects, Swordplay, Hand to Hand Combat, Weapons Handling
Water and Snow Skiing, Boat Handling, Precision Driving

FIGURE 6. Professional résumé.

JOHN JENNENS
(419) 535-9722

Height: 6'2"	Weight: 190 lbs.
Eyes: Brown	Hair: Brown
Suit: 44L	Shirt: 16½ / 34-35
Pants: 36/34	Shoe: 10½

THEATRE

"The Thirteen Clocks"	The Prince
"The Imaginary Invalid"	Father
"Night of January 16th"	Defense Attorney Stevens
"Cheaper By The Dozen"	Frank
"The Valiant"	James Dyke

TV COMMERCIALS / INDUSTRIAL FILMS

List available upon request

TELEVISION—RADIO

WKBN—TV (CBS), Youngstown, Ohio - Sports reporter and Anchor

WBKC—AM, Chardon, Ohio - News reporter and News anchor

TRAINING

Acting: Manchester College, North Manchester, Indiana

Commercial: Bowling Green State University, TV Commercial course
Terry Berland — TV Commercial Workshop

EDUCATION

Bachelor of Arts, Communication — Radio/TV/Film
Bowling Green State University, Bowling Green, Ohio

SPECIAL SKILLS & INTERESTS

Video Production (Videography, Editing), Voice Overs, Motorcycling, Automobile (standard and automatic), Truck Driver, Auto Restoration, Bicycling, Carpentry, Construction, Piano, Harpsichord, Trombone, Voice, Volleyball, Bowling, Baseball, Basketball, Hockey, Ice Skating, Tennis, Swimming.

FIGURE 7. An example of how a fledgling regional résumé can be constructed to look more professional.

nities. If you are pursuing work in a region where there are no union commercial opportunities (or if you don't plan to pursue these opportunities), it is the trend to list commercials you have already done to show you have experience, or to list agencies and production companies you have worked with.

After you've outlined your experience in the industry, it's time to list any industry-related *training* you've had. Begin with classes you've taken—scene study, improvisation, or cold-reading, for instance—and workshops. If the class or workshop was taught by a well-known coach, agent, or casting director, note that on your résumé as well. If you have a degree in theater arts, put it in your résumé (M.F.A. in Acting, Yale School of Drama, for example). Certainly include any voice and dance training.

In the beginning of your career, casting directors will be considering the extent and focus of your training as well as where and with whom you trained. Especially at the early stages of your career, it's important to demonstrate your devotion to the craft by developing the training portion of your résumé. Take ongoing classes, take part in community theater, and take every opportunity to audition (there's no better experience than on-the-job training). Before you know it, your fledgling résumé will become a focused, professional promotional tool.

Last on your résumé is a section listing *special skills*. Any special talents you have that might be useful in the business would be listed here. Acting-related talents are a good place to start—things like dialects and mime, for instance. List any musical instrument you play. Athletic abilities are extremely important (such as skydiving, horseback riding, martial arts, tennis, volley ball, baseball, and skiing). If you drive a car (automatic and/or stick shift), motorcycle, and/or truck (pickup to eighteen-wheeler), mention it. Almost anything else you do well—like electronics, photography, American Sign Language, foreign languages, and CPR, for example, can be noted in the special skills section of your résumé. If you enjoy working with animals and/or children and babies, this is a great place to mention it.

Note: If you say you can do something on your résumé, you had better be able to do it—and do it *well*. Limit the list to activities you can perform at an advanced or professional level.

❏ GETTING YOUR RÉSUMÉ PRINTED

Agents and casting directors go through literally hundreds of head shots and résumés weekly. The last thing they want to do is spend a lot of time looking through a poorly organized list of credentials. It is in your best interest to see to it that your résumé is attractively laid out, is easy to read, and draws immediate attention to your strengths as a talent.

Use the sample résumés in this chapter to help you lay out your own material. You can use a typewriter or a computer, or have your résumés professionally typeset. Keep in mind the following do's and don'ts when setting up your résumé:

Do:

1. Make sure the keys are clean and the ribbon is fresh if you use a typewriter, and take care to line up everything neatly on the page. Try using all caps to help distinguish headings from the rest of the material.
2. Use bold typeface for headings if you use a computer (or have the résumé professionally typeset). It's easy to read 12-point type. Try a slightly larger type for headings (14- to 16-point), with 24-point type for your name. Experiment a bit before committing to print.
3. Attach your résumés to your head shots with a stapler (or an adhesive that won't damage or show through on the picture or résumé) in all four corners. *Never* give an agent or casting director a head shot and résumé unattached. Doing so looks lazy and unorganized. The résumé can easily get separated from the photograph, in which case you are left with no way to be identified or contacted.

Don't:

1. Clutter your résumé with full sentences and nonindustry information. Think in terms of an outline of your experiences and abilities (see figs. 6, 7).
2. Have your résumés printed directly on the back of your

head shots. You should constantly update your résumé. It is better to print the résumé on quality white paper, trim it to the exact size of your eight-by-ten head shots, and attach it to the head shots as you need them (a small quantity at a time).

If you use a typewriter to create your résumé, you will most likely use a Xerox machine to make copies as you need them. Make sure the machine delivers good, clean copies (no streaks or spots, please). Clean the glass before each use and take care to line up the paper in the machine properly. If you use a computer and have access to a letter-quality or laser printer, you can make copies as you need them, making sure that the edges are clean (especially if your computer uses continuous-run papers).

If you have your résumés professionally typeset, the printer will give you a range of prices based on the number of copies you order. When ordering, keep in mind that you will be updating your résumé often. Try to negotiate a quantity that includes occasional updates as needed. Don't forget to ask the printer to print your résumés on eight-by-ten (not eight-and-a-half by eleven) paper. When using a computer or typing your own résumé, you will have to trim the résumés to fit your head shots yourself, using a paper cutter—not scissors—for a clean, professional look.

❏ UPDATING RÉSUMÉS

Your résumé should be updated regularly to include new credits, training, and special skills. If you are using a computer, simply insert the new information and delete less impressive notations, reformatting as necessary. If your résumé was professionally typeset, your printer will help reformat your material. Typewritten résumés will be created each time from scratch (it's almost impossible to realign a typewritten document well enough to "white-out" an area and retype information in the allotted space).

If you have a bit of white space (unused area) in your résumé that would comfortably allow insertion of new information, you may choose to neatly print in a line or two (in black pen to match the type) until you create a new document.

Note: When creating their original résumés, some actors leave a section at the bottom of the page to add updates. This allows them to continue (temporarily) using the résumés they have on hand.

❏ WHAT IS A COVER LETTER AND WHAT IS ITS PURPOSE?

A cover letter is a letter of introduction (fig. 8). Sent along with a head shot and résumé, a cover letter is a polite way to introduce yourself and to ask for what you want. If, for instance, you are looking for representation, you would send your head shot out to agents, requesting an appointment. Keep your cover letter brief and to the point. Using a contact name as a referral (mentioning the name of a colleague or mutual acquaintance) can be helpful in catching the attention of agents and casting persons. They will naturally gravitate toward someone who has been referred to them by a person they are familiar with and trust.

Some sample statements you might make in your cover letter include:

1. I've just graduated from . . .
2. I've taken a commercial workshop from . . .
3. I'm ready for work.
4. I'm in such and such a play.
5. I'm looking forward to meeting you.
6. I'd like an appointment.

Once you have created a good cover letter, you're ready to start sending out your head shots and résumés.

❏ TARGETING YOUR HEAD SHOT/RÉSUMÉ MAILINGS TO THE RIGHT PEOPLE

The first group of people you'll want to target your mailings to is agents and/or managers. In larger markets (Los Angeles, New York, and Chicago) as well as secondary markets (like

Alisa Harris
324 East Beaumont
New York, NY 10036
(212) 555-1234

Betsy Berg
Betsy Berg Talent Agency
5 East 60th Street
New York, NY 10036

Dear Betsy,

I recently graduated from Yale School of Drama. Comedy is
my strong point. I am a member of Gotham Improv
Theatre Group. Terry Berland saw me perform in a recent
showcase and suggested I get in touch with you.

I am looking for representation and would love to make an
appointment to meet you. Thank you for your time and
consideration.

Looking forward to hearing from you.

Alisa Harris

Alisa Harris

FIGURE 8. **Sample cover letter.**

Miami, Atlanta, and Dallas), industry bookstores carry directories that list talent agencies. You can get a list of SAG-franchised agents for any market by calling the national chapter in Los Angeles or by checking the phone directory for agencies in your regional area and asking if they are SAG-franchised (refer to the Appendix for SAG listings).

Casting directors also can be found in directories for both major and secondary markets. *Ross Reports* in New York, for instance, carries casting director listings. If you come from a smaller, regional market that doesn't have much in the way of industry bookstores or region-specific information, call your local film commission or union office to request a list of available casting people and/or production houses (some production houses do their own casting).

Compile a list of the people you want to direct your mailings to. Send a single head shot/résumé and cover letter in an eight-and-a-half-by-eleven envelope to each person on your list. Keep track of whom you send mailings to, when you send them, and any responses you get.

❏ FOLLOWING UP ON YOUR MAILINGS

Approximately two weeks after you do a mailing, follow up with a phone call to make sure the person received your package. Ask for an appointment. If the answer is no, thank the agent or casting person for her time, hang up, and make the next call. If the answer is yes, thank the agent for her time, tell her you are looking forward to meeting her, hang up and make the next call. It could take several months for an agent who is interested in you to call you in for an interview. You'll be making a lot of calls and appointments in this industry, so it's important to have on hand the proper tools to *(a)* keep in touch with the industry and *(b)* keep track of your activities, appointments, earnings, and expenses.

The next chapter will help you get yourself organized, motivated, and focused.

❏ **SUMMARY**

RÉSUMÉS

- ☐ 1. Prepare an attractive, easy-to-read, one-page résumé of personal/professional information including:

  - ☐ a. Name

  - ☐ b. Union affiliation (if applicable)

  - ☐ c. Agency representation (if applicable)

  - ☐ d. Phone number where you can be reached (answering service or agent)

  - ☐ e. Statistics (height, weight, hair and eye coloring)

  - ☐ f. Experience (credits in theater, film/TV, commercials, etc.)

  - ☐ g. Training (classes, workshops, college degrees, etc.)

  - ☐ h. Special skills (dialects, sign language, skydiving, etc.)

- ☐ 2. Get your résumé printed. Remember to print small quantities at a time, upgrading information as needed. Have your résumé printed on paper the exact size of your professional head shot, or trim it.

- ☐ 3. Attach your résumés to your head shots in all four corners (using staples or glue).

☐ 4. Create a cover letter to accompany your head shot/résumé submissions. Try to include the following:

    ☐ a. The name of a colleague or mutual acquaintance (if possible)

    ☐ b. A class or workshop you're taking (or degree recently earned)

    ☐ c. A production you're currently in (or have recently completed)

☐ 5. Compile a list of people (agents, managers, casting people, etc.) you want to target your head shot/résumé mailings to. Keep records of whom you mailed to, the date of each submission, and any follow-up notes.

☐ 6. Follow up on each submission (to make sure your head shot arrived and to request an appointment).

3

OTHER TOOLS YOU'LL WANT TO CONSIDER

Now it's time to consider a variety of tools that actors use to stay on top of opportunities in the industry. Agents and casting directors are not willing to chase you down to give you a job. It is your responsibility to make yourself accessible to them at all times, or they will simply call someone else. Being unavailable to receive calls and messages can result in lost wages, lost contacts, and lost opportunities.

Successful actors know the benefits of making use of today's advanced communication technology. To stay on top of things in their day-to-day quest for experience and exposure, they find the following tools indispensable.

❏ EQUIPMENT FOR KEEPING IN TOUCH

ANSWERING MACHINES

Unless you plan to camp out by the phone day after day, the best way to make sure you never miss a call is to purchase an answering machine. An invaluable communication aid, the answering machine takes calls for you when you're not available to do so yourself, allowing the caller to leave a message that you can retrieve later. Costs range from under a hundred dollars to several hundred dollars. A good dependable machine doesn't have to cost a lot and more than pays for itself in service rendered. If possible, consider the following options when purchasing an answering machine:

1. *Call screening* allows you to decide whether or not you want to take the call when you are home. Most basic machines have this option, but check to make sure. It can come in handy when you're studying or rehearsing material and don't want to be disturbed.

2. *Two-way recording* allows you to record both sides of the conversation. This is useful when you're given an appointment and don't want to hold up the agent or casting person while you write down all the information. Make sure the other party knows you are recording the call—it's the law.

3. A *built-in message retrieval system* lets you call your number from wherever you are to take your messages off the machine.

Patty Kallis, a Seattle casting director, had this to say about the importance of having an answering machine, "You'd be surprised how many people *don't* have an answering machine, and you can't do much of anything without it.

"Let's just suppose that I get a call requesting you specifically and that call comes fairly late in the day, with me needing you first thing in the morning—and you don't get in until two a.m. Ten o'clock (p.m.) comes and I still can't get you. I have to set my alarm for every hour on the hour. Do you know how unhappy I am with you when it's two o'clock in the morning when I finally reach you? And if the producer *wants* you, I have to make sure I get you.

"Now, if you had an answering machine, I would have left a message and I would assume you would check it at least once or twice in the evening. I've had people call me at three o'clock in the morning because that's when they got in, but at least I rested a little bit better knowing the message was on their machine.

"Sometimes I try to contact people who don't have a machine, and they lose. I don't try any further if I call once or twice and can't reach them. Why should I keep calling if you don't have a machine and you're not home? I'll try once or twice, then forget it."

ANSWERING SERVICES

Another option in some markets is to hire an answering service to take calls for you. If they are available, you can find such services in the Yellow Pages or in industry directories. Your local phone company may offer voice-mail services, which will take calls for you when you're not available to answer the phone. A monthly (sometimes weekly) service fee is charged, whereas an answering machine involves a one-time cost. All things considered, the purchase of an answering machine should prove to be more cost-effective and convenient than voice-mail and answering services. A little research should help you determine which option will work best for you.

BEEPERS

The beeper has become one of the most convenient ways for talent to keep in touch with the rest of the industry. Small enough to fit into a pocket or purse, this handy little gadget insures that you never miss a call. After someone calls your beeper number, a small beeping sound or pulse (if you choose this option) lets you know you have a message.

With a basic model, you simply press a button and the number of the person who called appears on a small screen. With more expensive models, the caller can leave a short message as well. You have the option of either returning the call right away or "saving" the number and calling back later. Agents love actors who use beepers. Beepers offer a convenient, low-cost method of keeping in close contact with the rest of the industry.

CAR PHONES

Having a phone in your car can be a convenient way to stay accessible to your agent or manager. If you break down on route to an audition or job, you can call ahead to let your agent know what happened while you arrange another way to get to work. The cost of cellular phones runs from around a hundred dollars to several hundred dollars and more.

Basic monthly service starts at around twenty-five dollars.

There are many options (your dealer will explain his company's specific packages for cellular phone usage).

Though convenient, cellular phones have one major drawback—you are billed for calls coming and going. This means that you pay for the call whether you are calling out or someone is calling in. One way to keep the phone bill down is to avoid giving your cellular phone number to anyone other than agents, casting people, and other important business contacts. Consider using your cellular phone primarily in emergency situations.

❏ RECORD-KEEPING SUPPLIES

Since making commercials is a business, it is important to keep accurate records. Keeping track of expenses, income, appointments, and audition information is crucial to your success as an actor. You'll also need to write thank-you notes and keep a journal on your goals and networking efforts (Chapter 6, Networking and Goal Setting, explains these essential tasks). The minimum requirements for keeping track of all of these things include:

1. Daily planner/appointment book—to keep track of auditions, callbacks, jobs, and other appointments. A section for notes, important calls, and new contacts is helpful.

2. Record-keeping materials—including a journal for keeping track of income and business expenses for tax purposes and a travel log to record mileage and other travel-related expenditures.

3. Networking/goal-setting journal—This can be any notebook or hardcover journal converted to detail your day-to-day, weekly, monthly, yearly, and long-term (five to ten years or more) goals, as well as whom you need to network with in order to accomplish them.

4. Thank-you notes.

The local office supply store should be able to provide you with a variety of stationery, record-keeping journals, and convenient-size travel logs, as well as standard tables on allowable business deductions. If not, try the business section of a good bookstore.

4

TRAINING

❏ **HOW CLASSES IN COMMERCIAL TECHNIQUE,
IMPROVISATION, SCENE STUDY, AND COLD-READING
PREPARE YOU TO DO COMMERCIALS**

Commercials have one thing in common with all other acting media—you (the performer) have to come off as real. The only difference in commercials is that the work is done in a shorter form and in a smaller space. Studying improvisation, cold-reading, and scene and monologue study provides a solid foundation for and adds ease and excellence to acting in commercials.

Classes in *commercial technique* teach you how to act out a situation in a fifteen-, thirty-, or sixty-second format. They should do the following:

1. Teach you how to analyze a script
2. Teach you to make the most of the physical space you're given to work with
3. Show you how to let out your personality
4. Eliminate self-consciousness in front of the camera

❏ **INTERVIEW WITH JOHN FIONTE**

Acting coach John Fionte, of Florida, briefly describes each form of study as well as the benefits of each:

In *improvisation classes* you are given the frame-work of a scene, scenario, or sketch—the gist of an idea. You make up your own lines, create your own relation-ships, and bring out your own personality. Improv classes help you:

1. Learn to loosen up, become less inhibited
2. Learn to think fast (and in this business, this is a definite plus)
3. Exercise the creative muscles in your brain

In *scene/monologue study*, you spend weeks or months working on the same material. Each time you approach it, you bring new levels to your performance. You learn to do in-depth research, script analysis, and background and relationship histories, which are really the core of an actor's work—creating "real" relation-ships.

The greater your knowledge of acting, the easier it is to do television commercials, because a TV commercial is actually a miniscene.

Cold-reading classes teach you how to audition, which is a unique technique. An actor can be brilliant in an acting class yet not be able to audition well at all. Cold-reading teaches actors to access the material quickly, pick out the clues given in the text, and then let their individual personalities come through in a committed manner.

❏ FINDING A GOOD COACH

In larger markets like Los Angeles, Chicago, and New York, it is fairly easy to find a good coach. In smaller, regional mar-kets, it can be tough. Word of mouth is always a great way to find out whom the better actors are training with. Ask for referrals from local agents, managers, casting people, and other actors.

If possible, audit the classes you're considering to see if you like the way the coach relates to the class and if you would fit in. Try to train with the best coaches you can afford, and know that if you come from a smaller market, you may need to go to a larger market periodically to get professional training.

According to Judith Jacobs, a Chicago casting director, "It's important to invest some time and money studying your craft. Be honest in assessing your strengths and weaknesses. It's very important to have good cold-reading skills. Then, you will begin to see more success in your career as an actor."

Seattle casting director Patty Kallis adds, "Information has to come when you're really ready to receive it. You may have several coaches, then one will finally get through. It doesn't mean all the other coaches were bad. It is generally more likely that you were finally ready to receive and apply the information given.

"No matter how well reputed a coach is, if the coach and the actor don't click, don't relate well to each other, you will not gain as much as when you are with a coach you get along well with and can respond to."

❏ COST OF TRAINING

How much should you expect to pay for classes? This varies, depending on the location and size of the class and the credentials of the teacher. In major markets, expect to pay a minimum of $40 per session with a commitment that varies from four to twelve weekly classes to a two-year program. A two- to three-day on-camera workshop with a well-known teacher can run $200 to $300. A few well-directed calls to several schools and coaches should give you a nice range to consider. Again, study with the best coaches you can afford.

❏ HOW OFTEN YOU SHOULD TRAIN

In this industry, training is a way of life. Anytime they're not actually working, successful actors are working out in class. To do well in any career, you must take the relevant courses, and then take refresher courses to stay current and to fine-tune your professional skills.

Newcomers to the business will spend the bulk of their time in class. You can expect to spend several years developing basic auditioning and performing techniques until you are consistently able to book work in the industry.

At some point, bookings will begin to take priority, with study taking place in between jobs. Just know that in some form or another, be it on-the-job training or formal classes, upgrading your skills must become a way of life if you are to become successful and stay on the top in this business.

❏ INTERVIEW WITH SANDY SHURIN

In the following interview New York City acting coach Sandy Shurin expands on the importance of ongoing training for serious actors:

Creativity as an ongoing process. The time to study is when you're working. The university level is just a taste of what performing is all about—that and a lot of theater history. After that, you want to get to a larger market like Los Angeles, New York, or Chicago, and into a school where you can really develop. Class is the place where one gets nourished and grounded, the place where creativity soars.

Finding a good acting coach involves looking for someone who is very current and does not try to make actors into something they're not. The coach should have a good eye for talent, using each person's uniqueness and raw ability to help develop him or her into a marketable commodity.

When actors first relocate to a larger market, it's important to realize that, first of all, they are coming in at ground one. They know a little bit (and that's great), but they really know more about theater history than they know about themselves. They have to learn that they are the instrument that *becomes* the character—that plays the role.

It's also important to know that when you first come

into the big city, you will have to humble yourself a bit. Observe. See how things are done in the larger market. Get good pictures and a résumé. Learn about writing good cover letters.

Start networking. Take advantage of the vast opportunities that come with being in a big city. Don't just spend your time looking for the bucks. Go to the unions. Go to union functions. Attend all the readings you can possibly get to. Attend lectures. Don't be afraid to ask questions. Find out where the agents, directors, and casting directors are. That's very, very important.

Be cautious when you are meeting people. Check to see that they are who they say they are. A few quick phone calls should set your mind at ease when deciding whether the people you're meeting are legitimate or not.

Regional people need to know that they're coming to a larger market to learn the ropes—to see what it's like to work with people at this level. There's always a new level to your creativity, to knowing how to audition, to learning what people in that market need from you.

Regional actors coming into a larger market need a certain amount of transition time before they really start to acclimate. You need to spend that time learning about your craft with your coaches. You're here to learn how to audition, to give yourself the opportunity to perform. As a writer, you would just take out your typewriter. As an actor, you have to create the opportunity to present yourself.

People who take their careers seriously work out, whether they are doctors, lawyers, teachers, or performers. They study, take courses, then take refresher courses. Study is a way of life in the big city. It's just like a gym—you go there to give your body a workout. There has to be a place for actors to work on their emotions, to develop their character muscles. That place is in class.

5

SCAMS

Unfortunately, there is a rather unsavory element invading the industry—one that feeds on the hopes and dreams of unsuspecting thespians—promising fame and fortune, separating you from your money, and then delivering little or nothing. These charlatans of show business are called scam artists. They're slick. They're smooth. And they're ruthless in the pursuit of a quick buck.

❏ WHY SCAM ARTISTS ARE SO SUCCESSFUL

Frankly, scam artists are very good at what they do. They often make an impressive presentation, citing the names of well-known agents, managers, production companies, and "stars," all of whom they claim are their close industry contacts. Scam artists prey primarily on young aspiring actors and parents who, in their excitement and enthusiasm at the prospect of getting involved in the business, forget to take the necessary steps to insure that the people they are dealing with are who they *say* they are and can do what they say they can do.

People who normally exhibit amazing common sense have been known to throw caution to the winds when it comes to making decisions concerning their (or their child's) potential career in show business. As scam artists become more creative and elusive, aspiring talent and their parents must become much more scrupulous in discovering which industry-related activities are legitimate and which are not.

❏ HOW TO SEE A SCAM COMING A MILE AWAY

By applying some commonsense rules, you should be able to avoid being taken by a scam artist. Before getting involved with anyone who claims to be able to help you build your career, consider the following:

1. **You should never have to pay someone up front to get work in the industry.** Think about it. If you were going to get a job at Burger King, you would never consider paying them for the privilege of working for them. You would never consider paying up front for an employment agency to get work for you. They would get a commission or fee *after* getting you a job. It's the same with agents and managers in the business. They make money when *you* make money, by taking a percentage of your income (SAG-franchised agencies, for instance, take ten percent of your earnings) as commission for getting you the job.

There is one legitimate reason for putting out money up front. Many agencies, especially in the print field, put out annual books showcasing their talent. This is acceptable practice, even though the talent pays a fee to be in the book (anywhere from fifty dollars for a place in a regional headbook to several hundred dollars for a full-page spread in a major-market agency book). Just know that the agency should be willing to represent you whether or not you have the money or the desire to be in their current book.

Do some research. Is the agency *really* obtaining work for its talent? Or is it a front for the book its owners are publishing? Call the Better Business Bureau, local production companies, or other actors in your region to see if the agency is legitimate.

2. **If anyone tells you that, for a certain amount of money, they will get you an audition, guarantee you work, or "make you a star," turn tail and run.** There are no guarantees in this business. As in other industries, talent people must invest a considerable amount of time and effort before they can hope for ongoing success. Anyone who tells you otherwise is full of beans.

3. **There is no reason you should have to disrobe to interview or audition for a job.** Nudity is prohibited by both the unions and the networks in commercials that audition and air in the United States. For auditions, you could be asked to wear a two-piece swimsuit (females) or a bathing suit (males). Other common requests would be for you to wear a halter top or an outfit that shows off your figure. When the commercial is filmed, there are ways to close in with the camera to imply nudity. This might be done in a shower or bathtub shot in an ad for a soap product, for example.

Steer clear of interviews and auditions held in personal hotel rooms at unseemly hours. Never put yourself in a position where you can be taken advantage of. Newspapers and magazines are full of frightening stories about young, inexperienced people meeting so-called agents, managers, casting people, or photographers who turned out to be kidnappers, molesters, rapists, and murderers. In some cases, failing to use common sense can result in personal disaster.

Even in a legitimate work situation, sexual harassment can be a problem. For example, one young model/actress was hired to do a print advertisement in which only her head and shoulders would show. During the photo session the photographer asked her several times to open her blouse. This young lady handled herself appropriately, refusing to open her top (why would that be necessary in an ad showing only her face?) and reporting the incident to her agent. The agent then called the client, who fired the photographer.

Individuals who harass and defraud talent can leave a bad taste in the mouths of those who have been taken. Such behavior demeans the efforts of legitimate industry professionals and reflects poorly on what is otherwise a terrific working environment. As aspiring talent become more scam conscious—making wiser, sensible choices, the negative publicity surrounding the industry will begin to dissipate. Use your head when deciding whom to work with, whom to trust. The payoff will be a career unmarred by frauds and tragedies.

Remember: If it seems too good to be true, it probably is.

❑ COMMON INDUSTRY SCAMS

Here are four things to avoid:

1. Ads in newspapers and magazines seeking talent of all kinds, no experience necessary. You go to these interviews and voilà! You are the most amazing talent and/or look these people have ever seen. *You* are going to be a *star!* Chances are, these folk are going to do one of the following:

- Ask you to pay to be interviewed by them for the opportunity of being represented by them *or* ask you to pay for the privilege of being seen by them
- Ask you to pay to be in a special publication that goes out to all the agents, managers, and casting houses (no one hires from these publications)
- Say how much work they could get for you if only you would pay them to supply the required pictures of you—no matter how wonderful your existing pictures are, they will not be suitable for whatever they are doing—and they just happen to have a photographer with them to take those pictures
- Tell you they think you're just wonderful, but you need a little coaching—and they just happen to have a seminar that will teach you everything you need to know.

All of this is usually a one-time-only opportunity. Only so many people will be accepted, and *you* (you lucky dog) are one of them. But you have to act fast. It's now or never.

Time to go. Leave the room. *Now!*

2. Agents or managers who offer to represent you as a talent without asking you to read something or, in some cases, without even having *seen* you. All you have to do is send in a small fee . . . This should send up an immediate red flag. Reputable talent agents simply don't sign up actors without having them come in for a formal interview to see if they have the right look, talent, and experience to be marketable to their clients. (And remember, you never should be required to pay fees up front.)

3. Photographers who come into town (often on the pretense of being a "big name" in some major market) and book sessions based on the premise that they are scouting for some big agency or are otherwise able to guarantee a connection resulting in paid work. Again, there are no guarantees. Although there are good test photographers who are brought into smaller, regional areas to photograph talent (by reputable local agencies and schools), they do not promise you work—they are simply there to help you develop your book (models) or to take talent head shots.

Be suspicious of so-called "famous" magazine photographers. Chances are, if they really shoot covers and tears* for major magazines, they wouldn't have the time or interest to come to regional areas to test models and shoot head shots.

In a common scam, a photographer comes into smaller, regional areas with slick ads and a lot of hype about who he knows and what he's done. The local talent lines up and signs up for a series of pictures, paying (of course) in full, in advance. If all goes well, the actors have a lot of fun and can't *wait* to see the results. They're happy. The photographer's happy. And why shouldn't he be? He's just made several thousand dollars, he's on his way out of town, and he's not coming back. The pictures? Well, if there ever was film in the camera, it was put there for show. The actors will grow a beard before they ever see any prints.

Make sure you know whom you're working with if you use an out-of-town photographer. If someone says he shoots or scouts for a well-known agency or magazine, get specific information (name of the agency or publication and a contact who can vouch for him).

4. A "major production house" coming to your town, auditioning talent for parts in a feature film. You're fabulous, an amazing talent—but not a member of the union. This creates a problem, but if you give them a few hundred to several hundred dollars, they will cut through the red tape, get you into the union, and you're ready for

---

*Tears (tear sheets) are pages from commercial print advertisements, editorials (fashion pages or covers), and catalogs that models tear out to place in their modeling book (portfolio).

work. No. *No. NO.* There are very specific conditions for joining the union. A simple call to the local SAG office (see the Appendix) will tell you how you qualify to become a member of the union.

In 1992, a group of scam artists calling themselves "Patrick Swayze Productions" went on a nine-month rampage, defrauding actors in numerous cities across the country by telling them that Mr. Swayze was producing a film, that they were auditioning for the film, and that for $250 to $450 they could get these actors into the union and into the film. Needless to say, there was no movie, these people had no connection to Patrick Swayze, and the actors never recovered their money.

❏ REPORTING AND INVESTIGATING SCAMS

If you suspect that a person or group in the industry is misrepresenting itself, don't hesitate to make some phone calls to check out its claims. Start with the Better Business Bureau to see if there are any complaints. Ask your local Chamber of Commerce if it registered with them.

Generally, anyone involved in businesses that exchange goods or services for money must have a business license. He or she should be able to produce a copy of that license, and you should be able to verify its validity with the government agency that issued it (look on the license itself to find out who to contact).

Scam artists are usually eager to get rid of someone who is too smart to be taken, focusing instead on those more likely to fall victim to their deceptive games. Those who are on the up and up will not object to you checking out their credentials, their contacts, and their prior business activities. So unless you are dealing with a well-known, reputable person or company, check things out before jumping into anything that seems even remotely suspicious.

If, in spite of everything, you find you've been "had" by a con artist, don't be embarrassed to admit it. Call the Better Business Bureau and the press about what happened. Doing so protects others from being scammed and will help make sure the offenders either make restitution or are prosecuted for their crimes.

If you are scammed, try to learn from the experience. Become a wiser, more conscientious consumer so no one can take advantage of you again.

Chris Farrell, a SAG-franchised agent in Denver, had this to say about one of the industry's more subtle scams: "There's a notice in the paper. 'Come down, pay twenty dollars [or more], get signed with an agent.' Obviously, these are not franchised agencies because it is illegal for us to charge to have a talent on file with us.

"When somebody makes you sign up to be listed with them and pay money, it's probably not a legitimate situation. If five hundred people come in and plop down twenty dollars each, they're out of town tomorrow with ten thousand dollars. This type of scam is going down all over the country."

❑ INTERVIEW WITH DAVID VANDO

David Vando, an industry consultant, gives valuable advice on how to avoid becoming a victim of modern industry scams. He is the owner of Model's Mart in New York City, which supplies educational material to actors and models and is an expert on the demands of working in the industry. David travels extensively around the country speaking at international modeling/talent conventions.

Traveling throughout the United States and Canada, one gets a feel for the types of activities that tend to repeat themselves in the industry, some of which are beneficial to young people breaking into the industry and some of which are not.

Young aspiring models and actors from all over North America are being victimized by a variety of different scams geared at both performers and at very ambitious, anxious parents who hope to get their children into the business.

In New York, there are ongoing problems with people trying to take advantage of young talent. Recently, I did some research while helping a number of government agencies in New York City and in Washington, D.C., to prosecute people who were running scams or operating illegal, improperly licensed agencies.

This is a significant breakthrough because up until now, this issue was sort of kept in the closet; no active government action was ever taken against these people. In New York, both talent and modeling agencies must be licensed, posting a ten-thousand-dollar bond that serves as a legal safeguard in the event someone brings a complaint against a licensed agency. This way, you would get paid for an illegitimate nonpayment.

Phony agencies create a major problem for the industry. They have no license and are not bonded so if you do business with them, you do so at your own peril. One of the first things newcomers to New York should do is to make sure that any agency they interview with is properly licensed with the city and state of New York. That's very easy to find out. Just call the Better Business Bureau of *any* state to find out if an agency is duly registered and/or licensed as required by state laws.

Agencies do not necessarily *have* to be franchised by the unions. However, if an agency is not SAG- or AFTRA-franchised, check whether it's a registered business and bonded (see "All About Agents" in Chapter 8).

Many scams play on your vanity. You are told that for a certain amount of money, you can have a big career. There is no such thing as instant success. Most people who are thought of as overnight successes have actually worked very hard at it for a very long time.

We are all guilty of letting our emotions and our excitement and our visions blind us, keeping us from using our own common sense. If someone asks you to pay to be "discovered," you should thoroughly investigate him or her. Legitimate industry activities don't work that way. Good agencies make money by finding work for you. Any other attempts to get money from you are very dubious.

An agency that is representing you and feels you need a better head shot can certainly give out the names of good photographers to consider, but you should be free to interview them yourself, making your own negotiations as to cost and the type of materials you need. Your agency may guide you, but it should not be part of a photographic studio or any other merry-go-round collecting fees from you.

You should be able to compare prices and talk to other performers to see who they've worked with. Speak to experienced actors about who the local scam artists are. Word of mouth is most helpful. Don't be afraid to ask questions. Be suspicious of anyone who doesn't want to answer questions about his business activities.

Check out people's credentials. It's one thing if you are allowed to participate in a talent search or a convention where only schools who are licensees participate. The purpose of these conventions is to educate new talent and, in some cases, allow reputable agents and managers to select talent for possible future professional development.

Any school that says "Come to my classes and I'll make you a star" is doing the student a disservice in the same sense as a fly-by-night scam coming through your city and having a one-night stand at some hotel. Good schools do not make promises they cannot keep. They can only give you the best training they can.

I went to Columbia University and they never made any promises to me. They made things *available.* Reputable corporations have sent people to interview students, but no promises were made. Be wary of anyone who says, "Give me some money and I'll make contacts for you." "I'll get you interviews." "I'll get you an audition." You are headed for a disappointment if you do business with these people.

The development of a show business career is a long process. People usually have to work very hard to get an agent. Agents usually have to work very hard to get them into their first interview. How do I know? Because I experienced it myself. It's never an easy process.

6 NETWORKING AND GOAL SETTING

Who you know, how well you stay focused on your goals, and whether or not you follow through have a tremendous effect on your career and its progression. It's important to surround yourself with a strong network of industry friends. You must also learn to set clear, attainable goals and take consistent, continuous steps to turn your dreams into reality.

❏ NETWORKING

It is no secret that successful people tend to surround themselves with a select group of industry friends and colleagues. Networking with the right people can move your career along at an accelerated rate. Who are the "right" people?

Fellow Performers. Associate with fellow performers who are motivated and active in the pursuit of their goals and who have a positive, outgoing nature. Hanging out with unmotivated people with negative attitudes will drain you emotionally and creatively.

Make it a point to spend time with people who are excited about their lives, who take advantage of the opportunities available in the industry, and who know how to make the best of a situation, no matter how crazy things get. Remember, the people you surround yourself with are a mirror of yourself and the way you relate to the world around you. Like attracts like. Take care to spend your time only with people who support you and whose efforts you admire.

Industry Professionals. Make yourself visible to the movers and shakers of the industry—agents, managers, casting directors, directors, producers, etc. Attend workshops and conventions where there are opportunities to meet and talk with people who may be in a position to help you build your career.

Make it a point to get to know everyone worth knowing in your market (and always have copies of your head shot/résumé with you). Be courteous to and appreciative of every contact. Even though the person you just met may not be able to make a direct impact on your career, he or she may be able to steer you toward someone who can.

Show sincere appreciation for anyone who does something nice for you. Sending thank-you notes to the agent who gave you an appointment, the casting person who called you in, the receptionist who was so helpful at the audition, or the coach who took a special interest in your career, for instance, not only brightens that person's day but also can help advance your career. Everyone wants to feel appreciated. Unfortunately (or fortunately for you), many people fail to properly thank those who have gone to bat for them. Thank-you notes are memorable. If you send one, the recipient will remember your thoughtfulness the next time your name comes up, and perhaps will be eager to do something nice for you again.

You'll never succeed if you spend your time at home on the sofa dreaming about your first Academy Award. Get out there and meet people, whenever the opportunity arises.

Mentors. Nothing helps young, aspiring talent catapult to success (talent and training aside) more than having a strong, successful mentor. A good mentor believes in you, sometimes (at first) more than you believe in yourself.

Mentors serve as role models, teachers, confidants, and friends. They shoulder the tears when you take a fall and give you a swift kick in the pants if you start to slack off. Having a mentor who is well known and respected can not only raise your self-esteem considerably, but also elevate your standing in the industry. People can't help but notice that this influential person has faith in your ability to do well in the industry. You'll find that with the right mentor, doors previously closed to you may suddenly begin to open.

How do you *find* a mentor? Generally, a mentor finds you. He or she may notice how hard you've been working, how much promise you seem to have. Mentors are often at a point in their lives where they have had a certain degree of success and now want to give something back. And, lucky you, they decide to take you under their wing and guide your career. That is one way it happens.

Another option is for *you* to spend some time deciding whom you would like to be your mentor. Look for someone you admire who has the personal and professional traits you desire and who, over time, seems interested in helping you develop your career.

Often, talent managers take on the role of mentor, grooming an actor into a well-rounded, marketable commodity. You may have a mentor who focuses primarily on one or two aspects of your career. A mentor may come into your life suddenly, bestowing his or her special gifts (lessons) upon you, and then move on to someone else who needs help more. Some mentors become lifelong comrades. In either case, if you're lucky enough to find a mentor, count your blessings and take care to make the most of the opportunities your "guardian angel" has to offer you.

❏ GOAL SETTING

There is no question of the direct correlation between success and the simple act of setting one's goals down on paper. Goal setting helps you to stay focused as you work on the day-to-day activities necessary to do well in the industry. Remember:

> *If you are failing to plan, you are planning to fail.*

There are numerous books and tapes on the subject of goal setting, all which cite the following tips for setting solid, achievable goals:

1. Make a habit of regularly writing down your goals. Studies show that the simple act of writing down your goals sets the wheels of success in motion. The process puts your dreams into clear focus so that you can prioritize them and begin taking action to bring each goal to fruition.

Use a journal to record where you want to be (and in what time frame) and who you need to meet and network with in order to accomplish your goals—and then break each goal into small, achievable steps. Review and revise your goals as necessary, working every day to complete some activity that will bring you closer to completion.

The Goal-Planning Sheet and Summary at the end of this chapter are designed to help you set up your networking/goal-setting journal for maximum results.

2. Break your goals down into the following categories:

- *Yearly goals*—Write a broad overview of the things you would like to accomplish over the next year.
- *Monthly goals*—At the beginning of each month, prioritize those things you want to get done over the next thirty or thirty-one days. Be more specific as you break down your yearly goals over the next twelve months.
- *Weekly goals*—Begin each week by writing down your goals for the next seven days. Be realistic about what you can accomplish in this amount of time and make sure that you spend time working toward the accomplishment of your most important achievements (it's easy to get wrapped up in the day-to-day stuff, neglecting the tasks that would really make a difference in your career).
- *Daily goals*—Little by little, you've been breaking your most important goals into smaller and smaller pieces (yearly, monthly, and weekly). Now divide your goals into even smaller "bites," planning something to do each and every day to move your career forward. As you complete each step on your daily "to do" list, you'll begin to notice that you are making strides in the major, annual goals you set for yourself.

Deciding what *specifically* you want, then consistently taking *action* to do the things that make you more marketable will provide the strong foundation necessary to create an ongoing experience of achievement.

As you write out your goals, it's important to know that you can't have it all, certainly not all at once. It's very hard to succeed if you are scattered, pursuing too may major goals at one time. For instance, it would be very hard to become a doctor and an actor at the same time. Becoming a doctor involves many years of study and practice. Becoming an actor requires equal dedication in time and effort to stand a chance of succeeding. Over time, you could certainly become both a doctor and an actor (the late Graham Chapman of Monty Python fame did just that) but it would be very difficult to pursue both careers at the same time.

You must prioritize your list of goals and be reasonable about what can be accomplished in a given block of time. Go over your list and as you attempt to decide which goals you are going to pursue (at this time), ask yourself:

1. Do I *really* want to accomplish this goal? Am I willing to make this goal a priority in my life, working every day in some way to make this dream a reality? Am I willing to pay the price of achieving my goal—to devote the time and effort necessary to make things happen? What am I willing to sacrifice in the pursuit of this goal (TV time, nights out socializing)?

2. *Why* do I want to achieve this goal? Be honest with yourself. Make sure the goal you set is chosen for the right reasons, that you are doing this for yourself, that it's something you *need* to do—not because someone else wants it for you. You will have to work very hard to achieve your goals. Do some soul searching to make sure that what you are trying for is something you really want.

3. What are all the wonderful things that will happen if I am able to achieve my goal? For instance, "If I lose weight, all my favorite clothes will fit, I'll look better on-camera, etc." Visualizing all the fabulous results of achieving your goals will inspire you to follow through.

4. What are the not-so-wonderful things that will happen if I *don't* achieve my goal? Spend some time contemplating the results of *not* taking consistent action to see your plans through to completion. "I didn't follow through on a connection I made at the casting. As a result, the part went to someone else." "I never did sign up for that cold-reading class. As a result, I was visibly inexperienced at the audition." Just thinking about what you felt like when you didn't achieve a goal, then comparing that to the way you felt when you did, should motivate you to take action *today* to complete one of the vital tasks you've listed on your goal sheet.

> *When you get right down to the root of the meaning of the word* succeed, *you find it simply means to follow through.*
>
> —F. W. Nichols

As you work your way through your list of goals, you may over time find that certain goals no longer seem important to you. Your priorities can (and do) change. Be flexible when that happens. Review your goal sheet periodically and update it as needed.

Also pay attention to which efforts are producing positive results for you—and which ones aren't. Revise your strategy when necessary. Keep doing whatever *is* working; stop doing whatever isn't. Be willing to try new things (No guts, no glory) and be willing to make mistakes along the way. Realize that behind every setback is the opportunity to learn and grow.

Be willing to do whatever it takes to accomplish your goals. Take classes, get out and meet people, work on your public image, eliminate the "negatives" from your life. Make the time to plan out your life—and no excuses. There is always time to do the things that are really important to you.

If you're not doing something on a regular basis to make your dream a reality, it could be that you don't *really* want this goal at all. Only you can decide how badly you want to change your present circumstances. A bit of soul searching as you review your progress should provide you with the answers you need. Remember:

> *If you do not take the time to write down specific goals and consistently* act *on them, you will wind up working for someone else who* did.

There are no shortcuts to greatness. Greatness comes with consistent effort and begins with the little things you do each day as you build your career, step by step. Take charge of your life. Take charge of your career. Stay focused and determined to succeed, and before you know it, your wildest dreams will begin to become reality.

❑ SUMMARY: SUPER SUCCESS STRATEGIES

STRATEGIES FOR CONSISTENT GOAL ATTAINMENT

1. Write your goals on paper and refer to them regularly. Doing so keeps your goals in clear focus. Studies show that people who write their goals out on paper tend to achieve much more than those who do not.

2. Be specific about what you want to achieve. Rather than writing, "I want to make lots of money," determine exactly the amount you want to make and give yourself a framework of time in which you feel you can realistically earn that amount of money. Giving yourself a deadline helps to keep you on track. The more specific and detailed your plan of action, the better the chance you will reach your goal when you plan to reach it. For instance, if you are currently making $5,000 a year making commercials, perhaps an attainable goal might be to be making $10,000 one year from the date of starting the exercise. Once you've decided how much you want to make and in what time frame you want to make it, be very specific about what you are going to do in the next year that will allow you to boost your sales up to the level you've aspired to. Make a list of things to do that will help you achieve your goal, refer to the list at least once daily (preferably first thing in the morning and again in the evening), and try to do something every day that will bring you closer to reaching your goal.

3. Review and revise your goals regularly, as needed. Keep your goals in plain sight and review them often to see what's working, what's not, and whether or not the goal needs to be revised before it is truly attainable. Maybe your goal was not realistic. Maybe you need more time to attain it. Sometimes the desire for a goal diminishes and another goal takes priority. Goal setting should be an ongoing process.

4. Associate with achievers. Watch the company you keep. Surround yourself with supportive, positive people. Find people who are doing what you would like to be doing, who inspire you to achieve and maintain a level of excellence. Avoid those who find a million excuses for not achieving their goals. If you are surrounded by people who don't support your desire for growth, find a new group of friends and colleagues who do. Your success depends upon it.

5. Take consistent action in attaining your goals. NO MORE EXCUSES! Whatever you want to do, get off your butt and get to it. No matter where you are now—no matter what your financial state, your educational level, or where you live, start with whatever resources are available to you and *get going*. There will never be a "perfect time," a "perfect" set of circumstances. The best time to begin is now. Even a small effort, when consistently applied, will create phenomenal change. In fact, the simple decision to write and act on clear, precise goals produces a certain positive momentum. All things are possible. You *can* create the kind of life you want if you invest regularly in these simple, highly effective goal-setting techniques.

GOAL-PLANNING SHEET

TO DO LIST	NOTES
	NEW CONTACTS
IMPORTANT CALLS	**THANK-YOU NOTES**

> *I know of no more encouraging fact than the unquestionable ability of man to elevate his life by conscious effort.*
>
> —Henry David Thoreau

II

TAKING YOUR ACT ON THE ROAD

7

THE KEY PLAYERS IN THE INDUSTRY

Now it's time to meet some of the key movers and shakers in the commercial industry. They are instrumental in the advancement of your career, so it's important to know who these people are and how they fit into your life as a performer.

❑ AGENTS

The agent is the person who represents you, who secures auditions for you. He or she accepts bookings for you, negotiates money and the terms of employment, receives the payments you get from the booking, and distributes the money (minus his or her commission) to you. The agent protects you according to the guidelines of the unions.

If you have any questions or complaints, your agent is the one to straighten them out for you. Some problems or issues that could potentially arise include:

- While on a shoot, you find out the commercial is running (airing) in a different way from what you were told when you booked it.
- You were booked as an extra and you are now recognized in the commercial. You feel you should be upgraded to a principal.
- You are no longer under contract for a commercial and a friend of yours calls and says the commercial is running again.

While your agent should keep a record of your bookings and products that are conflicts (products you are under contract for), ultimately it is your responsibility to keep your own records.

❏ MANAGERS

It is the manager's job to help you shape your overall career. You might, for instance, be doing a lot of commercials, then decide it's time to move more into film. Your manager should be able to tell you if your timing is right and, if it is, introduce you to film opportunities.

With your manager's help, all aspects of your career (theater, film, commercials, etc.) should be considered and a plan of action put into effect. Your manager is someone else on your side, taking your hand and offering personalized attention and guidance as you develop your career. Managers have fewer clients than agents, so they can take the time to develop talent. They also guide agents in negotiating money for actors. However, managers cannot directly secure bookings.

❏ CASTING DIRECTORS

The casting director is the one who calls the actor in to audition, either directly or through an agent. He or she is responsible for the initial selection of actors from all available talent. The casting director also directs the actor during the taped audition, then presents this audition tape to the creative team.

A casting director may be the first person of importance to see your work. If he believes in you and likes your work, he will call you in on any audition he feels you are right for, even if you don't have an agent. In this case, the casting director could be instrumental in introducing you to an agent. Although you can obtain auditions directly from the casting director, ultimately, you have more exposure to auditions when you have agency representation. Many casting directors will call your agent with different character descriptions, referred to as "breakdowns," which results in expanded opportunities to audition for actors who have agents.

A casting director gets no payment or commissions from an actor.

❏ PRODUCERS

The producer is the person who puts together all the elements of the commercial's production and is one of the members of the creative team who has a say in who gets booked for the job.

❏ DIRECTORS

The director is the one who actually directs the spot. Often, the director's opinion on which talent will work best for the spot holds sway (for more on producers and directors, see Chapter 11: "The Selection Process").

Now that you've been introduced to some of the key figures in the industry, you'll discover in the next few chapters how each is involved in the day-to-day workings of your career.

❏ ALL ABOUT AGENTS

Agents are always looking for talented individuals who have the potential to book jobs and make money for them. As a talent, you are most marketable when you are properly trained and prepared to go out on auditions. Being prepared means having your marketing tools in order, especially your professional head shot and résumé.

Chris Farrell, an agent in Denver, notes, "It is in the actor's best interest to have an agent because an agent acts as a go-between, making sure the person gets paid and that it's the appropriate amount of money. This way the talent isn't put in the uncomfortable position of bickering about money when problematic situations occur. The agent can step in and be the bad guy. It puts the talent in a little less vulnerable situation. The agent knows what the rates would be and a talent might not. The agent is always looking out for the talent's best interests."

A licensed agency is franchised by SAG and is required by both SAG and AFTRA to obtain a license from consumer affairs. "Franchised by SAG" means the agency represents actors only on union jobs, and puts up a bond so that it is able to handle the talent's money. If an agency doesn't follow the rules and regulations of the union, the union can take away its franchise. The actor is thereby protected by the rules and ethics set down by the union.

Many small regions do not have SAG agents because there is not enough, if any, SAG work available. Regions that have a fairly equal amount of union and nonunion work have both union and nonunion agents.

Most actors in most regions are registered with and may be sent out by more than one agent within a given market. In Chicago, this is called being *multi-listed*. In New York and other areas, it's called *freelancing*. The other way of being represented is to sign an exclusive agreement, meaning that a single agent represents you. Los Angeles is a *signed* town—an actor there can only be represented by one agent.

HOW TO FIND A GOOD AGENT

There are several methods by which talented people find good, reputable agency representation. The major union markets are New York, Los Angeles, and Chicago (see the chart in the Appendix indicating opportunities in all other regions). Each market has directories of talent agents. The Yellow Pages business directory is another source of industry names and numbers. Ask other actors about agents they have dealt with. Call the nearest SAG branch office (see the Appendix) for listings of licensed agencies in or near your area.

Check out any agency that is not SAG franchised. Call the Better Business Bureau and make sure it has a business license. Call production companies, ad agencies, theaters, acting schools, and other actors to see what they know about the agency.

Wichita agent Gregory Bouldin suggests calling local TV stations to find out which companies advertise locally, then contracting the ones who do a lot of advertising and asking where they get their talent. Bouldin adds that appearing in plays and showcases enable agents to see your work.

In the beginning, do mailings and get to know anyone and everyone who could possibly help you. Once you have a list of people to contact, the standard procedure is to mail your head shot and résumé to each of them, following up with a phone call a week later to request an interview.

It can take some time before you find an agent you're happy with *and* who wants to represent *you*.

❏ DO YOU WANT A MANAGER?

With a manager, you have another person working on you
behalf, and this can be beneficial. A manager is often mor
willing to work with newcomers in the industry, taking a mor
personal interest in developing budding careers. Agents neec
people who are ready to work. They are generally too busy
booking people for jobs to spend time developing talent. A
manager, on the other hand, might advise newcomers on all
aspects of their career. A good manager acts as a business
consultant, a middleman between agents and talent, a mentor, a confidant, and a "shrink." Make sure your manager is
well connected, which would mean more potential opportunities for you. Competition is fierce in this industry, so the more
people you can get behind you, the better.

The New York and Los Angeles markets are more man-
ager-oriented because the industry is much larger there,
which makes it easier to get lost in the shuffle there than in
smaller areas. A good manager in the major markets can be a
real asset.

The down side of having a manager is that you have to pay
him fifteen percent when you get booked in addition to the
agency commission. So experiment a little when you first start
out. Go out there without a manager and see how it goes. If
you are not getting the results you want after a while, try getting a manager and see if things improve. If working with a
manager means you are working more, then the extra commission is well worth paying.

❏ CONDUCTING A DYNAMITE INTERVIEW

So . . . you've done your homework, you've researched the
available agents in your area, you've done your mailings, and
you've followed up with a call to each a week later. Congratulations! You've gotten your first request to come in for an interview. Most commercials call for a clean, casual look, so
dress that way. However, if you are *only* the corporate or upscale type, dress to suit your type.

QUESTIONS TO ASK *BEFORE* TAKING ON AN AGENT OR MANAGER

When meeting with agents and managers, keep in mind that ultimately you are interviewing them as much as they are interviewing you. Make sure you are comfortable with the person you are dealing with and that you are satisfied with their answers to the following questions:

1. Are you a SAG-franchised agent (or a member of the National Conference of Personal Managers)?
2. Who do you represent (clients and/or talent)?
3. What can I expect from you as an agent/manager?
4. What do you expect from me?
5. What kind of contract (if any) would I be signing?

You should discuss with an agent (and especially a manager) what, at this point, you want out of your career. He should be aligned and attuned to you and your needs. If the agent or manager doesn't have the same aspirations for you that you have for yourself, he should tell you what direction *he* sees for you. If you do not like what he suggests, he is not the right person to represent you.

It might take several meetings for you to express your desires and goals to an agent or manager and for him to respond.

Here are a few tips from the pros on attitude and presentation at that all-important meeting.

Laura Fogelman, agent, Los Angeles: "You have about five minutes to win people over and knock them out during the interview. You have to be positive, upbeat, and keep the conversation going. If you are boring, you are dead in the water. That's it. I have people who come in to my office and sit in a chair, wait for me to ask questions, and give me one-word answers. It takes two people to have a conversation. One-word answers give me nowhere to go. Find things to talk about. It's easier for us if someone comes in and is very conversational and chatty. It makes us want to talk more.

"Also, actors have to look interesting when they walk in the door. They have to dress the part. I don't mean upscale. They just have to have themselves put together. They should have a sense of style. The girl should be unique and interesting, in a way that makes people want to look at her. I have seen girls come in in coveralls and look fabulous because they have a whole 'look' down pat. Have a sense of style and look confident when you walk in the room."

Kathy Hartigree, agent, Atlanta: "Personality is very important. If a person doesn't have a flexible, pleasant personality, the indication is that they're going to be hard to work with. It is also important that actors understand the industry. If they say things in their interview that make me aware that they don't understand how the industry works, I am concerned because we're dealing in professionals here."

Jane Schaffmaster, agent, Detroit: "If you have any questions, ask them. A lot of people are afraid to ask questions. Two or three days later, they'll call and say, 'You know, I really wanted to ask you this at the time . . .' *That's* your time . . . at the interview. Also, actors can seem particularly intimidated when asked to read copy. A lot of theatrical people are very big, very loud when they come in. When given the direction to pull back, keeping it one-on-one as if talking to an old friend, they do it loud again.

"Remember to bring your head shots/résumé. Be prepared. Dress accordingly. We do industrials and commercials and the people we use are very all-American; they look, for the most part, very generic. When we see people coming in with their hair ratted, eight-inch heels, red lipstick, we can't see what they look like. It's an interview and we need to determine where to place them, so they should dress for the market they're working in."

Traci Danielli, agent, Florida: "I expect talent to show up and be on time. Also, it's important for actors to just be themselves. Don't try to be something you are not. Don't try to impress me by throwing around important names or bragging about the work you've done. Don't be negative or make excuses. I have heard every excuse in the book. I know it's hard, but don't be nervous. Just relax and be yourself."

❏ KEEPING IN TOUCH WITH YOUR AGENT

Once you have found an agent, ask him how often and when you should be in touch. Some agents want you to call in every so often. Others prefer you not call them unless you have some specific business to discuss. Calling every five minutes to see if they have anything for you is generally regarded as a nuisance—don't be pesky. Unnecessary calls tie up the phone lines and frustrate the agent.

Your agent's function is to be on the phone all day working with casting directors to secure appointments for you with production companies and ad agencies, negotiating contracts, and straightening out any problems or issues that come up. Consider a typical day in the life of an agent, as described by Mark Bonney and Michael Powell of Marquee Talent Agency in Dallas:

> It takes communicating with the casting director, preparing a breakdown consisting of either lists of actors or photo submissions (sometimes both), faxing suggestion lists back to the casting director, calling appointments out to actors, taking confirmations from actors, and giving confirmations or cancellations to casting people. Then there is the callback stage of taking appointments from casting offices, giving out calls, getting confirmations, and giving confirmations to the casting office. The same procedure happens for a booking, which of course is what the agent and actor are waiting for. Throughout the course of a job, an agent could spend a total of eight hours and receive only one booking. One commission on a scale job is $24.33.

Understanding what agents do can help you realize that although it is important to stay in touch with them, you must do so in a manner that is productive for both you and your agent. For example, send your agent picture postcards when you're appearing in something, when something important is happening in your career, or just to say hello. This way, you are keeping your face in front of the agent without taking up valuable time that could be spent arranging auditions and bookings.

❑ HANDLING CONTRACTS AND AGREEMENTS

SAG-franchised agents use a standard union contract to sign their talent. Always read it over and don't be afraid to discuss changes you desire. The answer will be yes or no. You sign a one-year contract, which is renewable for three years after the first year. Nonunion agency contracts should be gone over carefully before signing. Be sure to ask questions about any points that seem vague or unreasonable. You do not have the protection of the union with a nonfranchised agency, so be especially cautious.

The two main points to check for in a nonunion contract are commission and the "out clause." Beware if the commission is over twenty percent. The standard nonunion commission is ten to twenty percent. The out clause is the way you can get out of the contract. Look to see under what circumstances you can be released from your contract. It should also indicate how often the agent must get you out on auditions in order to meet the requirement of sole representation. Have a lawyer look over the contract to see if there are any other legalities that would be unacceptable to you.

❑ WHY ACTORS MIGHT WANT TO DROP THEIR AGENT

The number one reason actors want to drop an agent is that they are not being sent out on enough auditions and bookings. They think if they were with someone else, they would have more opportunities. Sometimes, it's simply a case of the-grass-is-always-greener mentality.

The people who jump around tend to be the ones who are having a difficult time booking jobs. The agent could very well be submitting the actor for auditions, but the casting director or whoever decides who gets to audition is not choosing that actor. Or the actor might not get the job because her audition techniques are not honed enough to have the competitive edge.

An actor may choose to leave his agent if he disagrees with the agent as to what types of castings he's being sent out for. The actor will tend to blame the agent and decide to jump to another one, believing that he will book more with the new agent.

Kathy Hartigree notes, "Most people resign from our agency because they do not feel they are getting enough work. What everyone must remember is that *getting work is not what an agent does*. Auditions and interviews are what the agent is responsible for. Performers must understand it is *their* responsibility to win the job once the agent gets them into the audition or interview."

If you are not happy with your agent, arrange a meeting to discuss the issues. If you cannot come to a reasonable conclusion, it may be time to hire another person to represent you. Keep in mind, though, that your agent still gets residual payments for any jobs he secured for you while you were represented by him. Other than that, most agents agree that if you are truly unhappy, it is better for all concerned that you move on.

❏ WHY AN AGENT MIGHT WANT TO DROP AN ACTOR

The number one reason agents want to drop an actor is repeated unprofessional conduct. For example, if you do not show up on time, do not show up at all, try to bypass the agency by giving your phone number to a producer or ad agency, or are difficult to work with.

You must trust the agent you are working with and be able to take constructive criticism. Agents generally do not drop actors because they are not booking. They expect it could take a year or more to book something. As long as you are selected to come in and audition, you are enthusiastically auditioning, your craft is honed, and you have a positive attitude, your agent will stick with you.

❏ THE UNIONS AND THEIR JURISDICTIONS

The unions, SAG, AFTRA, and Equity, represent the industry; each union has its own contract. You may call each union and request a contract. Each union governs specific areas of the business:

1. The Screen Actors Guild (SAG) governs actors and extras appearing on film and in voice-overs. This includes motion pictures (whether shown on television or in movie theaters) and television commercials.
2. The American Federation of Television and Radio Artists (AFTRA) has jurisdiction over live and taped television shows and commercials, soap operas, disc jockeys and other radio performers.
3. Actors' Equity Association (Equity) governs performers and stage managers in live theater.

WHY JOIN THE UNION?

In regions where the work is split fairly equally between union and nonunion work, actors will be faced with the choice of either joining the union or not. According to Nevada agent Jaki Baskow, "Actors may choose not to join for the first couple of years. After they've built up résumé credits, they join the unions, almost without exception. Producers want to pay the actors next to nothing for a nonunion commercial, and actors can get really tired of this, as do the agents."

If you are seeking work in a region where most of the jobs are union commercials, you'll want to become a member of SAG and AFTRA as soon as possible. Membership in either of these unions is an indication that you are not "green." It means you have already done the work it takes to become a member. Agents will feel they are taking less of a chance on you because you have already proven yourself.

Benefits of joining the union include:

1. *Protection*—Union contracts establish minimum (scale) payments for talent performing in all industry-related

media under their jurisdiction. They also make sure that performers on union jobs are employed under reasonable working conditions. The unions determine work standards and establish guidelines for the education of children in the business. SAG-franchised agencies must follow the rules set down by the union. If there are problems with franchised agencies or on union jobs, the union is there to make sure the talent's interests are protected.

2. *Health insurance, pension coverage, and cost-of-living adjustments* (COLAs).

HOW TO JOIN THE UNION

The easiest union to join is AFTRA. All you have to do is fill out the application, pay the membership, and voilà—you're a member.

There are basically three methods by which performers become eligible for membership in Equity.

1. If you are hired to appear in an Equity production, all you have to do is bring your contract to the nearest Equity office and pay your membership initiation fee.

2. If you are a member of another union, SAG or AFTRA, for instance, and have fulfilled certain work criteria (one principal role, one "under five"* AFTRA job, or three days of extra work), you can join Equity by bringing in your contracts or written verification from the parent union† and paying the appropriate fees. *Note:* Your parent union dues must be paid up before you can join Equity.

3. The Equity Membership Candidate Program (EMC) involves working your way into Equity by finding a job with a participating theater as a production person or an understudy, depending on the specific theater. To become eligible, you must accumulate about fifty weeks of this kind of work.‡ Notify the union when you become eligible to join.

*An "under five" is a speaking role of less than five lines.
†The first union you join is your parent union.
‡The fifty weeks do not have to be consecutive. Sometimes you can test out after forty hours. Check with Equity's current requirements for the EMC program.

There are several ways to join SAG. Most common are:

1. Getting a job on a union project. After you do one union job, you become "Taft-Hartleyed," meaning you can do as many union jobs as you want for the next thirty days, after which you must join the union and pay your dues before you do another union job. If you don't, the production company will be fined.
2. Getting hired as an extra on three union jobs. Check with your local SAG office. Rules and regulations regarding extra work vary from state to state.
3. Entering SAG through your parent union. Check with SAG for current requirements. Again, your dues for the parent organization must be paid in full before you can join a sister union.

In a right-to-work state, companies cannot refuse to hire actors because they do not belong to the union or because they do not *want* to join the union. The biggest misconception union actors have about working in a right-to-work state is that they can do both union and nonunion work. Union actors who work on nonunion projects are violating Rule One of the agreement they signed when they joined the union. Right-to-work states are Alabama, Arizona, Arkansas, Florida, Georgia, Indiana, Iowa, Kansas, Louisiana, Mississippi, Nebraska, Nevada, North Carolina, North Dakota, South Carolina, Tennessee, Texas, Utah, Virginia, and Wyoming. In union commercials, you cannot be under contract for two competing products (such as Tide and Wisk detergents). One advertiser would never want the same person on the air advertising a competitive product.

❏ INTERVIEWS WITH CAROL INGBER AND AL ONORATO

Now that you have become familiar with the roles of agents, managers, and unions in the business of making commercials, you may want to read the following interviews, which explore the nuts and bolts of these jobs. Carol Ingber, of Ingber and Associates in New York, and Al Onorato, who works as a talent manager in Los Angeles, offer these insights:

CAROL INGBER

What does it mean for an actor to sign with an agent? What is freelancing?

To *sign* with an agent means the talent signs a SAG and AFTRA agency contract to be represented exclusively by that particular agent for one year. This means the actor cannot go out on commercial auditions for any other agency. After the initial contract, the actor has the option to sign for either one, two, or three years.

The reason people feel they need to be signed is so that they have a business relationship with someone who will groom them and take care of them. My first responsibility as an agent is to my signed clients. If a casting director calls and gives me a time slot for an actor, I'm going to give the time to my signed clients first.

Freelancing means an actor can work with multiple agents. In New York, actors can freelance. In Los Angeles, however, actors must sign exclusive contracts with one agent.

What do you look for when deciding whether or not to represent an actor?

I look for someone who has a good attitude, someone who treats people with respect regardless of their position in the business. If one of my assistants says to me, "I just got off the phone with so and so who sent in a picture. She really sounds nice on the phone," I'll make a point of remembering that person. In an industry where today's assistant can become tomorrow's agent, it pays to be respectful to anyone you work with in the industry.

I treat talent in a professional manner and I expect the same in return. I'm not interested in people who either show up late or not at all. If I leave a message for them, they should not wait twenty-four hours to return my call. I expect actors to tell me when they are going out of town (booking out*). It's

*When talent "book out," they give the agent or manager dates when they are not available for work.

important for agent and talent to work as a team. Our work together involves a fifty-fifty partnership.

If you sign a talent who doesn't book right away, how long will you continue to represent her?

When I believe in someone, I'll continue to work with her as long as it takes. I have a client who has been with me for six years and she just booked her first network spot. I have had clients who have booked right away, but I also know that it can take a solid year before a good streak starts.

There is no longer a statistical rule as to how many times it takes to audition to book something. This is because of the competition factor. Now there are fewer auditions to go out on and more people in the field, so the competition is stiffer.

What is the actor's job in developing his career?

To be professional. To take classes. This is his part in the teamwork with the agency. When talent are not up to par, they have to listen to their agent. If their agent says they have to do something, they must *do it!*

What do you look for in a head shot/résumé?

I like to see that an actor has done some theater work. I look for a picture that sort of hits me. I may be attracted to something in the cover letter. It's hard to define specifically what makes me want to call someone in. Something in the presentation grabs my attention and makes me want to meet the person.

Any thoughts about what should be in the cover letter?

Don't write a two-page letter. Every agent knows why you're writing us. Make it short and sweet. I get more than thirty pictures a day. I want to be able to read the note fast.

Do you expect actors to have a demo tape?

No. I don't look at them. I would rather get an idea of the actor's potential from observing the person in front of me.

What do you look for in a general interview?

Actors come across best when they are just being themselves, but if I ask an actor where he comes from, I don't want a fifteen-minute dissertation. Let the agent guide you. There are certain things we need to get out of that first meeting. What you think is important may not be. Say what you need to say and allow your personality to come out. Don't respond to the agent's questions with one-word answers, but don't go on for a long time, either. Try not to come across as desperate or overanxious.

Are there pet peeves actors should avoid?

Actors who don't want to accept early audition calls are high on my "peeve" list. I have to be in my office at 9:30 A.M., after going out to the theater and returning at 1:00 A.M. If I have a client in the show, we may go out afterwards, yet I still have to be in the office at 9:30 A.M. If I am not, you will have a problem with that. And if I can do it, *you* can do it too.

Actors with bad attitudes don't go over well with agents. You see this in actors who don't return phone calls, don't tell their agent when they'll be out of town, and blow off auditions. Some actors treat commercials lightly, as a secondary interest, yet commercials can be a powerful venue for actors to showcase their talent. I have seen a lot of clients who have gone on to TV and film because they were good in a commercial and were noticed by someone. Actors have been written up in *Newsweek* because of a sensational commercial they appeared in. I have gotten calls from Spielberg's office and Neil Simon's office, asking about actors they've seen in commercials. Commercials can definitely lead to better things.

Will you work with someone who isn't in the union yet?

Of course, It's very exciting when an actor gets his first booking and is waivered* into the union. Commercials are the

---

*Being *waivered*, or *Taft-Hartleyed*, is basically an entry into the union. The waiver allows you to work on as many union jobs as you want within a thirty-day period, after which you become a "must join." This means that you must be prepared to join the union for the next job you get after the waiver.

way for many people to get into the union. I am interested in talented people with an acting background. This includes people who have studied in small colleges in the Midwest as well as students from Yale or Juilliard.

How much can someone earn from a single commercial?

An actor can make anywhere from $443.25 to $40,000 or more from one commercial. I have a client who has made six figures from a spot that has been running for six years. In fact, I have known many actors who have appeared in commercials that have run for years and have easily made six figures.

What is the most important piece of advice you think you can give?

Believe in who and what you are. Hang in there and don't give up. Always be honest with the people you are working with. You'll get a lot further if you make a habit of being honest with yourself and with others in the business.

AL ONORATO

What is the difference between an agent and a manager?

The basic difference is that SAG-franchised agents are licensed and managers are not.

Agents are interested in finding jobs for their clients. Managers are interested in shaping their clients' careers for the long term. Also, agents generally handle a lot of people, while a manager has to be selective. For instance, an agent may handle a hundred people. A manager would have perhaps twenty-five.

A manager puts a lot of time and effort into nurturing and building the career, whereas an agent doesn't have time for that kind of personal attention. If, for example, someone is going to an audition, a manager would work with that person on the material, doing as much preparation and getting as much information on the audition as possible and following up on the results. It is also up to the manager to try to get feedback as to how an audition or a meeting went and how the talent is doing in one-on-one situations.

How does someone find a good manager?

Get out and talk to people. It's like finding a doctor, a minister, or a dentist. Many times, you just have to go on instinct. Ask managers for their ideas on building a career. Ask what types of people they handle. You might inquire about other people in the business they network with. The word *clout* comes in here—if they need to get someone on the phone—be it the casting director, the head of a studio, or a network executive, can they do it?

Is there a point when doing commercials might be a detriment to someone's career? When she should stop doing them?

If you're in television and you want to make a move into the movie industry, it can be a detriment to be too well known as a television personality. It's the same principle with commercials.

If you're building a career, you want to be seen enough to make people want to see more of you, but avoid being overexposed in one medium. Visibility is very important in the beginning, then you want to stop doing things so that people will want to see more of you.

9

THE AUDITIONING
PROCESS

❏ GETTING AUDITIONS

FINDING OUT ABOUT CALLS

In the primary markets (New York, Los Angeles, and Chicago) as well as in the secondary markets (Dallas, Miami/Orlando, and Atlanta), the best way to find out about auditions is through an agent. Agents are aware of most of the calls and will set up an appointment for their clients. Trade magazines such as *Back Stage* (New York) and *Drama-Logue* and *Back Stage West* (L.A.) also provide information on auditions, but most of the auditions listed are "open calls" or "cattle calls." This means that you'll have no specific appointment. The auditions are open to the public and you'll probably have to wait a very long time for your turn.

In smaller, regional areas, actors may audition through agents and/or they may send their head shots/résumés out to local casting directors and production companies. As casting director Patty Kallis says, "It is easier to call ten agents and ask for ten different people than to call a hundred people directly." It is perfectly acceptable in any market to do direct mailings to casting people and production houses. However, agency representation should be your ultimate goal.

HOW AN ACTOR IS SELECTED TO AUDITION

The typical casting call scenario begins with a casting director getting a call from a director or producer. The art director, producer, and writer present the casting director with a *storyboard*, which is a frame-by-frame pictorial layout of how the commercial is to be shot (fig. 9). The casting director makes a list of people to call in—people he has either worked with before or selected from photographs/résumés he has on file. Then the casting director gives the character breakdown to the agents. Each agent submits her ideas (people she feels fit the part) to the casting director. The casting director goes through the lists and decides whom to bring in for the audition.

The casting director calls the agents to discuss their choices. If an agent feels strongly about an actor who was not chosen to audition, the agent will go to bat for that actor, trying to convince the casting director to call that person in. While you might have all the right elements defined in the character breakdown, it's possible that you won't be selected because the casting director already has enough people from your agency.

Having your picture and résumé in front of the casting director helps a lot. Casting people also refer to two union-produced directories to find actors—*The Player's Guide* (New York) and *The Academy Directory* (Los Angeles). Make sure that the directory listing you use is a legitimate one.*

WHAT TO DO WHEN YOU GET THE CALL

Once the casting director has decided whom to call in for the audition, he notifies the agents. The agents then call the talent to let them know they got the audition and to give them important information about it.

Always have a pen and pencil ready by the phone. It is important to be prepared to take notes the second you receive the call. This is a very fast-paced business. It is a mark against you if you are not prepared to move smoothly and quickly as agents run off the important facts about the audition. Nothing annoys people in this business more than having to repeat themselves (or wait) because you weren't prepared to take

---

*Beware of other "directories" produced by people who take your money, claiming casting directors cast from these publications when, in fact, the directory is only produced as a money-making venture and is not a legitimate source for casting directors seeking talent.

OPEN ON A COCO'S CHEF AND A COCO'S MANAGER SEATED AT A CUTTING BOARD TABLE. MANAGER HAS AN ADDING MACHINE. CHEF HAS A PILE OF FRESH VEGETABLES.

MANAGER: Mr. generous Coco's Chef here has created something new for dinner.

CHEF NODS SMUGLY.

Calls it his Three Course Dinner.

CUT TO ECU SLOW TRACKING SHOT OF ENTREES

He gives you a choice of six of our most popular entrees, ...

TRACK TO FULL SCREEN ECU OF TERIYAKI CHICKEN.

like Teriyaki Chicken

SETTLE ON FRESH RED SNAPPER.

or fresh Red Snapper...

FOLLOWED BY SOUPS AND SALAD,

plus hot soup or salad, ...

FIGURE 9. Typical storyboard. (EVANS HARDY + YOUNG INC.)

THEN A COUPLE OF APPETIZERS

and *your choice of four delicious appetizers ...*

AND A FEW DESSERTS.

or six tempting desserts.

*CUT BACK TO MEN. AS MANAGER TALKS,
CHEF PUSHES ONE TOMATO FORWARD.*

*Then he says to sell it all for just $7.99.
to which I say...*

*HE THEN CHOPS IT IN TWO, FORCEFULLY,
WITH A LARGE CLEAVER AND LOOKS
MEANINGFULLY AT MANAGER.*

SFX: Chunck!!!

Good idea. Very good idea.

CUT TO FULL PRODUCT SET-UP.

SUPER: $7.99. COCO'S.

AVO: Coco's Three Course Dinners,: Just $7.99.

MANAGER: (VO) Very, very good idea.

their call. And if an agent forgets to tell you something, be sure to ask.

You should be given the following information about the audition:

1. The date of the audition.
2. The time of the audition.
3. The date of the shoot, Never audition if you are not going to be available for the shoot. It is a horrendous waste of everyone's time.
4. The product the commercial is advertising.
5. Any conflicts (if the job is a union commercial). Never assume what the conflicts are. When you accept the job you will actually be entering into an agreement where the conflicts are unwritten, yet you are legally responsible to be free of them. Have your agent tell you specifically in what categories of products the ad agency is asking you to be free of conflicts. There can be surprises; for instance, you might not realize a detergent has a whitener in it, creating a conflict not only with detergents but with other products containing whiteners.
6. If there is any food involved. If so, ask if you will be required to eat the food. Never attend a food-related audition (when eating is involved) if you cannot eat the food. If for instance, you are a vegetarian and the commercial involves eating a pepperoni pizza at a shoot, you will not be able to pick the pepperoni off.
7. How the audition is going to run. Terms like *network, regional, spot, test, dealer, seasonal,* and *cable* give you some indication of how much you could make (see Chapter 13: "How Much Can I Make?").
8. What to wear. If the agent doesn't know, consider the product being advertised and who you are in the spot, then dress for that part.

❑ THE DAY OF THE AUDITION

WHAT TO WEAR

Dressing for the part improves your chances of getting the job. If you're supposed to be at a party, dress up a bit. If you're supposed to be cleaning a bathroom, dress more casually. In general, if your agent doesn't give you detailed instructions, wear casual, clean, and comfortable clothes. Jeans are okay, but stay away from all-white clothing. White causes the camera lens to close down (it perceives white as light, which confuses the metering system), making you look dark and hard to see.

Don't wear all black either. Black is a serious, dramatic color, contrasting with the happy, playful energy of commercials. If, however, black is called for by the character (such as a poet at a reading, or a guest at a cocktail party), *do* wear black. Otherwise, wear colors that enhance your skin tones, making you look fresh and healthy.

Stay away from clothing that distracts from you. Big, bold prints and busy patterns are definitely not recommended. Keep jewelry simple and at a minimum. (Notice that in commercials, women in supermarkets or at home cleaning, cooking, or playing with their children do not wear jewelry that stands out in any way.)

Men should stay away from neck chains. Gold necklaces can be interpreted as slick. This would be inconsistent with a character such as a warm dad, guy-next-door, or anyone portraying vulnerability. If you wear an earring, wear one only if you feel the character you are auditioning for would actually wear one, for example, if the character is a musician, slacker, or someone with a "street" attitude.

WHAT TO EXPECT WHEN YOU GET THERE

Be on time, or even better, be ten to fifteen minutes early. This will give you time to find which studio your audition is in, relax, warm up your voice, and look over your script (if applicable). Come in with a positive attitude, knowing good commercial technique. Have your head shot/résumé with you. The

FIGURE 10.

SAG / AFTRA
COMMERCIAL AUDITION REPORT

THIS FORM MUST BE FILLED OUT IN INK

PAGE_____ OF_____

COMMERCIAL PERFORMERS:
▸ Print your name.
▸ Print agent's name.
▸ Circle applicable interview.

TO BE COMPLETED BY CASTING DIRECTOR

(X) WHERE APPLICABLE
TELEVISION ☐   ON CAMERA ☐   OFF CAMERA ☐   RADIO ☐   AUDITION DATE

INTENDED USE   UNION: SAG ☐ AFTRA ☐   Person to whom correspondence concerning this form shall be sent:
(Name & Phone Number)

CASTING REPRESENTATIVE NAME   COMMERICAL TITLE - NAME & NUMBER   ADVERTISER NAME

PRODUCT   JOB NUMBER   ADVERTISING AGENCY AND CITY   PRODUCTION COMPANY

INSTRUCTIONS: Circle the name of performer hired if known.   Mail one copy to SAG OR AFTRA on the 1st and 15th of each month.

TO BE COMPLETED BY PERFORMERS

NAME (PLEASE PRINT)	SOCIAL SECURITY NUMBER	AGENT (PLEASE PRINT)	ACTUAL CALL	TIME IN	TIME OUT	INITIAL	CIRCLE INTERVIEW NUMBER	SEX (X) M F	AGE (X) +40 -40	ETHNICITY (X) AP B C LH I	PWD (X)
							1st 2nd 3rd 4th				
							1st 2nd 3rd 4th				
							1st 2nd 3rd 4th				
							1st 2nd 3rd 4th				
							1st 2nd 3rd 4th				
							1st 2nd 3rd 4th				
							1st 2nd 3rd 4th				
							1st 2nd 3rd 4th				
							1st 2nd 3rd 4th				
							1st 2nd 3rd 4th				
							1st 2nd 3rd 4th				
							1st 2nd 3rd 4th				
							1st 2nd 3rd 4th				
							1st 2nd 3rd 4th				
							1st 2nd 3rd 4th				
							1st 2nd 3rd 4th				

This recorded audition material will not be used as a client demo, an audience reaction commercial, for copy testing or as a scratch track without payment of the minimum compensation provided for in the Commercials Contract and shall be used solely to determine the suitability of the performer for a specific commercial.

The only reason for requesting information on ethnicity, sex, age, and disability is for the talent unions to monitor applicant flow. The furnishing of such information is on a VOLUNTARY basis. The Authorized Representative's signature on this form shall not constitute a verification of the information supplied by performers.

Asian/Pacific — AP   Latino/Hispanic — L
Black — B   Native American — I
Caucasian — C   Performer with Disability — PWD

casting director will not always collect it, but always have it with you.

There will be a *sign-in sheet* (see fig. 10, SAG/AFTRA Commercial Audition Report) in the reception area. Do not sign in right away. Wait until you've had a chance to freshen up a bit, relax, and look over your script.

Expect the waiting room to be full of people who are your type. Expect to see a *script* and/or a *storyboard*. Dialogue often will appear on the right, and any direction, on the left.

The casting director will usually take a *Polaroid* of you (fig. 11) and give you a *size card* to fill out. (Do not be distressed by your Polaroid; it is used purely for reference.) Then sit down and wait to be called in. Use this time to go over the script and perhaps get familiar with the other actors. You'll tend to see the same people at many auditions, so becoming friendly may be useful.

FIGURE 11. **A sample Polaroid.**

WHAT TO DO AFTER YOU ARE CALLED IN TO THE AUDITION ROOM

In a typical audition room setup (figs. 12–19), expect to see a camera, a television monitor (which is positioned so the screen is not visible to you), lights, and a *cue card.** Generally at the first call (audition), the casting director is the only person in the room with you. There may be a camera person or assistant in the room also.

Read over the cue card first. Get used to the handwriting and the sentence structure, which may be different from your typewritten script. Keep track of any words that have been changed or added.

THE ACTUAL AUDITION

When you enter the audition room the person running the session (a casting director or a session runner) should give you basic or specific direction regarding the attitude and read expected for the particular situation. He may ask you to rehearse once. You should rehearse out loud as if the tape were running. This way, the casting director can give you any adjustments, notes, or "tweaks" he feels are necessary.

Then your audition will be taped. You may hear the following words and phrases during the process:

1. *Take your mark.* There is a mark on the floor; standing there will place you in the proper light and at the correct distance from the camera.

2. *Roll camera.* This means the camera is on and recording—taping the audition.

3. *Action.* This means it's time to say your lines.

4. *Cut.* The camera is no longer recording.

You may be taped once or twice. Do not try to determine whether or not the director liked you based on the number of tapings. The creative team has predetermined how many takes are necessary. The next time you'll hear about the job is

*A cue card is the script written in large letters and placed near the camera lens. This eliminates the need for actors to memorize copy.

FIGURE 12. **Find which studio your audition is in.**

FIGURE 13. **Sign-in sheet, storyboard, and any directions outside room.**

FIGURE 14. **Analyze script in reception area.**

FIGURE 15. **There will be a mark on the floor for you to take your place in the correct light and focus.**

FIGURE 16. **You will face your cue card which is set up next to the camera.**

FIGURE 17. **First call directed by casting director.**

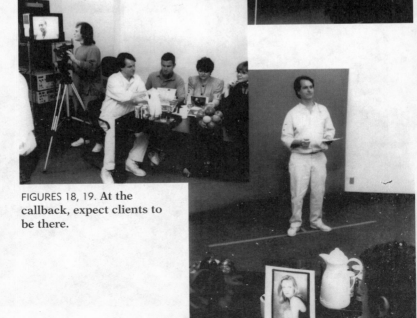

FIGURES 18, 19. **At the callback, expect clients to be there.**

when (or if) you get a *callback*. Getting a callback means that you are asked back to read again for (usually) the director, producer, art director, and writer.

WHEN YOU CAN EXPECT TO BE INFORMED IF YOU GOT THE JOB

Usually you'll know within a week or two after the first casting session if you got a callback. Generally, the auditions are completed within four to five days, with callbacks taking place the following week, but this varies considerably.

Two to three days after the callbacks, there is a preproduction meeting at which the choice of talent is introduced to the client for approval. The shoot is generally scheduled approximately three days to a week later. But nothing in this business is carved in stone—you could conceivably get a call and shoot the next day.

❏ THE COMPETITIVE EDGE

Now that you know how the auditioning process works, consider these seven ways to make sure you come out on top:

1. Know commercial technique. Know how to analyze the script quickly and make you and the situation you create in the audition seem one hundred percent real and honest. (Chapter 10 sets out specific techniques for auditioning.)

2. Maintain a positive attitude. It's not always easy to keep a positive attitude when you walk into a room full of people who look a lot like you and may have more experience. Keep in mind that the casting director needs you—you make him look good. He is expecting you to do a good job because he has either seen you in a show or been impressed by your résumé, or your agent has convinced him that you would do a good job. Your agent needs you. She only makes money when and if you book the job. The creative team wants you to do a good job because they want a wide selection of strong talent to choose from. It's like a puzzle, and you have the missing part that brings it all together.

Just by getting this audition, you've already passed a screening process. You've been given this time slot over many,

many other people. So stay positive throughout the audition, even when the unexpected happens.

3. Always expect the unexpected. Things do not always go as planned in this business. Being able to go with the flow is a crucial trait successful actors cultivate. For instance, you may worry when you see the crowded reception area. Chances are the casting director has set up the audition to run smoothly (not to be overcrowded), but some unplanned event has caused a backup. For example, the casting director may have been asked to bring people in four at a time, then on the day of the audition, the creative team decide to see people two at a time. This will cause a backup. Or, the first group of actors to be auditioned is late, causing a backup.

Sometimes a backup is unavoidable. The casting director may get a call in the middle of the audition, meaning he or she has to leave the room—perhaps to deal with some problem that has come up that has nothing to do with you or your audition. This creates a backup. It is important not to let such happenings affect your attitude. At any audition, you should always seem pleased to be there, from the moment you walk into the room until after you have left the site.

Also, if you sense any negative vibrations in the audition room, focus on the fact that you are not the cause. It could be that the art director and the producer are disagreeing about something creative, or any number of concerns. Don't assume that it has anything to do with you.

You may find it difficult to keep a positive attitude when you find out how quickly the auditioning process goes. You wish you had more time. Realize that what is asked of you in the auditioning room is all that is needed of you. Don't make yourself crazy trying to analyze your performance after you leave the audition. Just give it your best, then go on to the next thing.

4. Always expect to be put at a disadvantage. Be prepared for such things as the session being canceled. Maybe the character you came in for has been changed. The cue card may be difficult to read. Props that could make it easier for you to audition may not be available. Do your best to take each thing as it comes without getting visibly discouraged or frustrated. It's all part of being professional in this industry.

5. Be flexible. Be open to change and direction. For example, you've figured out how you're going to do your copy. You get into the room and the casting director gives you an entirely different set of directions. You must be flexible and say, "Okay."

If you aren't flexible, when things change, you'll become frustrated and will not be able to give a good audition. Avoid showing frustration and *never* show anger. Do not present yourself in a negative light.

6. Convey the feeling that you are intelligent. Being knowledgeable about the business and knowing commercial technique lets the creative team know that you are an intelligent professional and serious about your career.

7. Give the feeling that you have an unending well of creativity. Leave the creative team with the impression that you have much more to give, even after the camera has stopped rolling.

10

THE TECHNIQUE

❏ GETTING STARTED

ENTERING THE ROOM

It is important to realize that you are essentially auditioning from the moment you enter the room. Since commercials are basically playful and upbeat, you should walk into the audition room with a positive, happy energy. You must be comfortable enough to smile confidently.

With film or television auditions, you usually get about ten or fifteen minutes for your audition. You come into the audition room, chat with the casting director, then get into the mood and read one to four pages of copy. In commercial auditions, the pace is much faster. Your auditioning time slot is only about five minutes, depending on whether or not there is copy and how much copy is involved. There is no time to waste. Be ready as soon as you enter the doorway.

If you are auditioning with other people, you want to appear that you are comfortable with them right off the bat. Doing so will create a favorable impression with the person directing you, setting the mood for a positive auditioning experience. You also should appear excited and delighted to be there—and why wouldn't you be? This is the moment you've been waiting for, the chance to audition for a commercial spot!

To win at the commercial game, you have to *be* the character one hundred percent. You want to feel as though you are experiencing (or reexperiencing) the situation and avoid appearing "removed." You *must* look completely involved in each commercial scenario. In order to achieve this, the first thing you must be familiar with is the space you are given to work with.

COMMERCIAL SPACE

You have a certain amount of space to work with in front of the camera. It is very different from space used in film, theater, sitcoms, and soap operas. Most beginners automatically assume that the physical space they have to work with is fairly small. It *certainly* is smaller than the space available to you in the other media. But there is a way to expand the space and play in it.

The commercial space is like a sandbox. Its parameters seem small, but you can really play in it. You can bring a friend into it. You can make sand castles and mud pies. You can throw sand out of the sandbox or up into the air. You can run into the corners, dig holes and tunnels, and jump up and down in your sandbox. All of a sudden, what you thought was a relatively small space doesn't seem so small after all. There isn't much room to walk around, but there is plenty of space to play and release your personality.

The following exercises will help you see how you can expand the space you are given and give your performance more dimensions. Have a friend or family member tape your practice sessions with a video camera so you can review your performance afterwards.

EXERCISE 1

Pretend you are reaching for something on a table. Try doing it two ways: First, stand firmly in place, extend your arm, and pick something up from the table. This shows one dimension.

Now, reach for something on the table by putting one leg in front of the other and tilting forward. This gives the feeling that you have just walked over from somewhere else and have not quite finished getting to where you are going. You are still *in frame* (visible on the monitor) and have given the space more dimension by this forward movement.

While you are giving this small space more dimensions, you are building in time beats for yourself—giving yourself opportunities to express your personality. This is important since what the client is buying is your personality. There's only one way to give yourself time and that is to be familiar with the space. Giving the space different dimensions helps you gain the edge needed to win in commercials.

EXERCISE 2

While on-camera, try looking over to your side. As you'll see when you look at the tape, you have given the viewer the impression that you are looking over at something. You have now expanded the space to another dimension simply by looking slightly off-camera.

Now, record yourself looking off-camera and laughing at what you see. Look back at the tape and see how your mind conjures up images of what might be going on. Record yourself looking off to the side and appearing curious about what you see. Play this back and see how the viewer might be affected by your performance.

To effectively expand the space, you must really "see" what you are imagining. To do this, you must go into great detail as you imagine each scenario.

BODY LANGUAGE

Try leaning forward and saying something to the camera. See how leaning in implies closeness, creating a sense of intimacy with the viewer. The slightest body tilt can change a relationship on-camera.

EXERCISE **3**

Work with a friend. Stand next to each other with your bodies facing straight forward toward the camera. Look at the camera, then look at each other. Now, look back into the camera. Because your bodies are facing the camera, your primary relationship is with the viewer.

Turn your bodies in slightly toward each other and look at each other. Your primary relationship is now with each other.

Keep your bodies turned toward each other and turn your faces to the camera. Now, the viewer is your secondary relationship.

Turn your bodies straight toward the camera again. Once again, your primary relationship is with the viewer and your secondary relationship is with each other.

It's important to know how your body position can affect your relationship to the camera (the viewer) because you can use it to enhance your performance. You have control. You can make certain choices.

Now, stand together and nudge each other with your elbows. Something else happened to the relationship—a sense of mischief or fun, perhaps. The slightest movement can mean something different. In some ways, commercial space is microscopic and unforgiving. Everything you do in this space is important to the message you are conveying.

❏ IN THE AUDITION ROOM

TAKING YOUR MARK

There will be a mark (usually a piece of tape) on the floor for you to stand on. This is called *taking your mark*. Your mark will place you in the position for the best lighting and camera focus during the audition.

WORKING WITH CUE CARDS

In any unionized state, a *cue card* is required by SAG. A cue card is the script written out on a large sheet of paper in large print. The cue card should be placed so that it is easy to read while looking into the lens of the camera. This makes it easier for your eyes to sweep across the cue card while looking (often) into the camera.

Sometimes a cue card is placed in a position that puts you at a disadvantage during the audition. If, for instance, someone places the cue card underneath the camera lens, you will have to look down at the cue card, then up at the camera, then down again at the card, etc. Reading a card that is placed next to the camera lens is much easier. The slight back-and-forth motion of your eyes as you read the cue card and look back to the camera is acceptable and expected. If the cue card is hard to see because you forgot your glasses or it is placed much too far away from the camera lens and you see it can be easily moved (if it's on an easel, for example), don't be afraid to ask for it to be moved.

As soon as you enter the audition room, look over the cue card. Make sure you can read the handwriting. Look for any changes in the script. A word may have been changed. Being comfortable with the cue card will make it easier to move your eyes smoothly from the cue card to the eye of the camera. Try to look at the camera as much as possible.

Here's what you can do to practice:

EXERCISE 4

On a large piece of paper (a 26½-inch × 34-inch artist's pad, for instance), write down copy taken from a magazine ad. On a separate piece of paper, draw a circle approximately the size of a camera lens and place it next to the copy. Position both sheets of paper at eye level on a wall in front of you. This will simulate cue card copy and the lens of the camera. Practice moving your eyes from the copy to the lens (eye of the camera).

MEMORIZING COPY

If you are auditioning in New York, Chicago, or Los Angeles (where cue cards must be provided under SAG law), it is best not to waste energy trying to memorize your script. If you memorize the script and words are changed on the cue card, it could throw you off.

Another problem can surface if you haven't completely memorized the material and your eyes go blank as you try to remember the words. The cue card is there so you don't have to be concerned with remembering the script. Your energy can best be put to use preparing your character, analyzing the script, and making your performance as real as possible.

RELATING TO THE CAMERA

Think of a laser beam running from your eye to the center of the camera lens, into the back of the television monitor, and out through the monitor to the person viewing the tape.

The way for you to relate to the camera is to look directly into the "eye" or center of the lens. Relate to the camera the way you would to a long-cherished friend. You want to come across as open, friendly, and approachable. It's easier to avoid being intimidated by the camera if you pretend it's someone or something you feel warm, friendly, and familiar with. The camera is no longer a cold, intimidating piece of plastic and metal—it's your very best pal, your favorite aunt, someone you like very much—someone who likes you too. Make the camera someone you can be vulnerable with, someone you can let your personality out to.

Unless otherwise indicated, talk to the camera as if you are talking to one person. Keep in mind that if you have a background in theater and stage, you may (at first) tend to be too "big," projecting your character and lines the way you would on stage when you are performing for a theater full of people.

In commercials, you need to have a one-to-one relationship with the camera, as when you are talking with someone who is right next to you.

HOW YOU ARE "FRAMED" (HOW YOU LOOK IN THE CAMERA)

For auditions, assume that you are framed from the midchest up or waist up. Never ask, "How am I framed?" You do not have to be concerned with the technical aspects of the audition. You should be acting from head to toe, no matter *how* you are framed.

If, for instance, you are supposed to appear tired, not only should your face look fatigued, your body language should say "I'm pooped" as well. Your responsibility is to act properly within the context of your mark.

Generally, the person directing you will be standing somewhere near the camera. The monitor will be facing him. He can either look and talk directly to you, or he can look at the monitor while talking to you. The director usually looks at the monitor because things look different on the monitor than they do to the naked eye.

Before the camera starts rolling, if the director is speaking to you and relating to you by looking at the monitor, the way to relate (or look) back is to look directly into the eye of the camera. If the director is looking at you while speaking to you, look at him when you speak to him. However, as soon as the camera starts rolling, begin relating to the camera.

When the camera is rolling and someone is interviewing you from off-camera, ask the director if you should respond by looking directly into the camera or off-camera. Usually, the answer will be into the camera. It's okay to ask, just to be sure.

In two-person auditions, the person running the camera wants to frame you so that both faces can be seen clearly with the shoulder and chest areas visible as well. The chest area indicates the energy of the whole body. In commercials, body language is important. The following exercise will help prepare you for two-person auditions.

EXERCISE 5

Stand about four feet from a friend. Notice that on the monitor you appear to be much farther apart. You appear unfriendly.

Now stand close together, facing the camera with your arms slightly brushing. Generally, this position might feel a bit too close for comfort (perhaps even a bit intrusive). On the monitor, however, you look comfortably close and friendly.

REHEARSING AND TAKING DIRECTION

Usually you will get a chance to rehearse before the tape starts rolling. Rehearse out loud the same way you plan to do the commercial for the camera. That way, the person directing you can give you any adjustments or notes (changes in the way the material is to be presented).

As an actor, it is important that you be open and willing to take direction. Do not comment on or critique any direction you may be given. Be accommodating when you are given adjustments, maintaining your positive attitude the entire time you are in the audition room.

You should be like a piece of putty, molding yourself to the director's instructions. After you do what is asked of you, you may suggest doing it again with an idea you have.

In some cases, you might not get a rehearsal because something totally spontaneous is wanted from you. If this happens, just try to relax and give it your best shot.

SLATING YOUR NAME

The first thing you'll be asked to do after the camera begins rolling is to slate your name. This means to say your name (first and last). During the slate, you should be smiling and looking very pleased to be there. Your personality should already be radiating energy, flowing right up through your body and out to the viewer.

When you slate, look right into the eye of the camera and speak clearly with an upbeat, positive attitude. After you say your name, maintain your smiling, happy persona for a solid beat (moment) while continuing eye contact with the lens.

Staying with the camera a beat or so after slating gives you a moment to collect your thoughts before you begin to deliver the script. It also gives the viewer a chance to hear and register your name and face.

Good Slate. A good slate involves keeping solid eye contact with the camera before, during, and after the slate. It means maintaining a consistent, upbeat attitude. Basically, what you're saying as you slate is, "I'm really pleased to be here."

Bad Slate. One way to get a bad slate is to let your eyes dart over to the side. This makes you look nervous, not confident. Another way is to allow your eyes to look down toward the floor and back up. This looks as if you are insecure and don't know how to use the camera.

If you are slating with another person, the second person should wait a full beat before saying his or her name. In a two-person shot, sometimes the person directing you might point to you when it's your turn to slate. Sometimes, on a tighter shot, you'll notice that the camera will be on the first person slating, then move over to the second person.

Here's what you can do to improve your slating technique:

EXERCISE 6

Practice slating in front of the camera. While you are saying your name, dart your eyes off to the side (off-camera). As you play back the tape, notice how distrusting you look when you do this. If you were to say hello to a friend, then dart your eyes away, it would appear to your friend that you were hiding something or that you were distracted. Ths is exactly what happens if you dart your eyes off to the side while slating.

TRUTH IN THE EYES

The eyes are very important in this medium. They can make you come across as truthful and trustworthy—a must in commercials. To do this, create active, detailed visuals that give the effect that you are actually seeing something.

EXERCISE 7

Practice looking blankly into the camera, then create a visual that represents something delicious to look at. See every detail of the visual you choose. When playing the tape back, notice the difference in your eyes when you give yourself an effective visual. Truth in the eyes can give you the competitive edge, making the difference between booking and not booking the job.

VISUALIZING AND REACTING

Your reaction allows you to show your specific, individual attitude and personality. You want to create opportunities for yourself to show attitudes. One way is by reacting to something after you look at it.

Remember to *look . . . see . . . react . . .* whenever you are given the opportunity to visualize something. It is not enough just to *look.* Actually *see* what you are looking at. You do this by using the sensory and visual exercises presented in this section. Then it's time to *react.*

EXERCISE 8

Imagine you're *looking* at a dog licking a baby's face. See the baby in vivid detail. See him laughing. See what he looks like, what he is wearing, etc. See him sitting on the carpet. Notice the color of the carpet. See the puppy in complete detail. Finally, see the puppy licking the baby's face. *React.* Chances are, after giving yourself visuals like these, you will be smiling and reacting with certain facial expressions. These reactions let special traits—your unique personality—come out.

Don't be afraid to take the time to really "look" at the visuals you've created. Some people don't take enough time to really *indulge* in that beat. You must allow yourself to get into the moment and really experience it. You want to expand the space you are given. Give it dimension and apply your personality.

It is very important to create visuals for yourself. No matter how much direction you receive from the script or the director, you must keep giving more and more information to yourself. *Sensory practice* involves pulling from memory the visuals and feelings you need to project in order to do an effective job with the script.

Sense memory exercises involve recalling sensations of touching, feeling, and smelling that are stored in the memory. When you recall them, you are recreating an exact experience of these sensations, rather than coming from a purely made-up mental image.

EXERCISE 9

Close your eyes. "See" a glass a water on the table. Sit in front of the glass of water. Create a situation in your mind that will make you feel very thirsty. Maybe you've just finished jogging in very hot weather. You can't wait to quench your thirst with a cool, refreshing drink of water. Now, open your eyes and "see" the water. Reach for it, drink it, and allow yourself to indulge in the feeling of satisfaction. *Look, see, react.*

Develop your ability to use visuals and sensory work to fine-tune your auditioning skills. Strive to get to a point where you feel you're actually there—jogging in the heat, seeing the puppy and the baby—whatever the scenario.

Everything must seem honest. If you are miming reaching for a glass, your hand should look as if you are picking up a glass. Your arm should show intention (look like you want the water) and move toward the glass like you intend to pick it up. If you are picking up a piece of pizza, your hand should look like you are actually picking up and holding the pizza. You might even use the other hand to hold up the end of the slice to prevent the imaginary cheese from sliding off.

When picking up something small, like a tiny piece of chocolate, your hand and fingers should be positioned as they would be if you were really doing it. Practice on-camera reaching for many different objects, from very small pieces to larger, bulkier things.

EXERCISE 10

1. Think about sucking a lemon. Close your eyes. *See* the lemon being cut. Bring it to your mouth and suck on it. Feel your mouth start watering and puckering up from the tart sensation of the lemon juice hitting your taste buds.

2. Open up a can of cat food. Really smell the odor of the cat food.

3. Reach for a little piece of candy. Watch how your hand holds it. Think about the way the candy will taste when it gets to your mouth. Put the candy into your mouth and savor the rich, delicious flavor.

4. The winning lottery numbers were just posted. Pick up your lottery ticket. Begin rubbing off the numbers, one by one. *Feel* the excitement build as you realize that each of your numbers matches one of the winning digits. *React* to the realization that you have just became a lottery millionaire!

Another way to do this exercise is to build up to the moment when there's only one number left (you have all the others). You rub off the last one (the excitement builds), then react to the disappointment of discovering that you did not win after all.

❏ ANALYZING THE SCRIPT

Now that you are familiar with the camera and you have your sense memories warmed up, it's time to learn how to analyze a script.

Every script, every improv, every situation in a commercial audition is an opportunity to express your personality. The creative team is looking for a personality to help bring their vision to life. Your job is to let out your personality within a small working space and in a very short amount of time (fifteen, thirty, or sixty seconds). When you are given the script, ask yourself, "Where are the opportunities within the script to show the creative team various aspects of my personality?"

Generally, the outline of a commercial's "story" goes something like this:

1. *Some form of frustration and a problem to be solved are introduced.* Since commercials are generally lighthearted, any frustration shown has humor in it.* By adding humor to the situation, you become likable and approachable and the viewer will smile at you.
2. *You discover a product.* Life becomes grand and your outlook is much brighter.
3. *There is a statement about your discovery* and how it has changed your situation.
4. *Your satisfaction with the product is restated.*
5. *A final comment (called a button line) ties up the story.* This final statement provides an excellent opportunity for you to release your personality.

Figure 20 shows an example of a very basic commercial script. Use the following steps to analyze this script:

1. *Read the script over* to get familiar with the material.

---

*As the character, you should choose frustration over anger. An angry person is not approachable or amusing. A frustrated person is approachable. We can laugh at and with a frustrated person. Commercials are like sitcoms in this way. People in sitcoms are frustrated, not angry. They are likable, funny, and approachable, and we would be comfortable having them in our home. They are not a threat.

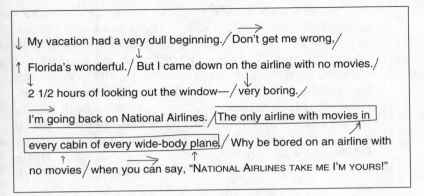

FIGURE 20. **How the script might look.**

2. *Identify what you are selling.* In this case, the "product" is National Airlines. It is important to know that you are not expected to "sell" the product. The commercial script is designed to do the selling. All you have to do is let out your personality.

The *sell line* is the first line that mentions the product name. Underline this sentence—in this case, "I'm going back on National Airlines." This does not mean you are expected to hit it hard or to sell hard. Underlining the sell line just lets you see where the sell comes in.

Notice also that the frustration comes right before the sell. It builds so that when you introduce the discovery of the product, there is a sense of relief from your frustration. This sets up the sell. The delivery of the sell is relatively simple. You simply become delighted and brighter or have a feeling of conviction because you have discovered this wonderful product.

3. *Find any specific "sell" information.* You will notice that there is not a lot of it. In this script, the applicable line is "The only airline with movies in every section of every wide-body plane." Put a box around this area so you can see it clearly.

4. *Divide the script into "beats,"* or moments of emotional or attitude change. Label each beat or attitude change with a slash mark (/).

You will want to show a lot of emotional changes within the context of the script. Think in terms of creating a woven blanket. Each change of emotion or attitude represents weaving a different color into the blanket. In this case, the more colors, the prettier the end result. Although you want to make strong choices, it's more effective to make changes with smooth transitions. The arrows indicate emotional changes. Down arrows indicate frustration. Up arrows indicate feeling bright. Forward arrows are a cue to the actor to speak with more conviction. Double underlined words are to be "punched up" (with more personality). Markings are individual. Develop your own markings so that the script has meaning for you.

5. *Divide the script into a beginning, a middle, and an end.* Doing so helps you realize that a basic script is not very long. Take it one step at a time. You'll notice that the beginning has only three lines, the middle has five, and the end only two. Tackle each section in the same way you would undertake skiing down a large mountain. Instead of looking at the enormity of the task of getting to the bottom, break the mountain up into smaller sections, then proceed down one section at a time. Before long, you find that you have accomplished your goal with relative ease.

6. *Decide where you are physically.* Remember to use active visuals, not passive ones. For example, an active visual would be running on the beach and feeling exhilarated. Just sitting on the beach and feeling nothing is passive. You want your audition to feel real—to be multidimensional. If you don't specifically come from someplace and go someplace, you are in a void.

In this case you could choose the airline terminal. See what it looks like in great detail and hear the sounds.

7. *Define your attitudes,* using very strong visuals. Create a very real situation for yourself. It should appear that you are either experiencing what is happening or that you are reexperiencing the situation.

Make particular choices. Have specific intentions and stay with your intentions.

8. *Establish relationships.* Know who (or what) you have a relationship with in the script. Give them (or it) a detailed history. Remember to stay playful (unless the script clearly calls for something different).

In this script, relationships are with (a) National Airlines, (b) the people you were with when you were in Florida, and (c) the person you are telling your experience to.

It is best to choose one particular person to speak to—someone you are extremely familiar with and with whom you can be loose and playful.

Remember that the creatives are looking for a definite personality. If an idea comes to you that is not consistent with your personality, don't stop yourself. Use it. Be open to discovering and exposing the many layers of your personality.

The following are examples of active visuals that will help you prepare for attitude changes. The script has been broken down into beats.

> *My vacation had a very dull beginning /*

The first line expresses a sense of frustration. Think about how you will create that sense of frustration within yourself. And even though you are frustrated, you must also give the viewer the sense that you are likable and playful.

For instance, think about the way you would feel if you planned a vacation in Florida and it didn't go the way you had envisoned. You were going to surf in crystal blue waters. You could actually *see* yourself riding the crest of the waves with the sun reflecting off your fabulously tanned body. This was your dream vacation and you couldn't wait to go, but when you actually got there, it *rained*. You found yourself in your hotel room with nothing to do. What a bummer.

Visualize the entire scenario. *Be* there. Coming from this visual, you can really say the line with frustration. You can *feel* the frustration.

> *Don't get me wrong /*

Make your attitude a little brighter. You are coming out of frustration, relating directly to the viewer.

> *Florida's wonderful /*

Your attitude is even brighter now. Visualize what you like about Florida—the huge waves and the beautiful, clear water.

> *But I came down on the airlines with no movies /*

You're going back into a sense of frustration. Think of it raining. Sitting in the hotel. You are stuck inside. You have one week of vacation all year and it's *raining*.

> *2 1/2 hours of looking out the window /*

Now you're going deeper into frustration. Think of yourself sitting in the hotel room. Think of all the things that are going wrong. As you say the line, look three-quarters away from the camera as if you are looking out a window. *Look, see, react*. Then turn back to the camera and react with humorous boredom and frustration:

> *Very boring /*

Your frustration is deepening. Your whole vacation is ruined. It's so bad, it's funny. Now, you're setting up the typical sell—frustration right before the discovery of the product that will make everything right again.

> *I'm going back on National Airlines /*

This is your sell. This is brighter. You have your solution. You've made a discovery. Keep in mind that brighter doesn't have to mean louder or even "big" and happy. To hit hard on the sell line is old-fashioned. In this case, you can be emphatic, knowing, or enlightened.

To prepare your attitude, you might imagine that you are trying to book a flight to sunny Florida. You call one airline and get a recording—you can't get a human being to come to the phone. You call a different airline and are cut off in the middle of the call. A third attempt to yet another airline finds you put on hold indefinitely. Finally, you call National Airlines and a customer service representative picks up the phone and helps you right away. Life becomes so much easier.

> *The only airline with movies on every section*
> *of every wide-body plane /*

This statement reinforces the prior statement.

> *Why be bored on an airline with no movies*
> *when you can say . . . /*

Here is the put-down. You are being condescending to the other airlines:

> *National Airlines, take me—I'm yours! (End)*

This is the button line. You can make it coy, big, embarrassed, shy—whatever you want.

These techniques can be applied to almost any script. In short, when you're working through a script:

1. Find humor.
2. Use active visuals.
3. Experience and reexperience the situation.
4. Find visual references—*look, see, react.*
5. Deliver the script as though you are talking to your best friend.

Don't beat yourself up if you didn't get every word right during the audition. Although you should try to get the words right, that's not what the audition is all about. You can make a mistake and still book the job. It will be obvious to the people selecting you that you are good, but your tongue got tied. You will probably be asked to do it again. Now, if you keep messing up again and again, you probably won't get booked. It would be obvious that you are unable to do what is asked.

❑ LEAVING THE AUDITION ROOM

Be sure to leave the audition room the same way you walked in—looking confident, positive, and happy to have been asked to audition. Thank everyone for bringing you in and don't critique yourself. You've given a good audition. Now it's time to find out how the selection process works.

THE SELECTION PROCESS

❑ THE CREATIVE TEAM

It's time to meet the creative team and find out what part they play in the selection of talent for commercial work. It takes at least eight people to decide who gets the job. Here's who they are:

The producer is responsible for putting together and keeping together all the elements that make up the production of a commercial. These elements include budgeting, selecting the director, coordinating the decisions of all the people involved, and making sure the production is on schedule, including editing of the final spot.

The producer is one of the people on the team who actually has a say as to who will be booked. If a producer knows your work and requests that the casting director include you in the audition, the casting director will definitely do so. It is a big plus when a producer is familiar with your work.

The art director is the person who visually conceives the spot and makes it come alive through drawings and visuals. In short, he or she is responsible for the way the commercial will look. The art director works very closely with (or is part of the team with) the writer.

The writer puts the message of the commercial into words. The writer and art director have to be in total alignment as to the message they want to get across.

The creative supervisor oversees the activities of the art director, writer, and producer.

The creative director is responsible for the work of all creatives in the advertising agency, and thus sets the tone for the entire agency (various agencies are known to be "on the cutting edge," "hip," conservative, etc.).

The director, of course, directs the spot. The director is hired for his creative input—his ability to enhance the spot. If a director has worked with you before and feels you are right for the project at hand, he will most likely make sure you are called in to audition. This gives you a chance to work with people who were previously unaware of your work. Many times, at the end of the creative selection process the director ultimately decides who will be presented to the client.

The account executives from the advertising agency serve as the liaison between the client and the agency. It is their responsibility to talk directly to the client, relaying the client's needs to the agency. They are the ones who look at the final selection of talent who will be presented to the client at a preproduction meeting; their agreement that the client will probably "buy" the actor is essential.

The client(s) are the executives who represent the product that is being advertised, be it Pepsi, Charmin bathroom tissue, or a Whopper. All selections of talent are presented to them and they have final approval. (The clients and the account executives are sometimes called "the suits.")

❏ HOW THE TALENT ARE SELECTED

The creative team collectively decides who would be best for the job, and the client makes the final decision (fig. 21). The casting director has very little to do with the actual selection process after the auditions are completed, although she might be asked to comment on a specific talent's acting ability and performance ability.*

Realize that the creative team is trying to be just that—creative, and turn out a nice piece of film. At the same time, they need to sell the product, meet legal specifications, and anticipate the client's tastes—knowing that ultimately, it's the

---

*In film, television, and theater, the casting director is more actively involved in the selection process.

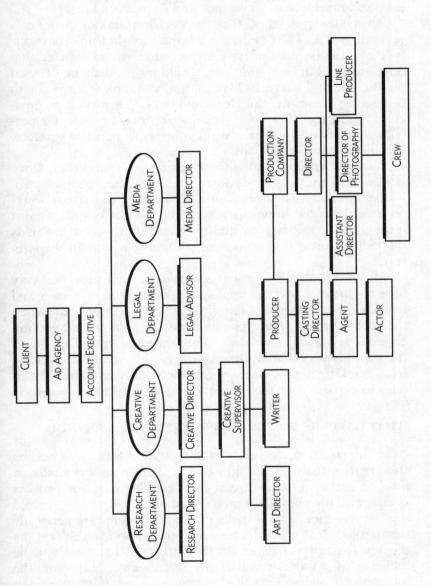

FIGURE 21. **Key players in the industry.**

client they have to please. The client has to approve the final look and production of the spot as well as the actor(s).

Always keep in mind that the decision-making process is very subjective. The writer, for instance, might think that your type of face is not the type of face that would be cleaning floors in the kitchen—that you would more likely be dressed up at a cocktail party. In his opinion, you look too upscale to be used in a commercial cleaning floors. The producer, however, might feel that your face *doesn't* look upscale. Or perhaps the producer may not want you simply because you look like his ex-wife. It happens.

All you can do as an actor is give a good audition. Once you've done that, it comes down to a "look" and people's subjective opinions. The final choice could come down to a "look" or it could come down to acting ability. But one thing you have control over is your ability to audition well, and this is the factor that will give you the competitive edge in the long run.

Many times, the way you are asked to audition has very little to do with how the final spot is done. You may be asked to do a broader range of emotions at the audition than when the spot is actually shot. The team needs to know that you are capable of handling whatever they throw at you. The day of the shoot is very demanding, so the creative team shies away from booking actors who are fairly one-dimensional. Thus it pays to expand your technique to show many dimensions.

WHAT HAPPENS TO YOUR TAPE AFTER THE AUDITION

After the audition, one copy of the audition tape is viewed by the creative team at the ad agency; then a copy is made or *dubbed,* and sent to the director to view. The selection process occurs and the actors are then called back.

The selection lists of the agency and director are generally compatible. It is possible, however, that if you weren't on the agency list but you *were* on the director's list, you will be called back. If the two lists are significantly different, the agency will realize that the director is envisioning the commercial in a way that is not consistent with theirs and will call the director to discuss his choices. The director will explain why he picked each actor. Generally, the agency will go with the director's choices, agreeing that the person should be called back.

Here's a scenario of how you might be eliminated from a callback list for reasons that have nothing to do with your performance: The agency and the director are going through their lists of actors selected for callbacks. The director is interested in seven people whom the agency has shown no interest in. Both sides discuss six people, and then the agency gives in to the director on each person and agrees that each will get a shot at callbacks.

Now they discuss the seventh person on the list (which just happens to be *you*) and the agency is beginning to feel that they are losing a bit of control. At this point, the agency argues against the seventh person (you), saying that they don't think you are right for the job.

Maybe the agency feels you're too quirky (different) for the spot. The director argues that the quirk is actually good for this particular job. The agency says they already have two actors for the spot who are quirky and would prefer that more of the people called back be more conservative. The agency argues strongly, expressing an interest in gaining more control. Ultimately, the director "gives you up" because he already got most of the people he wanted for the callback.

All callback choices are auditioned again. The director is there to direct the actors. The writer, art director, and producer are also there to experience the actors' performances. They want to see how well each actor takes direction, to envision how the actor fits into the original concept, and to see what the actor brings to the concept. Final choices are made. Following is an example.

The commercial involves a family consisting of a mom, a dad, and two teenage daughters. The Polaroids of each actor are laid out on a table. The two daughters tentatively chosen are blond cheerleader types. Next to those two choices are two alternate teenage daughters. One is blond, the other is brunette and "edgier" than the blondes. The art director says, "Look what happens if we replace one blond teenager with the brunette." Because of the differences created by the alternate daughter, the family dynamics have changed. The team decides this combination of teenage daughters is more interesting so the brunette gets booked instead of the second blonde.

The decision was not based on the actress's performance. All performances were good. The final selection came down to a viewpoint concerning the feeling the creative team wanted to project with the look of the family.

PRESENTING THE CALLBACK SELECTIONS TO THE CLIENT

Finally the preproduction meeting takes place, with as many as twenty-two people present. Every aspect of the production day is discussed, including the final selections of talent for the commercial. The creative team presents the actors to the client showing the callback tapes on a monitor. With luck, the client nods and the producer calls the casting director, giving the okay to book the talent. All personalities involved in the selection process are satisfied. Whew! What a feat.

TIME BETWEEN THE FINAL SELECTION OF TALENT AND THE SHOOT

Usually, casting begins two weeks before the actual shoot date. On rare occasions, casting will start two months before the shoot. But there are no rules. Many times, casting is done one to three days before the shoot.

❑ UNDERSTANDING THE HISTORY OF A COMMERCIAL

As an actor, you must realize that each commercial has a "history" that the creatives help to develop. The history might consist of where the family in the commercial comes from, as well as their interests, relationships, and economic state. The type of furniture the family would own (including the type of fabric) is indicated, along with the type of clothing each family member would wear, and how they relate to one another.

It is amazing how effective commercials can be, especially since they are only fifteen seconds to one minute long. In that short span of time, a commercial can create a myriad of emotions—sadness, envy, joy, humor, and curiosity.

In many ways, the commercial is the ultimate form of storytelling. In the most economical structure possible, we meet characters, identify with their struggle, then watch them change and grow in a narrative complete with introduction, climax, and resolution—all in thirty seconds. Moroever, the advertiser accomplishes the task of showing us that, like the characters in the story, we too can solve our dilemmas by purchasing the product.

Now that you are familiar with the people who create, direct, and produce commercials and have an understanding of how talent is selected, it's time to give you a more extensive look at what to expect concerning callbacks, bookings, and commercial shoots.

❑ THE CALLBACK

Congratulations! You have given an impressive audition and the creative team has called you back to have another look.

In the past, two to six people were called back per character. Now callbacks consist of as many as nine to fifteen people per character. The good news is there are more opportunities to get called back. The bad news is there is more competition.

Keep a positive attitude. Keep feeling special. You *did* get called back. Now the selection process begins again, and the same subjectiveness applies as in the auditions.

INFORMATION YOU SHOULD BE GIVEN WHEN YOU GET A CALLBACK

When you get the phone call to notify you of a callback, you should receive the following information. If you don't, *ask*.

1. When and where the audition is being held. If you do not know how to get there, ask for directions. You don't want to be late. It's a good idea to get the phone number of the place you're going to so if you *do* get lost, you can call to get instructions.

2. The shoot dates. You might be put on *avail* (availability) or *first refusal* for the shoot days, travel days, and weather days,* if there are any. An avail or first refusal is a handshake agreement between the actor, agent, and casting director by which the actor guarantees that the client will have first option on his time on the specific dates set aside for the commercial shoot.† This way, when the creative team sells the actor to the client and the client says yes, the casting director can book the actor with every confidence that the actor will be available and will accept the booking.

If another client wants to book the actor for the time of the avail or first refusal, the agent has to go to the casting director who has the actor on avail or first refusal. The casting director then goes to the client, giving him first choice of either booking the actor or releasing him. If the client releases the actor, the actor is then free to accept the other booking.

3. What to wear to the callback. You do not have to wear the same clothes as when you first auditioned, even if the wardrobe description is the same as for the first call. If, for instance, the first call was casual and so is the second, you would still wear casual clothes, but you could wear a different outfit. Of course, if you are asked to wear the same thing you wore for the first audition, do so.

Sometimes, however, the situation changes. For example, the creatives might have chosen you for a different character than you first auditioned for. You could be asked to dress differently.

4. How the spot runs (is "aired").‡ You should have been told at the original audition how the spot was running. At this point, the information should be reiterated. You might hear terms such as *national, network, spot, dealer, cable, seasonal,* and *regional* (see Chapter 13).

5. Type of Contract. You might also hear that a *standard contract* is desired by the client. This means the contract re-

---

*If it is an outdoor shoot, you can expect to be put on avail for a "weather day." This means if the shoot is rained out (or if any kind of bad weather occurs to delay the shoot), you have reserved the day specified to reschedule the shoot. There are also rules pertaining to payment for such a day depending on how many hours in advance the shoot is canceled due to weather. These rules can be found in a SAG guidebook or by calling your local union office and/or your agent.

†In New York, the procedure is referred to as first refusal, in Los Angeles, avail.

‡The places it runs are also referred to as *markets*, the places the spots will be shown on the air.

mains as written with nothing crossed off the back. On the back of your contract (in small print), there is a section that gives the client the right of use for theatrical (movie theaters), foreign, and cable usage at scale payment. This is a very acceptable practice and should not create a problem for the actor.

6. Moneys and payments involved. If there are moneys involved other than scale (basic union fees), this is a good time to confirm the amount to avoid possible misunderstandings at the time of booking or at the shoot, when you are signing your contract.

There are, for example, situations in which moneys are guaranteed per *cycle* for the actor. A cycle is thirteen weeks. This means that the actor would receive an agreed upon amount of money (guaranteed) every thirteen weeks. For more on talent payment, see Chapter 13.

7. Conflicts. The actor cannot be under contract for a conflicting product.

WHO WILL BE AT THE CALLBACK

Part or all of the creative team will be at the callback to direct and observe the actor. Among the people who might be present are the *producer* from the ad agency, the *writer*, the *art director*, the *director from the production company*, and the *production company producer*.

It is common to have at least five people watching you audition at the callback. The person who will actually be directing the shoot will most likely direct during the callback. This gives the director the opportunity to see how flexible you are and to see if you and he can get along well. It also gives the director a chance to see how his concept of the direction is actually going. It's unlikely that he'll go heavily into this at the callback, but he will get a sense of what is (or is not) working.

Many times, the director will pick something unique to your personality from your performance and build on that with you. Something special in your audition that sparks interest from the director could be the deciding factor in whether or not you get booked.

HOW YOU SHOULD CONDUCT YOURSELF AT THE CALLBACK

As always, it is important to be on time for the callback. Your appointment was scheduled specifically for the director to have a certain amount of time to work with you (and another person if you are paired up with someone for the audition). It is important to take direction and be flexible and amiable. Give a good audition and leave the room with a positive attitude.

WHAT THE CREATIVES ARE LOOKING FOR

What is the purpose of a callback? It's another chance to see how actors perform. Naturally, something in your performance may be slightly different from the first time. Callbacks give the team time to work with actors to see how flexible they are and how broad a range they have. If there are two or more actors in the commercial, the creatives can observe the chemistry (or lack thereof) between them. They can see if there is something special and very personal the actor can bring to the performance and they can watch the actor apply new ideas that the team may have come up with since the first call.

The team gets to determine how much they like the actor personally. Would *they* feel comfortable working with the actor? Is the actor cooperative? Florida casting director Lori Wyman notes that during callbacks directors want to make sure that the actor is not a prima donna, that she is not going to be difficult to work with or disagreeable. They want to know that the actor will be fun and easy to work with, and that they'll *want* to spend the day with this person.

Don't put pressure on yourself to do anything particularly different. Remember, if you understand the script and the circumstances of the spot you're appearing in, and know your technique, your focus will be on being the character in the scene. As with real life, something a little different might happen—perhaps a slightly different inflection in the voice, a slightly different attitude, or a slightly different movement. You are not expected to be exactly the same as at the first audition. So just be yourself and *do* be spontaneous at the callback.

If the situation calls for two or more people to work together, you might be mixed and matched. You may be called into a room with one person, then asked to wait and come back in the room with another person. Take notice of how your energies and chemistry change with different people.

Sometimes what you are doing will work better with one person than the other. This is normal and expected. If you are called in with someone you do not work well with, it doesn't create the best possible experience. But it also does not mean you won't get booked. If you are doing well and the other person is not good for the spot, the creatives can see it.

Many times, one person is booked and the other is not. No matter what occurs, keep doing your best at the audition. Don't play into the negative energies (or the bad choices) of the other person. Work with the person as much as possible without bringing yourself down. In fact, within the scenario, try to bring the other person's performance up to par.

❏ THE BOOKING

HOW MUCH TIME ELAPSES BETWEEN THE CALLBACK AND THE BOOKING?

It can take anywhere from one day to two weeks from the callback to the booking, but there are unending variables. In a standard situation, the creative team at the callback will make their selections, then present you at a preproduction meeting approximately three days later. Final approval is left to the client (the executives who represent the product.)

INFORMATION YOU SHOULD BE GIVEN WHEN YOU ARE BOOKED

The booking call consists of the time, date, wardrobe fitting (if applicable), and the location you should report to.

❏ THE SHOOT: INTERVIEW WITH BARBARA MULLINS

The following interview with Barbara Mullins, a commercial television producer, will help you become knowledgeable about and comfortable with the process of the commercial shoots.

What attracts the creative team to an actor?

We look for a certain quality that makes people stop and take notice. For example, do the eyes have life and sparkle? Does the actor seem intelligent? Does he seem to understand the script? Does she appear natural and genuine?

Sometimes an actor is chosen because he interprets the script best. The actor will then be made the core of the scene and the cast will be built around him. Sometimes the way two actors work together makes things happen. The creative team will have the actors spend a lot of time together on the day of the shoot before we actually start taping to see what might happen between them and use this relationship for the commercial.

What is expected from actors on the set?

Actors must have done their homework, be cooperative, and be prepared to listen and to take direction. They are expected to make a contribution—their input is important. Actors should come in with a sense of involvement and energy.

They should be aware of the totality of the spot, not just what their little piece involves. They need to know what they are trying to convey and whom the client is selling to. I think actors should know their lines beforehand. It's up to the agency producer to get the material to them ahead of time so they can memorize it.

Flexibility is important. Actors must be prepared to make adjustments in their interpretations of the script. The creative team is constantly working on ways to make things better, so if someone offers a good idea, why wouldn't we take it? We must deliver what we promised to the client, but there is always the possibility of another way to do it.

There are two main ingredients in a successful spot: the finest director and the best talent you can possibly get. The spot is nothing if you have a great director and bad talent (or vice versa).

What goes into the preparation for a commercial shoot?

The creative team does a lot of preparation before the shoot. At the ad agency, we draw up a storyboard, then sit with the director while he interprets it. Next, we create a *shooting board*, which is a tightly scripted, tightly drawn board laying out all the shots for the commercial. This is done after considering the input of the clients, the agencies, the account executives, and the directors.

The creative team, with the director, blocks out the shots with a more precise interpretation. There are hours and hours of meetings regarding locations, props, and how to shoot the commercial and capture a theme. Nothing is left to chance. We discuss the types of plates, food, clothing, and other props we are going to use. After all this gets into the hopper, the director will make up the shooting board.

What is the usual location of the shoot?

Actors can be called *anywhere* to shoot. Travel arrangements will be made with their agents. Be on time. If, for instance, you will be traveling by van with the production company and the departing time is 7:30, don't get there at 7:35. Time is crucial on a commercial shoot.

What happens the day of the shoot?

On the day of the shoot, dozens of people are present: the director, producer, copywriter, art director, film/shooting crew, makeup person, stylist, script supervisor (who is responsible for accuracy in keeping with the scripted words), and the clients. Expect to see up to six of the client's people on the site, including marketing managers or product managers.

Remember, the client is an ally; all of his needs should be met. We now have the luxury of videotape monitors off to the side so that everyone can watch the monitor instead of standing around and watching the actor. This has helped sharpen the team's eye for what is seen on the TV screen. On a sound stage, headsets are used to listen to the lines when it is not possible to hear the actors in their presence.

What happens when the actors first get on the set?

The producer usually introduces himself to the actors first. The agency producer or the second AD (assistant director) will give the SAG contract to the talent at the beginning of the day. This will confirm the start of a particular job. Then, a Polaroid is taken of the actors in their wardrobes so the team can refer to it later on.

What is expected of actors in terms of the contract?

The contract is given to the actors to be signed. They should be aware of the provisions beforehand, including how the commercial is supposed to run. All this information has been given to their agent.

Occasionally, the contract could look different from what the casting director discussed with the agent. In this case, the first thing an actor should remember is to maintain a professional demeanor, to call the agent, and to explain the situation. The differences are then worked out by the agent and the producer.

At what point is the product introduced to the actors?

The actors should be familiar with the product being used so that when it is put into their hands, it is not foreign to them. They should be asked whether they have ever worked with a product, for example, a computer. If not, they are given the product to become familiar with before the day of the shoot.

A technical advisor will be on the set. If the product is gum, the actor will learn to load* and chew gum; if it's a soft drink spot, she'll learn how to swallow and use the product in the correct way.

Is there anything actors should avoid while at the shoot?

First of all, when there is down time, the actors should observe what is going on, staying within the confines of the

---

*A technical way to put gum into the mouth for a commercial.

set and developing some camaraderie. The worst thing that can happen is for an actor not to be accessible because he is on the phone or out eating somewhere. Actors should let the assistant director and the agency producer know where they are at all times. If a shot comes up and an actor is not around, it creates a problem. Also, no family members, pals, or kids should visit the set. In short, the actor should always be there and committed.

Actors should be polite and courteous, relaxed and comfortable with everyone on the set. After all, they are the ones who are representing the product. All the focus is on them.

Finally, actors should not ask for things on the set. Do not ask, for instance, if you can have the clothing you wore on the shoot. If someone offers to give something to you, that is different.

How long does a commercial shoot take?

There is no standard time; a shoot can run fourteen to sixteen hours a day. How the commercial is being shot is a primary consideration. Factors such as location shooting and special needs (like a sunrise or a sunset) all affect shoot time. Consideration must also be taken for children (see Chapter 17: "Kids in the Business").

There is also a union rule requiring a twelve-hour turnaround for a crew. This means that twelve hours must elapse from the time you wrap (end) until you can start again. This may result in a later call time for the next day's shoot.

Usually, on a stage, you might have a crew call at 6:30 A.M. with the actors arriving at 7:30 to be put into wardrobe. The shoot might start at 8:30 or 9:00, once the lighting is set. A shoot is over when it's over.

If the shoot goes beyond twelve hours, people begin to get tired and wear down. Sometimes, the shoot is scheduled to go on into another day, but that is not always possible. The agency producer has the responsibility of keeping things going.

There is always a lot of waiting around on the sets. Different camera setups and shots are required, which results in a lot of down time for actors.

Is the commercial shot in segments?

An actor may shoot the spot from beginning to end in its entirety, or the commercial may be shot in segments. For example, the *master shots* (wide shots that show the entire scene) may require the same kind of lighting, in which case, the actor would be involved. Then we might jump to a shot that would appear third or fourth in the commercial. All the close-up shots might be done at the same time because afterwards all lighting and lenses must be changed. It's pretty rare for a commercial to be shot from the beginning straight through to the end.

How many takes might an actor expect?

Ad agency creatives want several different interpretations of the commercial script because they have a lot of people to satisfy. A shoot may involve anywhere from a couple of takes to twenty or thirty. An actor hits it at some point, then it goes in a different direction.

Who directs the actors? Do the actors have any input?

The director has primary contact with the actors on the set. The director is the sole focal point—the sole voice that actors should be hearing. If someone wants to request something from an actor, the request should go to the director.

Whether or not actors can give suggestions to the director during the shoot involves a lot of tact. There is protocol on the set. Actors should let the director direct, *then* they may be allowed to offer other interpretations.

Actors should *not* tell the director that they don't like something or don't want to do it. An actor could possibly say, "How about this?" or "Can I try something?" When everybody is cooking and contributing, an interpretation from someone other than the director is welcomed.

13 HOW MUCH CAN I MAKE?

The commercial industry is one of the most lucrative in show business. Performers from all over the country have financed college educations, upgraded lifestyles, and catapulted themselves into other areas of the business as a result of working in commercials.

A long-running national commercial can net over $200,000. Even a small, regional spot pays hundreds of dollars for a single day's work. Florida casting director Lori Wyman notes: "I know a talent who had one day of shooting for a network commercial for Wrigley's. It ran three years and he made ninety thousand dollars. That's for a single day's work. This sort of thing happens a lot."

Payment for commercial work is determined by factors such as:

1. How often the commercial runs
2. Whether it runs locally, regionally, or nationally
3. Whether it is a union or nonunion commercial

If you are doing nonunion work in a smaller region, you generally get "bought-out," which means you get paid a certain amount of money, and the client owns the spot and can play it as much as he wants. You don't get residuals (payments made to the talent every time the spot runs). Obviously, the potential earnings from this kind of commercial are limited.

With union commercials, however, there are different ways a spot can run so there are several ways an actor can be paid. Professional "talent payment" people, whose job is to handle payments to actors, follow an elaborate system and are checked by tracking methods that make sure everything is handled correctly. Talent payment expert Katie Stoll, of San Francisco, has provided an extensive look into how performers are paid for work on television and radio commercials.

❑ TELEVISION

SESSION

When a commercial is filmed or taped, the performers are paid a session fee as compensation for an eight-hour day of work. The session fee also provides the advertiser with the right to use that commercial for thirteen weeks and prevents the actor from doing spots for competitive products for the same length of time. To maintain the rights to use the commercial and to "hold" the actor, the actor is paid an additional holding fee every thirteen weeks (see "Holding Fees/Exclusivity" below).

A session fee for an on-camera performer is $443.25*
for an eight-hour day.
A session fee for an off-camera performer is $333.30 for
a two-hour recording session.
A session fee for an *extra* performer is $240.00 for an
eight-hour day (unlimited usage).

Performers receive a session fee for each commercial produced or each day of work, whichever is greater. For example, if five commercials are recorded in a two-hour session, five session fees must be paid. Session fees are usually fully creditable against reuse fees.† "Special provisions" cover any agreed upon details that do not appear in the standard contract. These include money above scale and special travel arrangements.

---

*Payments cited here are based on statistics available at time of publication.
†Reuse fees are paid every time the commercial runs (airs) or is used again after the initial run (airing).

Fees paid to extras vary depending upon the performance of the extra. They are paid a single fee, or *buyout*, entitling the advertiser to the use of that extra in the commercial for its broadcast life. In other words, extras do not receive residuals.

The current extra buyout fee is $240.*

The current hand model† buyout fee is $366.25.

OVERTIME

Scale session fees (regular union session fees) cover one eight-hour day. If the performer is required to work for longer than eight hours, overtime is paid as follows:

1. The ninth and tenth hours are paid at 150 percent of the scale session fee for one hour (the hourly rate is equal to one eighth of the eight-hour-day session fee). The current rate for the ninth and tenth hours is $83.11. This is called "time and a half."

For example, one hour of overtime for an on-camera performer is:

⅛ of the 8-hour session fee ($443.25 divided by 8):	$55.40
Plus an additional 50 percent of the hourly amount:	+27.70
Total amount:	$83.10

2. The eleventh hour and beyond are paid at 200 percent of the scale session fee for one hour. The current rate is $110.80. This is called "double-time."

3. An additional 10 percent must be added to the above hourly rates for performance between 8:00 P.M. and 6:00 A.M. This fee is called a "night premium." The hours subject to the night premium for extras are slightly different.

4. Performers are paid 200 percent of scale for weekend and holiday work. Recognized holidays include New Year's Day, Martin Luther King Jr.'s

---

*Payments cited here are based on statistics available at time of publication.

†A *hand model* is a person whose hands (only) are in the shot, for example, in a close-up of a hand opening a jar.

Birthday, President's Day, Memorial Day, Independence Day, Labor Day, Thanksgiving, and Christmas Day.

TRAVEL TIME

When performers spend time traveling to or from a shoot location, they are compensated for that time at the same rates by which they are paid for session time. Hourly or half-day rates may apply depending on the time of travel.

CONSECUTIVE EMPLOYMENT

Performers in any one commercial are paid for intervening time when they are not used. For example, if performers work on Monday and Wednesday but not Tuesday, they are paid a scale session fee for Tuesday in order to hold them for performance on Wednesday.

FITTINGS/WARDROBE

Time spent by a performer in fittings is considered to be session time and is paid as such. For example: If a *principal* (primary) performer spends one hour in a fitting, the payment due would be one eighth of the scale session fee for an eight-hour day ($55.40).

Performers are compensated for use of their own wardrobe at the following rates:

1. $25.00 for evening wear
2. $15.00 for nonevening wear

HOLDING FEES/EXCLUSIVITY

Advertisers must pay principal performers a holding fee every thirteen weeks in order to retain the right to broadcast the commercial during that thirteen-week cycle. The holding fee amount is equivalent to a session fee. The *holding fee cycle* begins with the earliest date that an on- or off-camera principal works and lasts for thirteen weeks. At the end of that time the next holding fee is due and a new thirteen-week cycle begins.

Holding fees also provide the advertiser with *exclusivity*, meaning that as long as an actor is being *held* to a certain product or service, she may not accept work in any competitive television advertising.

When a commercial is no longer held, the advertiser loses the right to broadcast the commercial and the performer is released from her employment contract and is free to accept competitive work.

Holding fees do not compensate the talent for any use of the commercial. However, holding fees are fully creditable against the use fees of a commercial.* For example:

Network use fees due:	$500.00
Less holding fee:	− 414.25
Total amount due:	$85.75

MAXIMUM PERIOD OF USE

The life of a commercial contract is usually twenty-one months with additional use periods obtained through *contract re-negotiation*. During the twenty-one-month period, the rights to continued usage are obtained through the payment of holding fees every thirteen weeks (as described above). At the end of the twenty-one-month maximum use period, the performer has the right to request a new rate. This process is called *negotiation*.

REINSTATEMENT

In the event an advertiser wishes to use a commercial after the employment contract(s) runs out, the talent agreements must be reinstated. This process includes making sure the principal talent does not have any conflicting SAG contracts for commercials for a competitive product or service, and negotiating a new payment agreement. If the performer has a conflict, he will not be able to enter into a new agreement for a competitive product.

*Holding fees may not be credited to cable cycles.

RESIDUALS

In addition to session fees, principal performers are compensated in *residual payments* for the use of commercials in which they appear. There are as many use types as there are ways to broadcast a commercial. Different and complex rate structures determine talent payment for each type, including network use, syndication use, wild spot use, cable use, foreign use, dealer use, and theatrical/industrial use.

Network Use. Residual payments for network use are based on the frequency of use. Performers are paid for each telecast during a thirteen-week cycle. The first network use date commences the thirteen-week network cycle. Rates are structured on a decremental scale, with the first use being the most expensive and use rates beyond the first decreasing in price per use.

Wild Spot. Residual payments for wild spot use are based on market weightings attributed to the cities in which the commercial is being broadcast. The unit weightings are based on population. New York, Chicago, and Los Angeles are referred to as *majors*, and because of their populations, they are more heavily weighted. The presence of majors, if any, plus the unit weightings of any additional cities, determines the dollar amount due to the performer. This payment covers unlimited use of the commercial in those markets for thirteen weeks. If additional markets are added midcycle, the payment must be upgraded to cover additional units.

Cable. For commercials used on cable networks, each principal performer is paid for thirteen weeks of unlimited use based on the total number of television households/subscribers receiving the cable broadcast. The rates for an on-camera performer range from $414.25 to $519.60 for each cycle of use. There are lower rates established for use on local cable systems with one million or fewer subscribers.

Demos/Non-air Commercials. There is no exclusivity required of performers in demo commercials, and the rates are $311.50 for an on-camera performer and $155.75 for an off-camera performer. Because there is no exclusivity, no holding fees are paid. In the event a demo spot is upgraded to a broadcast commercial, the talent must be recontracted under the appropriate scale.

❏ RADIO

SESSION

The session fee for an announcer/solo or duo is $185.00 per commercial. Lower rates are paid to group singers of three or more. Session fees are fully creditable to use fees. *Note:* AFTRA does not allow agents of performers to deduct their fees from scale earnings. As a result, most radio announcers are paid at scale plus 10 percent for session and residuals.

EXCLUSIVITY/MAXIMUM PERIOD OF USE

There is no exclusivity for radio performers. Radio performers do not receive holding fees and are free to accept work in competitive advertising during the course of their contract. The maximum period of use or *life* of a radio commercial is twenty-one months from the session date. Additional use periods are obtained through contract renegotiation.

RESIDUALS

Payments to radio performers are made when the commercial airs. As with television, there are several different use types and each type has its own rate structure. Some of the different use types are *network*, *wild spot*, and *dealer use.*

Network. Residual payments for network radio are based on the length of the cycle. Network radio cycles can be one, four, eight, or thirteen weeks in length. During the cycle unlimited use is allowed on any network programs on any and all radio networks for a single advertiser. There is also a limited use for thirteen weeks for either twenty-six or thirty-nine uses during the cycle.

Wild Spot. Residual payments for wild spot use are based on market weightings attributed to the cities in which the commercial is being broadcast. The unit weightings are based on population. The presence of majors (New York, Chicago, Los Angeles), plus the unit weights of any additional cities, determines the dollar amount due the performer. The payment can be made for either an eight-week or a thirteen-week cycle. The rates for a thirteen-week cycle are slightly higher than those for eight-week cycles. The eight-week cycle is designed to give advertisers a price break for those commercials intended for a shorter term of use.

Dealer Use. This is a flat rate for twenty-six weeks (six months of use) for broadcast time contracted and paid for by the dealer or distributor of a product (versus media buys made by the manufacturer).

Whew! As you can see, talent payment involves a very detailed and complex set of procedures. It is impossible to give you every possible payment scenario in a single chapter. However, the above topics cover the key considerations in getting paid for commercial work.

The next chapter discusses the pros and cons of working in regional markets and commuting for work, and how to tell when it's time to move on to a larger (or different) market.

14
WORKING IN REGIONAL AREAS

❏ **ADVANTAGES AND DISADVANTAGES OF WORKING IN REGIONAL AREAS**

Small, regional markets are important places to develop and nurture a fledgling talent career. Opportunities to appear in local commercials exist in all regional markets with a varying degree of work in national commercials, voice-overs, radio, industrial/corporate videos, commercial print, films, and television (including national searches for lead characters).

One reason a national commercial will be shot in a smaller region is for its location. These commercials are usually cast locally, with simultaneous casting in the larger markets such as New York or Los Angeles. Actor beware: You are up against some stiff competition. Producers don't mind flying someone in from a larger market to do the job. The best man will win.

In every state of the country, you can now find a high degree of professionalism that has evolved from sophisticated communication systems and mobility. In addition, many directors, producers, and agencies have relocated from larger markets to smaller ones because the latter suit their lifestyles better. Actors often make the same move, bringing with them new ideas, new photos, and a greater competitive edge. Agents and casting directors in all markets are communicating to a greater degree, and anyone who is interested can become more savvy to the workings of the industry, thus becoming more competitive commercially.

One of the benefits of working in smaller markets is less competition, which makes it easier to get an agent, book a job, build your résumé, and get your SAG card. In many regions, you can keep busy providing you are willing to audition in all areas of the business. One day, for instance, you might be working in a film, and the next day on a print job.

Gregory Bouldin, a talent agent at the Gregory Agency in Wichita, Kansas, says: "There is so much more competition in a larger market. By starting out in a smaller market talent people have a greater chance of being a big fish in a small pond and have more opportunities to build that résumé. Even in a small market like Wichita, a person can get a line on their résumé that says they've done an industrial for Pizza Hut. Working in a smaller market gives actors a chance to practice their craft and to get a small taste of the business."

Heather Laird, a casting director at Wright/Laird Casting in Kansas City, Missouri, adds, "You can gain a certain level of confidence working in a regional market that I think is *really* valuable. So many people end up in the L.A. market with very little experience, hoping to get 'discovered.' If people have an opportunity to work in a regional market, they are going to be a step ahead of ninety-nine hundred other people who just decided they want to be famous and walked out the door and went to L.A."

There can be some disadvantages to working in smaller markets as well. There is less work than in New York and Los Angeles, it's harder to find good coaches and classes, and you may have to invest a great deal of time scouting for opportunities to network and to find auditions. Savvy talent people make the most of their regional market by creating their own opportunities to build résumés and get experience and exposure. Kay Tanner, an agent at Genesis Talent in Atlanta, suggests that actors in smaller regions form their own theater groups. "There's puppet theater and other forms of theater that people can do to earn a living. It's not a great living, but it can be done. It's a way for actors to express themselves creatively too."

Jack Stevens, an actor from Jackson, Mississippi, advises actors to get pictures and letters to every TV station, every ad agency, and every film production company listed in the Yellow Pages. "In Jackson, almost everything is done in-house," he says. "People here do it on their own by checking in with the regional film office, by networking with each other, and by mailing directly to casting people in the area."

The reality is that there may not be much happening in your area. If you love where you live and don't want to leave, you will have to find another means of financial support. Commercials and other industry work can simply become an enjoyable part-time outlet for your talents and creativity. Be sure to set yourself up with a job that is flexible and allows you time to go to auditions and do commercials.

❏ COMMUTING

Another option is for actors to commute from smaller markets to larger ones. "There are a lot of people commuting from places like Milwaukee, Indianapolis, Minneapolis and even Detroit to Chicago for work," says Judith Jacobs, a casting director in Chicago. Some actors travel to and from Washington, D.C., Philadelphia, and Pittsburgh, or between Atlanta and Wilmington, North Carolina, for film opportunities. "Actors in Florida travel as much as four hours for an audition," says Suzanne Haley, an agent in Florida.

Others actually relocate temporarily in another market; for instance, actors from New York will go to Los Angeles for pilot season.* Of course, while they are there, they also audition for commercials. These actors are known as *bicoastal*.

By networking with other actors, you can find markets that would be viable for you. You would then want to find an agent in the other markets. It is accepted practice to have a different agent in each market. If the market you are commuting to is very close to your home region, check with your agent to make sure that your agreement with him does not cover the other market you are interested in. Doing so will avoid any

*A pilot is the first episode of a potential TV series. The network gives an okay to a production company to produce a pilot. Then, after it's shot, the network looks at it and evaluates its potential success as a series. If accepted, the show is given a time slot and the production company produces more of the series. Generally, pilots are cast and shot starting right after the first of the year. They must be finished and delivered by the end of April to be considered, with final decisions made between May and June.

unnecessary and potentially messy contractual issues with the agent you sign with in the new area.

Commuting can be expensive, so some talent managers suggest setting money aside for the year to cover the cost.

❑ MOVING TO A LARGER MARKET

If you have reached a point where you feel you've done all you can within your base area and want to do more—and if you're willing to relocate—it's time to consider moving to an area where you can get more work. The market you pursue depends on where your aspirations within the industry lie.

If your primary focus is on film and television, you will want to consider going to Los Angeles, since that is where most of those projects are done and there are many more opportunities to audition on a daily basis. There are auditions in New York, Chicago, and other places around the country for a national search, but if you *know* you want to make your living in film/TV, you should be based in L.A.

If your passion is theater, your base should be New York. There is also a good deal of work in soap operas and commercials in New York. Chicago is a regional market that is known for good theater as well as film and TV opportunities, as many searches are conducted in this area. There is clearly no one "right" place to be. Go where you feel most comfortable and content. It is important to balance your aspirations for your career with the rest of your life.

Before making the move to a larger market, make sure you have gotten as much experience as possible in your local area. Michael Powell, an agent with Marquee Talent in Dallas, says, "A good time to move to a larger market could be when you have exhausted all of your options—when you were going hot and heavy and that sting pulls off because you've become overexposed."

Actors tend to move on to a larger market when they become bored with what is available to them in their home market, or they may outgrow the kinds of parts they are getting and move to an area where more opportunities are available to them. They also leave for markets with more choices of training. Actors may feel instinctively when it is the right time to leave.

Heather Laird adds, "People who want to be actors get involved in the regional market and they do well so they don't stay. However, there are an awful lot of people who go to L.A., get some time in, and come back to their original market."

It is definitely a plus to have joined SAG (or become SAG eligible) before leaving for a larger market. Expect competition to be much stiffer. In New York and Los Angeles, it is not unusual to be competing against 125 other people for the same role, in comparison to 15 to 25 in a smaller, regional market. Also be prepared for more competition for agency representation. An agent may not want to represent you because doing so would create competition within her own agency.

"It takes a lot to make it in a large market," says agent J. D. Fryer, of Fryer Models of Alexandria, Louisiana. "You have to focus on one thing and that is, 'I am going to make it. This is what I want to do more than anything in the world—this is my dream.' If you don't have the attitude 'I *will* do this,' you will never be able to do it.

"People run into a lot of obstacles after relocating to a larger market. Being turned down at go-sees. Not getting the job. Going to the next and not getting that one, or the next one. They are used to being called in and just booked in a smaller market. You can't let that discourage you. You have to continue to follow your dreams . . . and who knows, in the next audition, you may get your foot in the door."

Lori Wyman, a Florida casting director, points out some of the hard realities of moving to a larger market, "Actors are enticed by the fact that they will have more of a chance to audition for a lead in L.A. or New York than in Florida. But if you can't get an agent and don't get auditions, what chance do you have? Everybody comes from somewhere. Your regional market can be a great place to get your feet wet, learn the business, learn the rules.

"I have heard it said that in Florida, we are the barracudas and in L.A., they are the great white sharks. Smaller markets are not as aggressive or as brutal. Actors get a little taste of it out here but out there it is thrown at them. Here, a strong talent might go out on every single casting that they would be right for. In L.A., that won't happen all the time. Actors come back frustrated."

Despite the challenges relocating to a larger market presents, if you are acting and hoping to etch out a full-blown career, eventually you might make the move. In the meanwhile, making the most of your regional market is a valuable part of the process.

❏ INTERVIEW WITH TOM JOURDEN

Tom Jourden has appeared in dozens of national television commercials. He has done commercials for Nutri-Grain breakfast bars, Eveready Energizer Batteries, and O'Doul's nonalcoholic beer. He is the host for Nordic Track infomercials and has appeared in hundreds of industrials, TV sitcoms, soaps, and episodics. Tom has recurring roles on *Days of Our Lives* and *The Bold and the Beautiful*. He offers some valuable insight into the issues facing performers who are considering the move to a larger market.

Secondary markets are great for learning about acting, studying, and getting some work. Atlanta is a perfect example. It's not as competitive in the area of industrials and commercials.

If you work in a secondary market first, you're going to understand what agencies do, what casting directors do. You're going to learn a little bit about taking head shots, hitting a mark, and how lighting works, and hopefully you'll get your union card and book some jobs. Even though it's not like the big markets, the experiences you have in a secondary market serve as training wheels. They give you a start.

In a secondary market, it's much easier to book work at different levels—nice little parts in films, parts in industrials, and commercials. You might be competing against eight or ten decent people in a smaller market, whereas in a larger market, you're competing against thousands and thousands who all look like you and might be better than you, especially if you're coming out to Los Angeles without training and experience.

After doing a certain number of industrial films and local commercials, you may feel like there isn't a whole lot more you can do without simply repeating yourself. At that point it may be time to move on, take the bigger risk and challenge—to learn and grow as an actor.

The worst thing that can happen in the big market is not having enough money. You end up getting to a place with great opportunities for commercial work and training, but you can't take advantage of them because you're working as a waiter somewhere forty hours a week and you don't have the time or the money to pursue leads.

I read a lot about acting in the area before making the move, and I talked to people who either were living in L.A. or had been there. I've learned that it's important not to put a time frame on your success. If you say, "If I don't make it in two years . . . ," you're not really committed to staying with it for the long term, and that kind of commitment is absolutely necessary in this business.

Whenever I go home or talk to friends, they always want to know either when I'm going to do something they can see or, even if I've just done something, when I'm going to be in something else. People not in the business have absolutely no idea how incredibly difficult it is just to get an audition, let alone a booking. When leaving a secondary market, you've got to expect those questions and be prepared to say, "I just met an agent . . . and that is a big deal." Make your victories a little different than they used to be.

One of the most surprising discoveries I found when I moved to L.A. was that there are a lot of *bad* actors in the big market. Yet for all the bad actors, there is an enormous number of good actors. In some classes, I observed actors pick up three pages from an Oscar-nominated scene or an Emmy-winning scene and after twenty minutes give a polished performance. It's hard to find the same level of competence in the smaller markets. But no one expects you to be that good, that quick, in smaller markets.

OPPORTUNITIES AVAILABLE

STATE	NEAREST MARKET	ON-CAMERA	VOICE-OVER	RADIO	CORPORATE VIDEOS INDUSTRIALS	COMM. PRINT	THEATRE	FILM	TV*
Alabama		x	x	x	x	x	x	x	x
Alaska		x	x	x		x	x	x	x
Arizona		x	x	x	x	x	x	x	x
Arkansas	GA, LA, OK					x	x	x	x
California		x	x	x	x	x	x	x	x
Colorado		x	x	x	x	x	x	x	x
Connecticut	MA, NY				x	x	x		
Delaware		x	x	x	x		x	x	x
Florida		x	x	x	x	x	x	x	x
Georgia		x	x	x	x	x	x	x	x
Hawaii		x	x	x	x	x	x	x	x
Idaho		x	x	x	x	x	x	x	x
Illinois		x	x	x	x	x	x	x	x
Indiana	IL, OH, KY	x	x	x	x	x	x	x	x
Iowa		x	x	x	x	x	x	x	x
Kansas		x	x	x	x	x	x	x	x
Kentucky		x	x	x	x	x	x	x	x
Louisiana	TX	x	x	x	x	x	x	x	x
Maine	MA				x	x	x	x	
Maryland	NY, Wash DC	x	x	x	x	x	x	x	x
Massachusetts		x	x	x	x	x	x	x	x
Michigan		x	x	x	x	x	x	x	x
Minnesota		x	x	x	x	x	x	x	x
Mississippi	LA, TX	x				x	x	x	x
Missouri		x	x	x	x	x	x	x	x
Montana	ID, UT, WA	x	x	x	x	x	x	x	x
Nebraska		x	x	x	x	x	x	x	x
Nevada		x	x	x	x	x	x	x	x
New Hampshire	MA				x	x	x		
New Jersey	NY, PA				x	x	x		
New Mexico		x	x	x	x	x	x	x	x
New York		x	x	x	x	x	x	x	x
North Carolina		x	x	x	x	x	x	x	x
North Dakota		x	x	x	x	x	x	x	x
Ohio		x	x	x	x	x	x	x	x
Oklahoma		x	x	x	x	x	x	x	x
Oregon		x	x	x	x	x	x	x	x
Pennsylvania		x	x	x	x	x	x	x	x
Rhode Island	MA, NY				x	x	x		
South Carolina		x	x	x	x	x	x	x	x
South Dakota		x	x	x	x	x	x	x	x
Tennessee		x	x	x	x	x	x	x	x
Texas		x	x	x	x	x	x	x	x
Utah		x	x	x	x	x	x	x	x
Vermont	MA, NY	x			x	x	x		x
Virginia	MD, Wash DC	x	x	x	x	x	x	x	x
Washington		x	x	x	x	x	x	x	x
West Virginia	NC, PA	x	x	x	x	x	x	x	x
Wisconsin		x	x	x	x	x	x	x	x
Wyoming		x	x	x	x	x	x	x	x

Percentage of opportunities vary with size of the market

* Television includes sit-coms, movies of the week and/or national searches for TV series

FIGURE 22. Opportunities chart.

15

VOICE-OVERS

Voice-over is another area in which you can find many opportunities to develop your talent, make money, exercise your acting ability, express yourself, and have a lot of fun.

❏ WHAT ARE VOICE-OVERS AND WHO DOES THEM?

A voice-over is the audio portion of a commercial (or other filmed or taped material)—the voice you hear. Talent fall in love with this medium because it doesn't matter what they look like and there are significantly fewer restrictions in it than in other areas of the business. Woman can go to auditions without makeup, it doesn't matter what kind of clothes you wear, and age is not a deterrent—you can be fifty and sound thirty. There are no ethnic restrictions. If your voice sounds nonregional, you are eligible for any and all nonregional-sounding parts.

Another plus is that when you record a spot, it usually doesn't take all day. In theory, you can record a commercial (which usually takes two hours) and have the rest of the day to go on other auditions or do whatever else you want.

Voice-over talent receive residuals for the run of the spot. They tend to have less of a chance of becoming overexposed. Because on-camera actors are visibly recognizable, clients may feel reluctant to use the same people too much and choose new faces or looks for their commercials. This can never be a problem with voice-over talent.

It can be a plus for certain types of talent to be able to do funny or cartoon voices. A grown man can do the voice of a magic rug or a wild animal—even a spoon, a shark, or a clock. Think of all the voices in the film *Aladdin*.

Many newcomers to the field have the misconception that having "a nice voice" is enough. This is not true. A voice is your instrument, but a professional voice-over is a combination of several elements—of how well you play the instrument as well as its tone and quality. The sound of your voice will place you in a category that defines you as a spinet or a grand piano. Whether or not you actually play Carnegie Hall has to do with your interpretive skills, your performance skills, and your personal point of view.

❏ VOICE-OVER MARKETS

The three major markets for voice-over are New York, Los Angeles, and Chicago. Secondary markets are Dallas, Florida, and Atlanta, with limited work in other states.

❏ TYPES OF OPPORTUNITIES IN VOICE-OVER

Television, radio, and film all offer many opportunities for voice-over work. The special characteristics of each are described in this section. Animation, another market for voice-over talent, is discussed at the end of this chapter.

TELEVISION

Television offers opportunities for network announcers, promos (promoting a show), animated cartoons, sitcoms, and action voices (any voices not appearing on-camera, for example, a talking parrot or voices coming out of a TV set—remember Carlton the doorman on *Rhonda*?).

In television, the picture is completed and edited first, then the creative team goes into the studio with the voice-over actor and lays down the track (records the voice-over) to the picture. At this point the voice must fit the time and mood of the finished (visual) commercial.

RADIO

Radio and television are very different media. Voices for television have the support of visuals, whereas in radio, the voice is the only thing that conveys the message; it must create the mood and produce a reaction, whether it be humor, frustration, intimacy, or curiosity.

Radio has no visual restrictions. This allows the creative team to be more flexible in the studio. They can change ideas as they go along. Because of this, flexibility on the part of the talent is demanded more frequently for radio auditions than for TV auditions. Radio spots allow more opportunities to react and relate with other characters. Technical ability, knowing how to take direction, and having a good sense of timing are essential in both media.

FILM

In film, there are opportunities in *dubbing*—replacing the original voice of the actor with another person's voice. Foreign films, for instance, are often dubbed over with American voices. That way, subtitles are not necessary when the film is viewed in English-speaking countries. A film also may be dubbed if the dialogue needs to be changed. If the original actor is not available, a person who sounds like him or her does the dubbing. The actual technique involves watching the picture and recording the words or sentences in sync with the dialogue being replaced.

Other opportunities exist in *ADR* (additional dialogue replacement), or *looping*. A loop group is where the actors "slug in" background sounds. For instance, in a huge office or crowd scene, the background noises may have to be "sweetened," or enriched with sound effects or music. The actors watch the action and supply additional voices as orchestrated by a director. They have to be very clear about what the scene is all about and technically correct. For example, if the scene involves a hospital, the actors may have to know some hospital jargon. They have to know regionalisms. If the film takes place in the South, they have to speak with a Southern accent. Actors who do ADR have to be very versatile.

MISCELLANEOUS USES

Miscellaneous opportunities include voice-over for interactive games, videocassettes, voices in toys and dolls, and books-on-tape. Voices for business applications such as automated recordings on answering machines (like those on automated billing services for department stores and utility companies), promos for TV shows, network announcements, and trailers* for films offer other outlets for voice-over talent.

❑ WHAT IT TAKES TO SUCCEED

In every market, there are a handful of performers with the tools to compete nationally. The right tools are training, a professional-quality voice-over demo reel, and the marketing savvy to position yourself properly on the national scene. It's a combination of awareness and training as well as skill. The big difference is professionalism.

The quality of delivery must be solid, sure-footed, and sophisticated, and should be defined by the actor's personality. The successful voice-over performer is original and freed-up creatively. The comedian Robin Williams is a great example. He is totally free. He has a way of looking at the world that comes through loud and clear, and there's no mistaking his personality—other people try to be Robin Williams imitations, but it's never quite the same.

According to Steve Garrin of Voice Works, "Timing, rhythm, being able to interpret copy, and being able to make the words come to life are essential. You can have a bad piece of copy and have a great voice-over artist who makes the copy come to life. But if you have great copy and a mediocre voice-over artist, then the copy just doesn't happen."

*A trailer is an advertisement for film highlighting selected scenes.

❏ HOW TO GET STARTED DOING VOICE-OVERS

The three major markets in the industry are New York, Los Angeles, and Chicago. The process of developing your talent and getting into voice-overs is similar in each market. You need to learn to give a good audition and to perform well under pressure. You also need a demo tape to use as your calling card.

If you are already doing on-camera work, you'll have an edge. You may already have an agent and might find auditioning for radio spots easy. Even so, you must learn to be patient if you really want to get into the field. It can take three to four years to get into the voice-over area from on-camera work.

TRAINING

If you are not a performer, you should take some sort of acting class so that you understand how to play and develop a character. Take a good class in voice technique so you know what to do when you get on that microphone.

Nick Omana, of NOVA Productions in Los Angeles, tells what training should accomplish: "After several workshops, you should know the difference between TV and radio reads, and about different energy levels. You should learn how to bring copy to life in a minute or a half-minute and you should learn how to do a 'donut.' A donut is a little hole or space in the music or picture that is provided. You have to be able to record copy in just the right amount of time to fit into this space. Depending on how many holes there are, it may be referred to as a pretzel. You have to be able to execute any direction given to you. You have to know the medium so you know what the creatives, who are directing you, are talking about when you get into the booth.*

"Remember, one three-hour workshop is not going to make a career. It's going to take a lot of practice time outside of class. You want to get to a point where you can compete with people who do this for a living everyday. In order to be

---

*The booth is an enclosed, soundproof area with a microphone where the talent record their words. It is separated from the creatives by a glass window. The creatives sit in the control room with the engineer, view the talent through the window or glass wall, and talk to them through an intercom system.

successful doing voice-overs, it has to be a passion for you. It can't just be a passing fancy. You have to have the kind of enthusiasm that will give you the energy to see it through the times when it is really tough. Developing a career in voice-over takes time."

DEMO TAPE

A demo tape is the voice-over performer's calling card. Like the on-camera actor's headshot, it requires careful preparation.

To get a demo tape that sounds professional, you cannot have a friend put it together. Find a professional by getting references from friends who have good demo tapes, or call local talent agents who represent voice talent. The producer of your demo tape will help you choose scripts that are best suited for you and will direct you recording the tapes. They will then edit any glitches out of your tape and finish it off with the proper music.

Always ask about studio costs. You will be charged for the time it takes to record and edit your tape. Your producer will also dub extra copies that you want to distribute as marketing tools. Meet the producer before agreeing to hire him. It is important that you feel comfortable with this person. Visit the studio. Shop around before choosing a producer. Be sure you choose a studio because they will give you a professional product, not simply because they are the least expensive. Studio time can vary from $25 to $150 per hour. Usually you can get a package deal for the entire recording of your demo tape.

"A good demo tape shows what you do best and nothing more," says Nick Omana. "If you have only four good pieces and the tape is under a minute long, that is perfectly fine if those four pieces are really strong. The level of quality has to show that you can compete against people in the market who are working every day. The spots should sound like they actually aired somewhere.

"If the spot requires music or sound effects, it should be mixed that way. It needs to have a basic flow to it. The pace should move. Blunt cuts are good, with a quick change into the next piece. It forces listeners to pay attention. Slow fades lull listeners, and they might zone out on you. A spot needs to start strong, stay strong, and finish strong.

"There is no sense in trying to bury a weak piece in the middle. A talent who is marginal in one area will not be called to audition. The creatives want someone who can nail the job and give 100 percent all the time. For the first tape, short and sweet is probably the best way to go—three or four strong pieces. You can build from there as your career goes on."

A demo tape is not only for the performer just entering the field; even the most seasoned voice actors have demo tapes. It is important to keep your tape current by upgrading it annually.

What About Demo Tapes for Advanced Voice-over Talent? "A ten- to fifteen-second clip of a sport is plenty to get across a style," according to Omana. "Put together the tape so it times out to two to two and a half minutes. The tape should show a range of what you do. You want to show that you can do variations on a theme. Some people have one note that is an identifiable style. They do this very well and get booked a lot for it. Some examples of styles are 'real person conversational,' 'light spokesperson,' and 'promo ad' types. You could also have different tapes to market yourself. For instance, you might have a separate tape for promo, another for character, commercial, narration, and animation."

How to Package Your Tape. In your demo tape you should always include a cassette insert card called a *J-card*. Your name should appear on the spine and front of it. Any contact number should appear on the back. A picture of yourself is not recommended. It limits people's views of the possibilities of your voice. The label on the cassette itself should be printed in the same type face as the J-card, not typed. This keeps your package consistent and professional looking. The design should reinforce your image in some way.

The promise on the package should reflect what's inside. "I saw a performer," said voice-over consultant Maurice Tobias, "who spent a lot of money on a CD, and the subtitle he added to his name was 'The Second Most Powerful Voice in the World.' When I played the CD, I expected there would be a voice explosion. Instead, the voice I heard was a dusty, midrange voice that was lovely but had nothing to do with power. At that point, because I was so disappointed at not hearing a James-Earl-Jones-type voice, I couldn't really appreciate anything about it."

Getting Someone to Listen to Your Tape. "You have to get someone to listen to your tape," says Steve Garrin. "You can take a couple of different routes. If you feel you have the skills and are ready to compete with people who have been doing voice-overs for a long time and are excellent at it, you can go out and find an agent. Another route would be to start at the bottom of the ladder and go to small production companies or small advertising agencies and try to market yourself there.

"This is a business. You are a salesperson. What you are selling is yourself. You have to know exactly what your strengths are and make people aware of them. The more people who know about you and what you can do, the better your chances of getting an audition or booking."

Who to Send Your Demo To. Garrin continues, "Find out which trade publications are available in your area. In New York, for instance, there is *Ross Reports,* which lists the casting directors, talent agents, and production companies. There are also producer's guides such as *Madison Avenue Handbook, New York Production Guide,* and *Back Stage Producers and Production Guide.* In Los Angeles, there is *LA 411* and *The Blue Book.* Your local papers will tell you about production going on in your area. There may also be trade papers in your market. In New York and Los Angeles, for example, you have *Variety* and *Back Stage.*

"In smaller, regional areas talent can also call local TV stations, production companies, and radio stations to find out how they get their talent for the local commercials you see and hear."

❏ MARKETING AND PACKAGING YOURSELF AS A TALENT

In any profession, marketing is everything. From your résumé to the work you do on a daily basis, it's all about marketing. It feels too commercial to a creative person, but the fact of the matter is that you are all in business for yourselves. You are all entrepreneurs. In this particular case, the voice is the product you are offering. The product has to have a unique stand, a unique identity that's presented in the tape.

If you are a beginner, the main thing to do is listen to what's being done to get some idea of general style, then work to develop your own spin on that. The better you present what you have to offer, the more rapidly you will move up in the business. And don't design yourself to sound exactly like the voice you think you most admire.

Another important part of marketing is keeping up to date. For example, current trends are for a "real read," using someone who is conversational, approachable—the guy-next-door type. There is also a trend to use "in-your-face," funny-edged, and tongue-in-cheek types. To see for yourself, simply turn on prime-time television and listen to commercials. Pay particular attention to cutting-edge venues like FOX, MTV, and The Comedy Channel. Then record yourself on tape and compare the style of your read with that in the commercials. Be willing to let go of your preconceived notions of what a voice-over read should sound like. Actors who stay on top of current trends in voice-over are more likely to book the job.

HOW LONG WILL IT TAKE TO BOOK YOUR FIRST JOB?

According to Garrin, "It's hard to say. Some people hit it immediately. They take a workshop and within six months they are out there and have three or four national TV or radio spots. Sometimes it takes years to do it. Sometimes people don't make it because they don't have the desire to get out there and stay at it. They send out tapes, then don't make follow-up calls. They just sit and hope someone calls them. You have to really *make* it happen. The more you work at it, the quicker you may succeed. It's a numbers game. You have to get the auditions. You have to be good. You have to practice."

Garrin concludes, "Just keep going. If you have a bad day, take the day off, get your head together, and go after it the next day. Don't think about it too much. Just do it. It's a crazy business. There are no rules as to who succeeds and why they do. A lot of it is luck. A lot of it is being at the right place at the right time. If you think about it too much, you'll probably talk yourself out of it."

❏ TAPPING THE REGIONAL MARKETS

In addition to major markets there are voice-over opportunities nationwide, even in the smallest of markets. Wherever there is advertising of any kind, there is voice-over. According to Maurice Tobias, the biggest resource in a smaller market is a radio station, where you can work either as a DJ, as part of the production department, or in the department of creative services, which writes and develops ads for the station's advertisers. You can then end up doing the voices for the commercials at the station. As a result, agents and companies who want to advertise may call the station or contact you directly, and use you on a freelance basis.

The second route is through little theaters. The person looking to hire a voice often contacts theaters because actors have well-developed voices. Acting classes and modeling schools are another resource for producers looking for talent. A lot depends on how sophisticated a market is. Another place to get a start is through professional workshops established by voice-over professionals. You can learn the skills, after which you can put together a demo tape and start sending it out to agencies and communications departments involved in advertising and/or narration.

❏ THE TAPING SESSION: INTERVIEW WITH BARBARA GOLDMAN

The producer is one of the principal people who decides who will get booked for a job. Barbara Goldman, radio and television voice-over producer in New York City, takes us into the studio for a look at what happens during a typical voice-over session.

What can an actor expect when he first arrives at a session?

Generally you are given the script a few minutes ahead of time to look over before you enter the booth. Depending on the climate of the session, you will either be sent right into the booth or you will come in and meet the client and everyone else in the room.

At a radio session, where there may be many characters in one spot, the actors may be called in at the same time to record the spot together because an overall timing is needed for the spot. You may then be asked to step aside so the creative team can concentrate on different performances in different segments of the spot. Many times, you'll have to wait around while the team perfects all the technical aspects of the spot—it's not a reflection on how well you're doing. After the spot is timed out, the announcer might be recorded and allowed to leave; then work begins with the other actors.

Who is in the studio for a radio voice-over announcer session?

A radio recording session will run most efficiently if one person talks to the talent. This person is usually the producer, or it might be the writer. The art director, clients, assistant writer, writer, account executive, engineer, and the producer could be at the session.

Many times radio work is done at the last minute, so all parties involved are needed there to move the process along. Something magical can happen in the recording session, something unexpected, so it is a good idea for the client to be there. Many changes, including ones involving legal issues, can occur, and actors usually have to record over and over again to cover all bases.

The actor can expect anywhere from three to forty takes. All takes are listened to. The first take might be the one actually liked best. It is played back for the talent, and the actor might be asked to do it again. You are expected to understand what you did in a particular take so you could recreate a very subtle nuance of it, if necessary.

Who is in the studio for a television voice-over announcer session?

Generally, the producer, writer, art director, engineer, and, in many cases, the editor are present. Ideally, the voice is the last element that is put on the spot. After the spot is shot and edited, the music is edited, and all the pieces put together, the announcer will be called in. Ideally, one person who can convey the message clearly directs the talent.

If the director is not getting the feeling he or she wants from the actor's read, perhaps the actor will have to chime in and help figure out what is wrong. An experienced actor may suggest a solution as simple as projecting a smile into her voice. Interpretation can make or break a reading.

What is expected of the actor in the studio?

If an actor gives one or two takes and feels that's all he can or will give, then it is not worth having him there. It may be the greatest performance of his lifetime, but if it's not what the client wants, it's not right.

The attitude and personality of everyone involved are very important. The actor should accommodate—not get in the way. An actor may feel he can read the line ten different ways and give them all to the creatives before being asked. That would be totally distracting. On the other hand, if an actor feels a line should be read differently than directed, he can find ways to approach that without resisting or offering too much.

The actor should not feel that he has to be the center of attention. He has to sense the climate in the control room, determine whether it is playful or serious, and whether or not there is room for some levity. Sometimes it's better simply to get the job done and get out of there.

The more people in the control room, the more likely it is to be a tense situation, simply because there are more people who have to be pleased. If it is a tense control room, the actor has to go along, do what's asked of him, and finesse a way to ask, "What if I try it *this* way?"

Actors have to realize that the people in the studio are under a lot of pressure to get the right outcome. It is the producer's job to accommodate the writer and the client. After the creative team finds what they want, actors are welcome to their way of doing it. But they should bear in mind that the creative team in the control room is not thinking just about the voice. They are thinking about all the elements of the production.

What do actors tend to struggle with on their first booking?

They have the ability, otherwise they wouldn't be there, but they seem to feel insecure about the procedure and, possibly, when to talk. It is not expected for a talent to be a time clock, bringing something in exactly to time. With the new technology, chunks can be taken out of copy. If the talent and attitude are there, the creatives will have the patience.

FINAL TIPS ON TAPING SESSIONS

Too Many Directors? Sometimes there is just one person in the control room; sometimes there is a bank of people. At some recording sessions, they all have input; at others, they just sit there. The most trying time is when five or six people on the creative team show up and each one has a different opinion of how the recording should go. This has to be conveyed to you and you have to satisfy all of them. These people are all part of the deal. Don't try to split the difference and make everybody happy. Communicate with the people who are directing you. Explain to them that you are hearing two different pieces of direction and you are not sure what they want. Suggest doing it one way and then the other way. This business is all about communication.

Too Many Takes? Nick Omana shares his experience of an extended taping session: "There was a time when I had sixty-seven takes. I went out to get a glass of water during a break and the engineer said to me, 'You're doing a great job. These guys usually do a hundred or more takes.' Producers want to make sure they have every base covered so they are going to work you every way to Sunday to make sure they have done so. As talent, we are always seeking approval after two takes. That doesn't happen very often."

Steve Roland, a voice-over talent, has this advice for newcomers, "To do well in voice-over work, you need a lot of versatility and diversification. Once you are booked and in the booth recording, you want to get the job done right. You should learn to take direction. Listen to the creative team. They are the ones with the idea—right or wrong. Usually, a smart director or writer will say, 'Is there any other way you hear or feel this?' Then you put it down the way you feel it should go."

❏ ANIMATION

There is tremendous growth in cartoons, creating expanded opportunities for voice talent. The bulk of animation is done in Los Angeles, the "mecca of toons."

Charlie Adler is a voice-over cartoon artist who has done many animated films including *Aladdin*, *Tiny Toons* for Steven Spielberg (playing Buster Bunny), *Smurfs*, and *Real Monster* for Nickelodeon. In *Cool World*, he played Brad Pitt's animated sidekick Nails, a neurotic spider. He has done over seventy series in the last nine years and over a hundred regular characters.

Charlie suggests that animation involves a much more definitive, broader use of acting abilities than acting on camera. With on-camera acting, the actor is seen. The viewer knows if the character is tall, skinny, fat, sloppy looking, handsome, or sophisticated. In animation, the actor has to paint the picture with his voice—to entirely create the look of the character with it.

"I have done a series called *Swat Cats*, Brock Peters was one of the villains and Roddy McDowall, Tim Curry, Sally Struthers, Brenda Vaccaro, Nancy Travis, and Jim Belushi played various characters. It was a wonderful place for people to come and do real, good work. The only difference between this and other acting media is that you are invisible, so nobody's watching you.

"This is an acting job. It is offensive when people out in the real world say, 'Oh, *I* can do a funny voice. *I* can do cartoons.' It's not about funny voices. You need to have a great ability to act and create characters. You need an incredible imagination and the ability to be very, very free. You must be very flexible, able to switch gears in a matter of seconds. Technically, you have to be very adept at many things.

"Yes, voice is important. Yes, having dialects is very important. The energy level is hyperspace in animation. It's like running a marathon every time you do a show. The ability to commit to a character and to be consistent requires some serious acting skills. Animation's not a medium for people who can't act."

HOW TO GET STARTED IN ANIMATION

There are an infinite number of ways to get into animation. For example, Charlie Adler has always considered himself goofy. He was the brat in school. He was the kid who never shut up, who made fun of everybody and lived in the principal's office.

Luckily for him, he had a talent that could be translated into acting. He went into theater and broke into commercials very early (at the age of eighteen). He learned how to work in front of a camera, which helped prepare him for voice-over and radio.

Adler's agent got him into an audition for an animated special that came to New York. She knew he was goofy, knew he had done a lot of improv and that he was good at satire. He went in, landed the spot, then recorded it in New York. After going on tour in a Broadway show, Adler moved to Los Angeles—the hotbed of animation.

"I told the agent I got in L.A. that I wanted to do cartoons. I had to go in and demonstrate to her that I knew what I was doing. I wrote forty characters, three lines per character, and insisted I audition for them. They listened to what I had to do. A week later, they got me a general audition for Hanna-Barbera using my material, my characters. I was given five minutes. I ended up doing twelve. Nobody stopped me and a week later, I had *Smurfs*. Two weeks after that, I had another series and three weeks later, another.

"There's a sense that in the voice-over world, as in many other businesses, there is a clique with the same old people getting all the work. This is not true of animation. A casting director in animation cannot hire the same people, so there is room for newcomers in the voice-over field. Creative teams are always looking for new voices. The trick is to be able to execute the technique as well as or better than established veterans."

HOW TO MAKE A CHARACTER COME ALIVE WITH A VOICE

Adler goes on, "Before the voice-over is done, the talent should be able to see a picture of the character. If a sketch is not available, a monologue in which several actions are taking place is necessary. One should not always expect these to be cohesive.

"You have to have a keen sense of the visual—of what is going on. A director or writer tells you what the action is, and you put all that information together—what you believe from the monologue and the piece, the physical characteristics you get from the picture, and what the director and the other people in the control room tell you they want in the way of sensibility and feeling.

"Do they want a mischievous person? A young person? An older person? Full-bodied? Angry? Edgy? A character type? Someone who is aggressive? Shy? Neurotic? These descriptions translate into an energy and a sensibility. A good way of hooking into a character might be to imagine you are doing children's theater, musical theater, vaudeville, or characters typical of those in *The Wizard of Oz*. In fact, one could say that those characters were living cartoons.

"You have to be very imaginative and very, very free. Paint your character with broad brush strokes. Take all these things into consideration, commit to a choice, and *go*. It's very improvisational and you really, really must fly.

"Let's say you finish the monologue and the director says, 'Okay, that was interesting but this character has to be a little crankier and he needs to have a little more weight. Look at the picture—he is a little heavier. And look at the upper lip— it's very, very thick and he has buck teeth. We want to get a sloppier sound and a more aggressive character. He is a little angrier.'

"Then all of a sudden the writer says, 'You know what? I think it would be very interesting if we went a whole different way with this guy. Let's try this. Instead of making him fat and aggressive, let's make him very thin sounding and neurotic.'

"Those are two huge adjustments to make. Now you have to take that monologue and adapt it to a different personality. You have to completely switch gears and you might have fifteen seconds to make this adjustment. You have to commit to the character and go with it. That's why I say it's very improvisational. That's how you get the job.

"Usually, you show up at work for a table reading, which is a rehearsal sitting. Sometimes you rehearse at a microphone. Every studio has a different setup for rehearsal. They have the full script with pictures of the characters. You have a read-through with the director, and he tells you every beat action* of the scenes. For instance, you know if there is a physical action. Does the character trip and fall here? Is the character getting up and reaching? Is he screaming here? Whatever.

"You do a read-through. You mark your script. This takes about an hour and a half, then you go to tape. It goes like a radio play and it moves like the wind.

"By the way, SAG allows the people booking you to require you to play three characters and get one payment with a ten percent bump up for the third character. That tells you right there that it is cost-efficient for a producer to hire somebody versatile.

"Let's say you are playing one character and you have two more that you are required to do. Of those two, you could have rehearsed a sixty-five-year-old Irish elf, which they have decided on ahead of time. Then, in between the rehearsal and the taping they could say, 'We never had the drawing, but play him as a fourteen-year-old East Indian boy. *Go.*' There it is. That's how it works."

---

*A beat action is a moment when an actor changes attitude, emotion, or physical movement.

16 MODELS CROSSING OVER INTO COMMERCIALS

❏ WHY MORE AND MORE MODELS ARE GETTING INTO COMMERCIALS

Models are breaking old stereotypes, becoming extremely savvy business people. "All looks—no brains" could hardly describe the streetwise entrepreneurs who work today's runways and appear in editorials and advertisements in major markets around the globe. And as America's baby boomers reach maturity and approach seniority, the industry has begun to tune into their needs. Whereas models used to have a career life span of little more than ten or so years, now a good model can work well into her forties and beyond—a direct reflection of changing demographics relating to the "aging of America."

Well before a smart model's career begins to wind down, she starts to invest her earnings or develop businesses of her own. Models are opening restaurants, designing clothing lines, endorsing products, and branching out into other areas in the industry. More and more models are exploring film, theater, and television, and one of the primary ways for models to get their foot in the talent end of the industry is through commercials.

Models who expand into television commercial work position themselves firmly inside the industry. An increasing number of models are taking acting classes to increase their chances of getting commercial work. As models become better prepared and well trained in commercial auditioning technique, they broaden their career and fatten their bankbooks. The residual income from commercial work can come in for years after the actual work was done, carrying the model through slow times and/or adding a lucrative financial base from which she can expand in both careers.

Most commercial agencies now have separate departments or are affiliated with model agencies exclusively to represent and send out models for commercials. Many of these departments have expanded even further into representing their talent for theatrical (film and television) deals. Model agencies recognize the growing trend of models crossing over into other areas of the industry and are quick to give attention to this lucrative segment of their businesses.

❏ HOW COMMERCIAL EXPERIENCE CAN BE A STEPPING-STONE TO TELEVISION AND FILM

Many times a beautiful person is needed in a film. The casting director or the film's director will see a model acting in a commercial and will trace him or her down to audition for the film.

Commercials can be a model's first opportunity for exposure outside the world of print advertising. As the first experience of acting on-camera, commercial work can help models learn to take direction, deliver copy on time, follow blocking instructions, and exercise expressions and emotions on film.

After acquiring some commercial experience, a model often discovers that she likes acting and pursues it more seriously by taking dramatic acting classes. The commercial experience gives her the insight and confidence to expand her career.

❏ HOW MODELING AND TALENT CONVENTIONS OFFER OPPORTUNITIES TO EXPAND INTO OTHER AREAS

From Toledo, Ohio, to Hollywood, California, aspiring models and actors vie for the opportunity to break into the business by attending one of the numerous modeling and talent conventions held annually in the United States and Canada. These events, running over the course of a few days to one week, draw casting directors, agents, and managers from major markets across the globe, each scouting new faces to appear in print, national commercials, televison, and film.

"When young people like Elijah Wood, Jessica Biel, and Ashley Bucille were discovered at IMTA, they were seen on the runway before they broke into television," says Helen Rogers, president of the International Model and Talent Association. The "million dollar" contract for IMTA's male model Joel West included Calvin Klein's *Eternity* commercials with Christy Turlington—West's transition from print model to television. Every star model would love to get a television commercial campaign for the exposure and the money.

Participants of such conventions have signed contracts with major agents and managers in both Hollywood and New York and have appeared in national commercials for McDonald's, Rice Krispies, Advil, Cheerios, Burger King, Jack in the Box, Coca-Cola, Calvin Klein, and many, many more.

❏ THE ROLE OF A GOOD MANAGER IN MAKING THE TRANSITION

Talent manager Vincent Cirrincione discovered and developed Halle Berry. Halle started out as a pageant contestant while she was still in her teens. She became Miss Teen All-America and was runner-up to Miss USA. A native of Cleveland, Ohio, Halle—who was only five feet seven—moved to Chicago, where she primarily did catalog modeling for various department stores. She had intended to study acting extensively but when she met Vincent and came to New York, he moved her acting career along so quickly she wound up getting on-the-job training instead.

"You can't expect to live in a small town and fly to a big city and have people take you seriously, until you're a big star," says Vincent. "I never heard Halle say, 'I can't do this or that.' She just did what she had to do. There was a time after her first movie when she lived on a couch in my office to save money on rent to invest in herself. She took the money and hired a publicist. When I gave her advice she understood and acted accordingly. Halle went out there to follow her dreams. She didn't just wait for it to come to her. There was a certain amount of strategy and serendipity."

Vincent's strategy included positioning Halle's career contrary to Hollywood's assumption that you can't act if you're a model. Up to this point, Halle had done a stereotypical part in a short-lived TV series about models called *Living Dolls* and guest starred on weekly sit-coms like *A Different World*. The new strategy led to her role in Spike Lee's *Jungle Fever* with Wesley Snipes, where she played an unattractive crack addict. This gave Halle a chance to show that she had more to offer than just a pretty face. One thing led to another and she got an Eddie Murphy movie and a TV series called *Queen*. The *Flintstones* followed.

Halle's crossover from modeling into film was made very quickly, and she was able to by-pass a television commercial career. But now Halle is a *Revlon* girl. Her career has come full circle. She got the *Revlon* campaign because she was successful in film and television, and she feels her background in pageants gave her the ability to talk to people and express herself well.

❏ HOW FASHION PRINT WORK DIFFERS FROM MAKING TELEVISION COMMERCIALS

In some ways, modeling for print is very similar to working on-camera in a commercial spot. You have to be comfortable being in front of the camera, you have to relate to the camera as you would to a dear friend, and you have to be able to take direction from the person behind the camera. You have to love the camera, and the camera has to love you.

In other ways, commercials present new challenges for a model. In print work, the photographer is trying to capture a moment. Clients wade through resulting contact sheets looking for a single shot or a strong series of images that will best represent the client and what they're looking for. Movements for print work are exaggerated, free flowing and stylized, often mannequinlike. A commercial is an active medium from start to finish. For an on-camera commercial, movements and expressions are more natural, usually with more warmth and approachability in the actor's demeanor.

Another consideration is space. Whereas on the runway or for print, a model has ample space to move and express herself, in some commercial work she will have to adjust to the limited space of the television screen. Movements for commercials in this case will be slight, yet expressive.

In print advertising, your primary promotional tool is the portfolio, consisting of a range of photographs containing your strongest images as well as tear sheets* from previous work. In the United States, commercially, your primary marketing tools are your commercial head shot, your résumé, and ultimately, a demo tape† showing samples of your work in commercials. In foreign markets, where the trend is to use pretty faces for commercial work, a model may get by without standard talent marketing tools. However, it is important to put together a proper head shot, résumé, and demo tape if you want to be taken seriously as a commercial actor.

❑ WHAT IT TAKES TO CROSS OVER

The transition from model to on-camera actor takes more than just a great face. When the model speaks, being physically attractive isn't enough. That's when knowing how to analyze a script and to audition can expand her career.

Suzette Vazquez is an agent for J Michael Bloom & Associates in New York City who represents models for commercials, TV, and film. She offers some insight into what it takes to make the transition from modeling to commercials and television: "When you see those good-looking people running down the beach in a commercial, it doesn't really take any acting qualities. Anything that they've already experienced through print work applies to on-camera work for commer-

---

*Tear sheets are samples of a model's published work (print ads, fashion spreads, etc.) torn fom the publications to put into a portfolio.

†Most of the time, a demo tape, or reel, is not requested for commercial work. However, it is always best to request and collect a copy of every commercial you do at the time of the shoot or soon after the shoot. You will then have the material on hand if you wish to put together a demo reel. This will give you the competitive edge on the rare occasion when a reel is requested.

cials. Whether they are just walking down the street and laughing with a friend or playing with a young child, it's about the look.

"There are those diamonds in the rough who have a personality that is amazing and it shows. Those are the ones who really push through. They do the commercials where there is copy. Many models don't really do commercials with copy because they don't have acting experience. So the ones who can act get to do commercials with copy.

"My advice to newcomers is to listen to what people are telling you. Be open to suggestions. If it's suggested you take acting classes, do it. If it's suggested you need a new head shot, do it. The process weeds out a lot of models who are not as hungry for the work as let's say, actors who have just graduated from Juilliard and will do anything to be on stage. Many models think they can just do commercials without knowing what's involved. This is wrong. Models who are serious about expanding into film and television should be taking acting classes."

❏ TRAINING

Although your modeling experience may give you a slight edge, the transition to commercials will be much easier if you invest in a good commercial auditioning workshop or class. There is a specific technique applied in commercial auditioning. Proper training will help you get comfortable with the procedure and give a good audition. Having commercial training with a good coach listed on your résumé also shows you are serious about learning and applying the craft.

❏ OPPORTUNITIES IN FOREIGN MARKETS

There are many opportunities for models, not only in the United States but in foreign markets as well. Clients from all over the world often want someone beautiful to represent their products, and not just cosmetics. European markets can become a virtual gold mine of opportunities for models with acting experience. "The trend is to use models instead of actors whenever possible," according to Italian model agent Alberto Righini. "Sometimes, it has something to do with the budget. The models are already there (in Milan) so they don't have to fly in special actors to do the spot. In Europe, models cost less than professional actors, which saves clients as much as fifty percent in salaries."

The trend toward using primarily models in commercials is evident in many countries. For instance, models from Scandinavia, America, Canada, and England go to Barcelona, Spain, to make money in commercials, then go to Madrid to do editorials—using money made in TV commercials to finance other career aspirations.

In Milan, models can enjoy a full range of work, from high-fashion editorial print (as opposed to catalogs) to television commercials. Greece does a fair amount of commercial work, and Australia and South Africa have opened up in recent years. England has a strong commercial market. "It's big business there," says Righini. "With computers and graphics and the ideas to do creative, innovative presentations, the English are the best by far."

HOW A TYPICAL AUDITION IN EUROPE DIFFERS FROM ONE IN THE UNITED STATES

In Europe, all commercials are dubbed over, so it doesn't matter if you can't speak the language. If there is a script, you are given a copy anywhere from the night before to an hour before, and someone will help you translate it into English and direct your facial expressions. You are just expected to mouth the words, so that when the voices are dubbed in, the audio and visual parts go together well.

❏ COMPENSATION

WHAT MODELS CAN MAKE IN PRINT AND COMMERCIALS IN THE UNITED STATES

In the United States, a day rate for catalog print modeling can range from $1,250 to $1,500. As the popularity of the model increases, so does her day rate. Top models can make up to $15,000 a day.

When models are booked on a commercial, most of the time they get their day rate for the shoot day and a guaranteed amount of money every payment cycle, which is every thirteen weeks (see Chapter 13). It's just a matter of shooting the commercial and then waiting for the residuals to start rolling in. Model agents, by the way, can command more money than noncelebrity actors. This makes appearing in commercials a very attractive prospect for them.

HOW MODELS ARE PAID FOR COMMERCIAL WORK IN EUROPE

In each country compensation is different. In Milan, for instance, the agent negotiates a set price for the talent, then discusses royalties. If the spot runs over many years, the agent negotiates for more and more money each year. Generally, the model is paid for the day, plus the royalty for the first year. Future royalties are paid to the model by most agencies, even if they are no longer in the country.

Most foreign markets don't have unions, at least not like America's SAG and AFTRA. Exceptions include Canada, which has a strong union, and Spain, which is developing a more structured format from which to book and pay for commercial work. Day rates in most foreign markets depend on the model's name and experience—and whether or not it is for a private channel, a local channel, or a national channel. In Italy, for example, day rates range from several hundred dollars for a small spot to two thousand dollars and up (base) plus royalties for a national commercial.

❏ INTERVIEWS WITH ELLE MACPHERSON, CARMEN, TIM SAUNDERS, AND PATRICK JOHNSON

Following are some inspirational insights and advice from professional models who have made the transition into commercials.

ELLE MACPHERSON

Elle MacPherson is an international supermodel who has done commercials for McDonald's, Biotherm (in Europe), and MCI. In addition to other companies, she has a lingerie company in Australia where she produces her own commercials. Here's what MacPherson recalls about her start in modeling:

In Australia I was awarded an opportunity to attend law school. But after graduating from high school, I decided to take a year off before going to college. I held a variety of jobs including waitressing in a theater restaurant and working in a pharmacy. A friend of mine, who was a model, suggested that I try it and possibly make a lot of money. "No way," I said. "No way ever. I could never do that." My friend then bet me twenty dollars that if I went to the agency with her, they would take me on. I thought, okay, that's twenty bucks, the equivalent of three or four hours' work. So I went.

When you are sixteen, you have weird perceptions of beauty. You haven't grown into yourself. I was a long drink of water, very tall. I didn't look like what I thought models looked like.

I gave the agent a snapshot taken by a friend. The agency sent me to have more photographs and the next thing I knew I was being booked for jobs. I worked for a year and a half in Australia. While on a skiing trip in America, I called an agent from Click in New York who had been pursuing me, started working with them, and never left the States.

I always had more of a commercial look than a high fashion look. I really didn't do a lot of fashion. I didn't work a lot for the magazines, except *Sports Illustrated*. I did a lot of advertising campaigns and TV commercials. I guess I work well on-camera. I feel like I need to move and I'm freer when I'm moving, so I'm better on-camera than I am in stills.

I never wanted to act. It was just one of those weird things. A script for *Sirens* came to my manager's attention and he suggested that I read it. I didn't want to read it because I didn't want to do film. I couldn't see the point. He suggested I read it anyway. The director was in town and wanted to meet with me. He said, "I think *you* should be the one to tell the director you are too lazy to read the script. That you don't care about doing a movie in Australia about a famous Australian artist and spending two months in the mountains with Hugh Grant. You should be the one to tell him that you won't even consider it."

So I read the script and changed my mind. I thought it would be really good for me to spend a few months in Australia and do something different. Working very hard in modeling made me feel burnt out. I did the film. It led to others, and my film career seemed to propel itself. Now I love making films and that's all I want to do.

CARMEN

Carmen is known for her longevity in the modeling world. She has been with Ford Models since they opened their doors approximately fifty years ago. Carmen has appeared in every magazine from *The New Yorker* to *Vogue* and is known for her work with Revlon and for the classic Vanity Fair lingerie advertisements as the "girl with no face." She is trying to help people redefine themselves at every age from fifty to seventy and beyond. Her longevity in the industry lends itself to some interesting insights. Here's what she has to say about it:

I take good care of myself. Life's a challenge as a human being, not just for models. It's a long trip. One has to have an overview of the whole trip. I eat when I'm hungry. I try to keep some balance in my life. I make sure I get a good night's sleep before I work. I drink a lot of water. I am always mentally prepared. I make sure I get good nutrition and maintain a high energy level. If you stay up all night at nightclubs, it's going to come out of your hide in the long run. And smoking is the worst thing you can do for your skin. Forget smoking. You have to opt for healthy choices.

Doing commercials takes natural ability, being able to apply one's inner life and imagination to the craft of acting. So I didn't find it difficult to move from print work to commercials. I found it challenging. The timing and what I am asked to do on the set is different.

Television commercial work is not as intimate as photography in a studio because there are so many people around. It is a different process. The hours are different. When you are used to one and you like the area you are moving into, you just pay attention and learn the trade.

Make sure that you keep on educating yourself because the work does not come to you. You have to keep developing your lust for life in general so that you have some inner life to bring to a job. What makes the difference between someone who gets work and someone who doesn't is the amount of passion you bring to your craft.

I would advise young people to stay in school. School really teaches discipline. It's very hard to pick up self-discipline on one's own. Reading is the single most important thing for youngsters to get into. Once you can read, you can learn by yourself.

It's very tricky for young people starting out to understand the personality of some of the people they come in contact with. For instance, if you are hired for a job and you know you are going to make money, and the photographer is on drugs and offers or insists you take the drugs to "make you more expressive," it's important for you to remember to do the right thing. It takes a lot of guts to gracefully get out of the way of something that is self-destructive but it must be done.

TIM SAUNDERS

Tim has been modeling with Ford Models since 1966. He got his start in London a year before signing with Ford. Tim has done 187 TV commercials including Sominex, Promise margarine, United Airlines, Cadillac, Bahamas Tourism, and Prell Shampoo. Here he describes the differences in shooting print and television commercials.

It's a very different job. In commercials you must be able to walk, talk, and chew gum at the same time. With print you don't. Each print job and commercial is different depending on what you are trying to sell. With fashion modeling, you are usually selling a garment and you are trying to make the clothes look good while giving them an attitude. In modeling you either look right for the job or you don't. You don't have to go deep down to any acting abilities to come up with a special look. You were chosen for the job because you look the way you do and the client wants you to be yourself.

In television commercials you are acting more. You are relating to either the camera or to another person you are working with. In both you have to have a presence. When you are booked for a print job, you are booked for a certain specified number of hours or days. With a commercial shoot the hours never end. If you are booked nine to five, you might work nine to midnight, and you are obliged to stay until the job is done. Print is not done this way. You are very often booked for one job from two to three and another from three-thirty to four. You can say your time is up and go on to the next job. If you are booked a half a day for a commercial, you cannot accept another job for the afternoon because the commercial might run over and you must stay. Commercials very often have more down time while sets are being lighted or camera angles being changed. You very often are in a hurry-up-and-wait situation. You can wait all day while other scenes are shot and do your scene at the end of the day.

PATRICK JOHNSON

Patrick has done over thirty commercials including Gillette, Red Lobster, Arid Extra Dry, Suave Shampoo, Head & Shoulders, and JCPenney. He is also a motivational speaker. Here he shares some of his insight into what it takes to do well in the industry.

I got my start in the industry when a friend of mine encouraged me to go along with him to enroll in a modeling school while I was going to the University of Arizona. The school asked me to meet Eileen Ford, who was coming in on a scouting trip. I didn't know who Eileen Ford was. I went with the agency to the IMTA convention and won Model of the Year in 1980. Several model agencies wanted to sign me. I went with Ford because they had a good softball team.

These conventions are not so much about winning. It's about a chance to pursue a dream. The only guarantee is that you'll have a good time if you allow yourself to. If this dream doesn't work, there are others. It's not about becoming a famous model. There are many avenues you can pursue other than becoming a model. A lot of people can't see beyond that.

I find commercials a little bit more challenging than print. I like challenges. I like the stimulus I get from the commercial environment. It is like a movie set on a smaller scale. I wanted to be a part of that. Commercials have moved me into other things. I wanted to be on a soap opera so I took extra work and spent time on a set to see what the actors, the set, and the atmosphere were like. I learned from the people who were working. I got a contract role on the soap *Loving* and have done films like *Aspen Extreme, The "M" Word,* and *New York Crossing.*

There is a thing in modeling called "The Golden Handcuffs"—being locked into modeling, working at two thousand dollars a day, or taking a trip half way around the world with someone else paying for it. This made modeling difficult to leave, even for a crossover into the acting world. You can be a model and work successfully in commercials, but if you are working all the time modeling you never have time to go to casting calls. You have to decide what you want and stay focused.

17

KIDS IN THE BUSINESS

In commercials, kids are big business. Appearing in commercials can create scores of extraordinary opportunities for children, including:

1. Significant income potential
2. Business opportunities that can be carried into later life
3. Personal development in communication, presentations, and team work
4. Visibility, which can help the child move into other areas of the business

❏ WHAT TYPES OF KIDS DO WELL IN COMMERCIALS?

New York children's agent Karen Apicella describes children who are suited to the business: "Kids who do well in this business are naturally outgoing. They don't have to be 'rehearsed' or 'energized' (by parents) before they go in to meet an agent or casting director. They're just fun-loving young people who are not afraid of strangers and can talk without being coaxed or coerced.

"Children can't be afraid to leave Mommy. I look for children who will talk, who can keep their attention focused, who can answer questions. Someone who is very spontaneous, very uninhibited, and not at all shy. All this is as important as looks.

"We get a lot of moms who say, 'Look, I have this beautiful

child,' but Susie is very shy. She gives one-word answers. She is always looking at the ground. She fidgets and is clearly uncomfortable. Seven-year-old Susie is not going to work because there are other children who are sparkling, outgoing, and lots of fun. They enjoy themselves. They look like they're having a good time. They respond to you. They're funny.

"It's important that you not only have a cute child (*everybody* has a cute child) but that you have a precocious child. That's what the agents look for, the one who stands out and is remembered."

Los Angeles children's talent agent Judy Savage discusses specific requirements: "The first thing I look for in a child is the passion. A child who wants to do this comes in for the interview and he's just so excited and 'alive'—he *loves* the idea of being in the business. The kid has to have a great look. This doesn't mean he should be gorgeous or beautiful. The look has to be, first of all, *blendable,* so he can blend into families. In most commercials, the adults are hired first, then a child who fits. For instance, a child who has sandy hair and a few freckles blends in with other actors who have dark, light, or red hair. They blend so it's easier to get them started.

"Next, you look for size. In L.A., we look for forty-two-inch six-year-olds to play four-year-olds and fifty-four-inch ten-year-olds to play ages eight, nine, and ten. We also look for twelve-year-olds who are not over five feet tall, thirteen- to fourteen-year-olds who are five-one to five-two. If they're thirteen and five-seven or five-eight, they have to play fifteen- to sixteen-year-olds because they're taller than everybody. It's almost always preferable to have older children who look younger."

Children who do well in the business read well. The earlier they learn to read, the better they'll do. Child actors who are very successful are always smart. Usually, the brighter they are, the more they'll work. They also have to have charisma. Kids who are suited for the business light up the room when they come in. Even with a three-year-old, the conversation during the interview should be so interesting that you'd rather be with the child than anyone else.

Note: Never beg, bribe, or bully a child to get him to perform.

Having to resort to such tactics indicates that the child is not interested in doing this. Children will always be better at something they enjoy doing.

❏ GETTING PICTURES

When children are under the age of five or six, agents generally don't suggest parents run out and get professional pictures done. At that age, children change so quickly that by the time you get an appointment with a photographer, have the shoot, get your proof back, order and receive enlargements, have any necessary touch-up work done on the print, get mass reproductions made, mail out the pictures, the child no longer looks like her picture. It's highly impractical to spend three hundred dollars on professional head shots of a child who will change before you have a chance to send the pictures out. To get younger children started, all you need are a couple of snapshots.

In a snapshot, agents look for the same things as in a professional head shot. You want a picture that looks like your child. No hats, makeup, big bows in the hair, Halloween masks, or food on the face—just a nice clean picture of your child looking like a child. Make sure the face is looking straight at the camera. The child should be smiling or looking like she's having a good time. Don't send in "crying baby" shots.

Once the child is a little older (age five, or after your agent suggests it), it may be time to think about a good professional head shot. A good commercial head shot is your child's most important marketing tool. Initially, you may send your child's head shots out to agents to request an interview. The agent sends the head shots out to casting directors in order to secure jobs for the child. As with adults, your child's head shot is his calling card.

In Chapter 1: "Getting Head Shots", you learned how to go through the process of finding a good photographer, selecting the right shot, and getting mass reproductions. That process is almost identical when preparing children for the business. However, you have one additional question to ask every photographer before you go to see their work: Do you specialize in photographing children for the industry? There is a big difference between commercial head shots for the industry, modeling head shots, and pageant pictures (figs. 23–25). Whereas photographs intended for commercial and modeling agents are done with simple lighting, simple clothing, no noticeable makeup on pre-teens and younger kids (and very light, clean makeup if any on teens), in pageant competition photographs, it is perfectly acceptable, depending on the pageant system, to use glamorized photos using makeup at almost any age, fancy dresses, and hats and accessories; gimmicky photos (using special effects, diffusion or soft focus, and "theme pictures") are also appropriate. Some pageants are judged by modeling and talent agents, so it is best to ask for guidelines before submitting entries. Agents and managers tend to frown on traditional pageant pictures. Some agents and managers have stereotyped views of pageant kids, seeing them as little automatons, too poised or rehearsed (lacking normal childlike spontaneity). Pageant moms have also gotten a bad rap in parts of the industry ("stage mothers").

Know that each style of photograph has a specific purpose. You would not wear a ballerina's tutu to a rodeo audition; neither would you use a typical pageant photograph for a modeling audition or for a commercial audition. To look professional, become clear as to the uses of each type of photograph and use the right photograph for each circumstance. It's important to find someone who knows what agents and casting people want in a child's head shot.

Not all photographers relate well to children. Try to find someone who photographs lots of kids and *loves* doing it. When you go to the interview, watch the interaction between the photographer and your child. If they don't seem to be hitting it off, it might be better to look for someone else. You're paying for these pictures and a successful outcome boosts the child's chances of getting work in the business. A great head shot is a collaboration between artist and subject; the result of the shoot depends on the existence of a very positive chemistry between your child and the photographer.

TIPS FOR A SUCCESSFUL SHOOT

1. *Kids look best in simple, kid-type clothes.* Denim shirts or jackets, overalls, and textured sweaters look great on

FIGURES 23, 24, 25.
Differences between children's commercial head shot, modeling head shot, and pageant head shot.
(PHOTOS BY DEBORAH OUELLETTE; MODEL: JACKELYN GAUCI)

kids, and they love wearing them. Stay away from busy patterns, frilly things, hats, bows, and large accessories that get in the way. Avoid distracting jewelry or props. Avoid glamourous hair styles and don't have your child wear makeup (other than corrective). Teens should look clean (not made up). Trust the photographer and the stylist to suggest what's best when it comes to preparing for the shoot.

2. *Make sure the child comes to the shoot well rested.* No sleepovers or late parties the night before a photo session. Do not let little ones fall asleep in the car on the way to the studio, or they will look sleepy or puffy during the shoot (they may also get crabby if they weren't ready to wake up). If you have a long ride, plan ahead for activities that will help the child stay alert and excited about the shoot.

3. *Bring some quiet project to keep the child occupied in the waiting room.* Avoid letting her run all over the studio and never leave a small child unattended.

4. *If the child is not well or having an off day, call and try to reschedule the shoot.* Your child will not photograph well if he's not into it. Give as much advance notice as possible as a courtesy to the photographer. Not showing up without calling to cancel is a definite no-no.

5. *Don't bring any negative energy into the shoot.* Leave problems at home. Children absorb emotional energy, positive and negative. If you have been lecturing the child or engaging in nonproductive conversation on the ride over, or especially in the waiting room, it may affect the child's session. Commercials are very happy and energetic. It is important that your child feels that way when performing in front of the camera.

After the shoot, thank the photographer and assistants. When your proofs come in, the photographer will usually help you select the best ones to enlarge. Reread Chapter 1 for help in selecting pictures, retouching, and getting mass reproductions of your prints for distribution.

❑ RÉSUMÉS FOR KIDS

Résumés for kids (figs. 26, 27) are set up pretty much the same way as adult résumés (see Chapter 2)—a single eight-by-ten page (which you will attach to the back of the head shots) that summarizes your child's statistics and experience in the business.

Unlike an adult résumé, children's résumés generally include their date of birth (never an age; it dates the résumé). An early résumé also includes eye/hair coloring, school productions (these show the child's interest in performing), achievements that imply drive and ambition, and any special skills the child may have (for a three-year-old, special skills might include reading and having a long attention span; for older kids, skateboarding, roller-blading, and scuba diving may be listed as special skills). With a little imagination, even a rank beginner can put together an attractive, interesting résumé.

Never lie on a résumé, especially about a special skill. Says Karen Apicella, "Anything you list on the special skills portion of the résumé, you'd better be able to do and do *well*. If you get called into an audition and you're asked to do something you listed as a special skill, then you can't do it, that leaves a terrible impression. Make sure your résumé is honest.

"Also, I don't like to see modeling or pageant experience on talent résumés. Many casting directors feel that pageant kids are overrehearsed automatons and they feel so strongly about this, that if they see it on a résumé, they will tend *not* to pick the child. I think pageants and modeling are wonderful accomplishments, but being in a pageant really does not connote becoming a well-rounded actor. On the other hand, acting experience of any kind is good.

"Mom may say, 'Well, Susie has only played a tree in the school play.' I want to see that. It shows she wants to perform, and performing is what it is all about. A child's ability to get out and act, whether in front of a camera or on stage, is precisely what I'm looking for. Include any experience of singing, dancing, or acting classes in the training part of a résumé."

Once you put together your résumé, have it typed or

RACHEL CAMPBELL

The Savage Agency
6212 Banner Avenue
Hollywood, CA 90038
(213) 461-8316

| Hair | Lt. Brown |
| Eyes | Hazel |

Height 44 in.
Weight 45 lbs.
DOB 10-1-85

FILM:

"Come the Morning" - World Wide Productions

EDUCATION:

Young Actors Space - Diane Hardin   Van Nuys, California
- Children's Workshop II - Currently Studying
- Children's Workshop

Young Actors Space - Diane Hardin   P.S. Images,
- Television Acting Clinic   Midland, Texas

P.S. Images - Phyllis Gonzales   Midland, Texas
- Child's Modeling and Acting Workshop

TX Talent Corp. Training Institute   Denver, Colorado
- Children's Workshop I (16 hrs)

SKILLS:

Horseback Riding   Gymnastics
Dancing   Computers
Swimming

FIGURES 26, 27.
Children's résumés.
(a) Fledgling child
résumé; *(b)* advanced
child résumé. (BOTH
COURTESY OF THE
SAVAGE AGENCY, LOS
ANGELES)

(a) This is a beginner's résumé. Even if there's not much on it, the theatrical people won't think you're professional without a résumé.

The Savage Agency
(213) 461-8316
Talent Agency
6212 Banner Ave
Hollywood, Calif. 90038

HARDIN/ECKSTEIN
PERSONAL MANAGEMENT
(213) 851-2337
(818) 344-6201

Ross Malinger

HEIGHT: SAG/AFTRA
WEIGHT:
HAIR: BROWN
EYES: BROWN
                                                           DOB: 7/7/84
FILM

SLEEPLESS IN SEATTLE   Star   Nora Ephron, director
KINDERGARTEN COP   Featured   Ivan Reitman, director
EVE OF DESTRUCTION   Co-star   Nelson Entertainment
LATE FOR DINNER   Featured   Nelson Entertainment

TELEVISION

GOOD ADVICE
DOWN THE SHORE
IN SICKNESS AND IN HEALTH   Series Regular
ROSEANNE   Guest Star   Tri-Star TV/NBC
DAVIS RULES   Co-star   FOX
WHO'S THE BOSS?   Guest Star   CBS Movie of the Week
BEVERLY HILLS, 90210   Guest Star   ABC
AMERICA'S MOST WANTED   Recurring   CBS
WAKE, RATTLE, AND ROLL   Guest Star   ABC
                            Guest Star   FOX
                            Guest Star   FOX
                                            Hanna Barbera

COMMERCIALS

List upon request

TRAINING

YOUNG ACTORS SPACE – Improvisation and Scene Study
JOAN MARICHAL – On Camera
BEST TALENT AGENCY – On Camera
THOUSAND OAKS DANCE COMPANY – Creative Dance

ABILITIES

SWIMMING, BICYCLING, HORSEBACK RIDING, BASEBALL, FOOTBALL, MOST OUTDOOR
SPORTS, COMPUTER GAMES.

ROSS IS CURRENTLY AN A STUDENT AND IS ON HIS SCHOOL'S HONOR ROLL.

(b) This is a very good résumé. It's easy to read and has all the important and relevant information.

printed on good quality paper. Order enough copies to attach one to each of your head shots. If necessary, trim the résumé to the exact size of the head shots (use a paper cutter, not scissors, for a cleaner look).

❏ FINDING AN AGENT

Now you're ready to start mailing out head shots to children's agents. Agency listings can be found in the Yellow Pages and in industry directories. Call first and ask if each agency has a children's division before mailing out snapshots or professional head shots. Be sure to enclose a cover letter (see Chapter 2) with each submission, requesting an interview. Generally, agents only respond when they'd like you to come in for an interview. If you don't get a response within two weeks, call each agency to make sure they received your mailing.

Once you've secured an appointment, the following tips may help you and your child get through the interview/audition process:

1. Review Chapter 8: "What You Need to Know About Agents, Managers, and Unions."
2. Make sure the child is well rested and fed before going in.
3. Do not coach the child as to what to do or how to behave at the interview. Let the child answer questions addressed to her and do not answer for her.
4. Dress the child casually, preferably in clothes she likes. The same choices and advice given for photo shoots apply to interviews and auditions for kids.
5. Resist the temptation to critique or analyze the child's performance during or after the interview.

After the interview, the agent will either offer to represent your child or tell why he isn't interested at this time. He may suggest waiting until the child is older or suggest that the child take a class or workshop that will make her more marketable.

❏ MANAGERS

Whether or not to hire a manager is a personal decision. For a child, having a manager can be an asset. Good managers tend to nurture and develop a child's career. They work with many agents, so you may get more calls.

While agents work hard to find jobs for your child (and many others), they are generally too busy to educate parents and kids about the business, to monitor the child's progress, or teach the family how to deal with frustration, rejection, or success. Many people, especially beginners, find that having someone mentor parents and child as they learn and develop is well worth paying the extra 15 percent.

Parents might consider hiring a manager at the point where the child has done many commercials and the family decides it is time to expand into film and television. If the child has a manager, it is the manager's job to place the child with a theatrical agent. The manager will guide the growth and movement of the child's career just as he would for an adult.

There are many managers who represent only children. Some handle both children and adults. Others represent infants. Many agents will not sign infants as clients because they change too quickly in looks and behavior. Another problem with representing infants is that parents often change their minds about the business when they discover the cost and time involved in launching and maintaining a child's career. An agent is reluctant to invest time and energy in a client who is not in it for the long haul. Dealing with overzealous or unmotivated parents or trying to educate them about the professional expectations of the industry can be time-consuming. Rather than sign on infants himself, the agent will contact managers who represent them.

The best ways to find a manager for a child is to ask other industry parents or your agent for names of managers in your area. Call the National Conference of Personal Managers in New York City. It is not a good idea to look for managers in the Yellow Pages.

❑ TRAINING

When children are young (four to seven), they can pretty much get by on their personality, reading, and charm. But by the time they're eight or nine, they really have to begin to know what they are doing.

Judy Savage elaborates: "I always say that if you are an incredible six-year-old—you read, you're smart, you're small, you're outgoing, you have the personality—your competition in the whole town is only about ten other kids that are that special (at that age). By the time you're ten, there are about two hundred competitors, and by the time you turn eighteen, there are about two thousand.

"What happens is that everybody who turns eighteen and has a passion for acting comes to California from all over the world to try to break into the business, and your competition absolutely magnifies. These other kids might have been taking acting, singing, elocution, speech, and every other kind of lesson you can think of since they were six years old. Also, when you turn eighteen, the competition comes from the legal sixteen- and seventeen-year-olds who have graduated from high school as well as young-looking twenty-five-year-olds, so it's tough."

A class or workshop* in on-camera commercial technique will help your child get comfortable in front of the camera while learning how to audition. Once the child starts getting calls for auditions, on-the-job training serves as the best teacher. Exposing kids to improvisation classes, acting classes, community theatre, and school drama programs can help them round out their talent and develop confidence.

---

*A workshop for children should bring out their individual personality and eliminate inhibitions. It should not try to mold or change a child or, worst of all, take away from the child's natural spontaneity.

❏ TIPS ON AUDITIONS

DO'S AND DON'TS

Do:

1. Respect your audition appointment time. Casting directors have a schedule to keep. Coming late causes confusion and creates a backup.
2. Sign in upon entering the reception area. Casting directors use this sheet to call performers into the studio. Forgetting to sign in could put you at risk of losing the opportunity to audition.
3. Take your child aside and begin going over the script after signing in. Resist the temptation to socialize with other parents and children in the reception area. You are better off attending to the business at hand. Concentrate on preparing your child to give a good audition.
4. Have your head shot and résumé ready to hand to the casting director.

Don't:

5. Overrehearse the script. It is important to become familiar with the material while maintaining spontaneity.
6. Wait until your child is called into the audition room to begin grooming him. When the casting director calls "Next!" the child should be fully prepared to go in and give a good audition.
7. Bring extra family members, friends, boyfriends, or performers to the audition.
8. Put makeup on your child. *Please!*

OTHER CONSIDERATIONS

1. Food auditions: Many auditions for children are for food, especially snacks, fast foods, and cereals. You will be told at the time of the audition call what the food is. If your child cannot eat the food because she doesn't like it or is allergic to it, please make sure to ask if the actor will actually have to eat the food. If the answer is yes, don't waste everyone's time by going to the call. Your child will be given the food at the audition to make sure she actually likes it. She *will* be expected to eat the product enthusiastically, take after take, and will have to eat more than the usual intake. If your child cannot eat the product, it's to everyone's advantage for you to say so *when you are called for the audition.*

2. Parents are not asked to come into the audition room. Part of the casting process is to see how a child behaves without a parent in the room. If a child is shy or insecure, or cries when his parent is not with him, he is not good commercial material. Always be nearby, however, either just outside the door or in a reception area.

Sometimes parents are allowed to "assist" when the audition calls for babies and toddlers. You should be aware that for very young children (age four and under), backup kids are always booked for shoots, just in case one or more children get tired, cranky, or otherwise unable to cooperate.

❏ COMMONSENSE SAFEGUARDS FOR SHOWBIZ KIDS

In a world where parents must take every precaution to assure their child's safety and well-being, it defies logic to watch how quickly well-meaning moms and dads throw caution to the wind when it comes to working in show business. The industry requires children to talk to people they don't always know well and to do so without their parents in immediate sight, so it's very important for families to keep their feet on the ground (and the stars out of their eyes) when making decisions that affect their child's immediate and long-term future.

Common sense is essential to guard against unscrupulous vultures who prey on show biz kids and their families. For instance:

1. Know that a minor (fifteen years or younger) *must* have a guardian at a shoot. If there is travel involved, the production company must also arrange (and pay) for the guardian to accompany the child.

2. Be alert if you are called to hotels, unsafe neighborhoods, out-of-the-way buildings, or any location late at night. It's not that auditions are not held under these

circumstances. Just use common sense when dealing with these conditions.

3. If you are going to an unknown casting office, be alert to the surroundings. Are there a lot of other guardians and kids there? Are other kids coming out of the room happy? Are the people who bring the children into the room friendly to them and their guardians?

4. Teenagers going to auditions alone must be alert. Females are not asked to wear less than a two-piece bathing suit at a legitimate commercial audition. No one should be asked to change into a bathing suit in the audition room. If an actor needs to change clothes, some kind of changing room should be provided. There have been instances in which Peeping Toms hid behind a two-way mirror and taped a clothing change.

5. Males *and* females should be aware of advances or threats by people who audition or hire them (people who seem to be in powerful positions). *No* job is worth compromising yourself and no legitimate job would ever involve unsavory behavior. You would *never* have to go to a producer's house or go out on a date with him.

6. *Trust your instincts*. If something doesn't feel right, *leave*.

❏ WHEN TO CONSIDER COMMUTING OR RELOCATING TO A LARGER MARKET

Most agents and managers agree that children should get as much experience in their own market (however small) before deciding on going to a larger market. Karen Apicella advises to audition as much as possible at home so a child can acclimate as quickly and as easily as possible in a larger market. "Also, the child should perform and learn the many disciplines involved before going to a larger market."

The child must listen to his parents. He must be able to move swiftly and in an organized manner, getting to appointments on time. He must tolerate the tedium of traveling from one audition to the next, waiting in the reception room until it's his turn to audition. At the callback, he may be asked by the director to do something over and over again. He may walk into a callback audition and have to perform in front of six clients. The child must be willing to come in early for a booking if need be, and he must be able to handle the pressure during tense moments on the set.

The demands on children in the industry can be considerable. They range from travel demands to disappointments when they don't get the job. It is certainly not for everyone. Yet some kids love the challenge, the demands, and the rewards that come with them. Inevitably, parents of serious child actors will decide whether or not to take the child to a larger market.

Deciding between the two larger markets (New York and Los Angeles) is a matter of personal choice. If the focus is entirely on commercials (which, by the way, is a good way to get your feet wet and to get comfortable with the industry), there are as many opportunities in Los Angeles as there are in New York. Look at both lifestyles and decide which you prefer. New York is a big, congested city where you would use public transportation. Los Angeles has a more outdoorsy atmosphere and everyone drives. Look into the costs of living in both locations. Is climate a consideration for you? One place won't have the magic answer—so do your research on both markets, then go where you feel most comfortable.

When regional kids come to New York or Los Angeles for the summer, they find themselves competing against hundreds of other kids from all over the country, some of whom have several summers under their belts. Then there are kids who come from the area, who were practically raised in the business. If your child is booking most of the jobs she auditions for (or is consistently called back) in her own market, she may be ready for a summer in a larger market. But competition will be stiff. The better prepared children are, the more experience they have, the better their chances of booking in places like New York and Los Angeles.

All experiences in your local market will prepare you for the larger markets. In the larger markets every aspect of the business is in larger proportion. There are many more agents, actors, opportunities, and disappointments.

❏ WHAT PARENTS CAN EXPECT

Judy Savage is the owner of one of the leading children's agencies in Los Angeles—The Savage Agency. "Most people come here not prepared enough, not trained enough, and with high expectations," says Judy. "They think that in three months of a pilot season, they're going to make it. The general rule is that it takes about three years to make it. There may be an exception. They may get a little thing here and there, but to get on a series or to get a movie, the time frame we're looking at is generally wider."

And whatever the time frame involved, the child always needs a parent or parents around. "It's very thankless to be a show biz mom," explains Karen Apicella. "Moms in this business don't get enough credit. You have to be very organized to be a good industry mom. If, for instance, you're with several agents and don't have a manager, you have to keep your facts very, very straight because if you don't, you could wind up in a mess.

"Say, for instance, you go out on an audition and book the job but can't remember which agent the call came from. The client will not know who to send your check to—and if it winds up going to the wrong agent, you will create an uncomfortable situation for all concerned."

Judy Savage adds: "The parent and the child have to become partners in this. There's never been a successful child actor without one committed adult (a parent or relative); somebody who literally has to give up her own career for ten or twelve years and devote all her time to this child (or children), because they have to be ready to go at any moment.

"The more you are available, the better your chances of getting started. Most of the time, we get a little bit of notice—a day, or we get the call in the morning, but there are lots of last-minute calls where they say, 'Be there in an hour.'

"So the mother has to be on call. You have to realize that it's going to be really hard on the rest of the family. You can expect not to get much respect on the set. When a child is hired, the mother has to be there, within sight and sound.

They would rather have you be a mute and sit in the corner and not know you're there. I did it for fifteen years and I know the feeling. You feel like you don't belong. You feel like a vegetable. You feel like you don't have a purpose. And yet, you know in your heart that this is something your children love and it's an amazing way (for most) to be with your children, and make some money for them. Some kids pay for their braces, cars, college, and houses, and a lot of them don't stay in the business, but they have that by the time they're eighteen or nineteen. A lot of these parents could never have afforded to give them that kind of lifestyle."

❏ COMPENSATION

Because of the many opportunities for children in commercials, a great deal of money can be made, depending on how many commercials the child books and how the commercial runs (see Chapter 13 on talent payments). The amount made can be as little as $443.25 or in excess of $100,000 a year.

HANDLING THE CHILD'S MONEY

It is very important to know exactly what you are going to do with the money your child earns in the business *and* what the law says you *must* do to protect the child's interests.

In California, for instance, the Coogan Law (named after child star Jackie Coogan, who wound up penniless when he came of age because his parents had spent all his money) was set in place to protect young performers from their parents' or guardians' lack of knowledge, inexperience, or outright greed. The Coogan Law mandates that twenty-five percent of a child's earnings be placed in trust so that when the child comes of age, he will have something to show for his efforts.

Even if there are no specific laws governing the way a child's earnings are used, know that when children reach the age of majority (eighteen in most states), they can ask their parents for an accounting of the money they earned while under age. Parents risk being sued by their children for mismanagement of funds if they cannot adequately account for the money.

In cases in which a child becomes the primary breadwinner for the entire family, courts tend to look with disapproval upon parents who charge the child's estate excessively for such things as chaperoning/chauffeur fees, food, rent, and schooling. Such expenses generally fall under a parent's normal responsibilities (most folks don't expect their kids to reimburse them for such things). If a child's money is used to buy property (like a bigger house, for instance), the youngster may even be able to sue her parents for the home, since it was her earnings that paid for it in the first place.

Aside from the obvious legal and financial problems that can arise from failing to launch a sensible financial plan for a child's earnings, the emotional and psychological damage done when children are put in the position of having to sue their parents to get what is rightfully theirs is nothing short of catastrophic. Wise parents will discuss financial planning with their accountant and their agent or manager and put a proper trust/investment package into place.

❏ WHAT IT TAKES FOR KIDS TO MAKE IT IN THE BUSINESS

Judy Savage comments: "It's going to take absolute passion, total belief in yourself and your child (it works both ways), and the ability to do it for the love of doing it—and not taking the rejection personally, which is such a hard thing. You have to get to the point where you can go into an interview for the pure joy of showing your work to the casting director. You get a high out of that. When you get to that point, you won't take the rejection seriously. And you can never let success go to your head. You have to stay humble and grateful because the minute you start becoming a legend in your own mind, you're almost destined to find yourself moving back the other way.

"Most of all, remember to hang in there. Some people struggle for four or five years without something significant happening in their careers. Take Mayim Bialik (*Beaches, Blossom*). Mayim had been going on auditions since she was three or four and never got a job because her look was hard to fit into a family. Then, when she was ten years old, she did the film *Beaches* and it made her overnight. Everybody wanted her. Since then, they've created one thing after another for her, but for the first seven years or so, she got nothing.

"Another one was Lisa Bonet of *The Cosby Show*. She was absolutely the most gorgeous child and she was talented. She went on interviews for probably ten years and never got anything. There was very rarely an interview for her because, for television, there are stereotypical parts written and if you don't fit into one of those stereotypes, it's very hard to get started.

"I tell these hard types, 'The harder you are to fit into something—the more unstereotypical you really are—the more likely you are to become a star one day.' Because it's taken them much longer to get started, they've had to spend many more years in theater and in training and in improv groups, so when they do get a role, they are ready to just blow the world away."

❏ INTERVIEWS WITH MAX CASELLA, ROBERT MEEGAN, PAT MEEGAN, ALAN SIMON, AND SUE SCHACHTER

The following interviews address specific issues and experiences that young people and their families go through while working in the industry. Actor Max Casella (Vinnie Delpino on *Doogie Howser, M.D.*), for instance, speaks of the advantages of being older, looking younger. Sixteen-year-old Robert Meegan (*Honey, I Shrunk the Kids*) advises young performers on handling celebrity as a child, and showbiz Mom Pat Meegan offers insights into what parents and families can expect to deal with when their child works in the business. Alan Simon discusses educating children on the set. Sue Schachter, a talent manager, wraps things up by helping parents decide when it's time to consider commuting (or relocating) to a larger market.

MAX CASELLA

How did you get started in the business?

I got started doing mime with a friend of mine in grammar school in Cambridge, Massachusetts. We would make up skits based on things we found in *Mad* magazine, then entertain people in the school hallway.

When I was twelve, I had my first acting experience playing Theo in *Pippin* at Cambridge High School. I began doing theater in Boston. As a kid, I became well known and booked a lot without auditioning. Acting was a lot of fun. Somewhere along the line, I made the choice to pursue acting as a career. I decided to go to New York and study.

I got into the American Academy of Dramatic Arts but was eventually booted out because I didn't exactly fit in. Not that this experience discouraged me. I always had this almost arrogant feeling that I *was* going to work. I knew it in my gut. Every time I would hear something like, "Well you know,

Max Cassella.

ninety percent of actors are out of work," I would get depressed for a little while, then I'd think, "Well, I'm special. I know I'm going to do well. I have something nobody else has. I *know* I'll be all right." This is the way you have to think if you hope to survive in a business where everyone is vying for one job. I have this blind faith in myself that I really have to thank my mom for. She has been always been one hundred percent supportive of me.

At this point in your career, did you consider acting to be a hobby or a business?

I always treated my career as a business. When I was trying to find an agent, I kept a record of the names, addresses, and phone numbers of the people I contacted. I sent out pictures and résumés with a cover letter explaining that I was interested in representation and requested an interview. I kept track of the date I sent things out, waited a week or so, then called the agent to follow up.

As you know, in New York, you don't have to sign with one agent exclusively. You can be with fourteen agents if you want to. I had five agents at one time.

In Doogie Howser, M.D., *you played a teenager, several years younger than your actual age.*

Yes. I have found that it is to my advantage that I look younger than my actual age. When you're older and you look convincingly younger, it's an advantage for someone to hire you because you bring along more experience than someone who *is* younger.

I may be able to bring some kind of new subtlety to the role that a real kid (in high school) maybe won't bring out because I'm looking back in. Also, there's the purely technical thing about the child labor laws. A seventeen-year-old can only work so many hours, has to have a tutor on the set, and has to go to the tutor every three hours. Whereas if they hire me, an adult who *looks* seventeen, they can work me like any other adult.

Did you get nervous at auditions?

You always get nervous *waiting* at auditions. I *hate* the

waiting part—in the lobby, in the waiting room. I've always felt it's like running your engine on idle. Your engine is revving and you're not going anywhere yet. Also, I hate it when actors talk to each other in the waiting room. I prefer to be left alone at auditions. I'm the type who goes on auditions, puts my head down into the pages, and waits.

After you got the part on Doogie, how did your life change?

There were a lot of adjustments. After I got the part on *Doogie*, I moved to L.A. I had to find a place to live. I had to get a car. I had a driver's license, but in New York I hardly ever drove so I didn't need a car. In L.A., everybody drives, so I made all the necessary adjustments.

The show became successful and I have become a "celebrity," and it feels great. At first, it's funny. You don't know how you want to present yourself to the people who are responding to your new-found notoriety, like on a talk show or to somebody on the street. You just try to be as nice a guy as you can possibly be. Then, you find out that you can't be so nice because people will take advantage of you. It's like they expect you not to have any kind of private life. For instance, I'll be at dinner and some guy will come over. I'll talk to him for a minute and the next thing I know, he sits down and won't go away. Finally, I have to ask him to leave. One time, I was sitting in a restaurant and this woman was holding a video camera over my table. *I couldn't believe it.* A friend of mine finally jumped up and said, "Come on . . . the guy's trying to have his dinner, Okay? What are you *doing?*"

I've never turned down an autograph in my life. What I'll say though is, "I'll sign it but, you know, I'm having dinner."

Would you still do commercials at this point in your career?

I do a voice-over for a Saturday morning cartoon. I would do a commercial, depending on what it was. Commercials are good to do. It's different for everybody. It depends on where you're at in your career. If you're a superstar, you wouldn't necessarily do one but it's a good way to make a living, certainly.

I know actors who make lots and lots of money doing commercials. It's also a good way to get exposure. Friends of mine have gotten great jobs as a result of the exposure they got appearing in commercials. Commercials play all the time. Somebody is bound to see them.

Emmanuel Lewis, the star of the sitcom *Webster*, got a series from doing a Burger King commercial, so if you're in the right commercial and you're the right face at the right time for something, that's all you need.

I tell anyone who wants to be an actor this: You have to be an actor twenty-four hours a day—observing people, observing things in life, thinking like an actor. If you're going to be an actor, it's not something you do . . . it's something you *are*. You're thinking like an actor every day.

ROBERT MEEGAN

How did you get started in the business?

It was something I always felt I could do. I would watch TV and memorize the commercials—the jingles. I talked to the TV more than I talked to other people. I loved talking along with the people in the commercials. My mom would say, "Go outside and get some fresh air," but I was always watching television or reading. I can't remember when I didn't want to perform. I nagged and nagged until my mom finally agreed to let me give it a try.

I started out doing print and commercials. I remember my first audition. It was a dream come true. I wasn't nervous. I was too young to understand the significance of being on TV.

When I went into auditions, I put a lot into it. Sometimes, I would just act like an idiot and they hired me for it. I couldn't understand why they would hire such a goofy little kid. It was fun. If I didn't get booked, I didn't feel rejected. I knew I would have another five auditions that same day. I would try to do it better next time.

Did you have to give up a lot of school activities?

I gave up *all* school activities. I never played sports when I was little. It was never something I wanted to do. All I did was go to school and go to work. My extracurricular activities

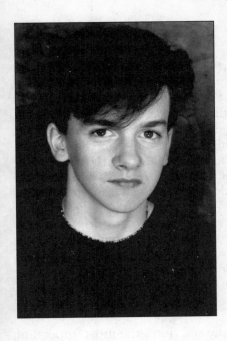

Robert Meegan.

consisted of going into the city, having fun, and acting like an idiot.

What was it like, being a "celebrity" while still in school?

A lot of people thought it was a big deal (being in the business), especially when I got into film. People would ask me for my autograph. All that goofiness. After a while, my friends got used to it. I have a great group of friends. The are "real" and protective. They never exploit me. They were my friends before I was doing this and they still are.

Looking back, how do you think performing has helped you on a personal level?

Because of my experiences in the industry, I learned to be comfortable meeting and performing in front of people. I became a lot more extroverted, a lot more independent. Because of my experiences traveling and working as an actor, I feel I can handle almost any situation that might come up.

What is it like on a commercial set?

It was always fun. Generally, the people on the set who work with small kids try to make the set fun. Not all sets are the same though. On one set you can be pampered, and on the next you are treated like dirt and you have to accept it. On one set, you may have a huge dressing room; on another set you have a dressing room half the size and you share it with four other people. You have to learn to deal with that. Sometimes it's hard for the parents. They may feel "My kid deserves more" because their kid had done two more commercials than one of the other actors.

The way you behave on a set has a lot to do with your parents, your upbringing. I've been with people who are real shy—who just do what they're supposed to do, and I've been with people who are totally "out there," going nuts and trying to prove that they are something they're not. I've also been with people who think that because they are in a commercial, they are Marlon Brando.

I think if you have fun on the set, that's the most important thing. If you spend all your time afraid to do something that might mean you'll never work again, you'll put so much pressure on yourself that you won't want to do it anymore. You need a lot of patience. There's a lot of hurry-up-and-wait in this business.

You must be able to take direction. Being an actor means you have to perform something that somebody else wrote and somebody else is directing. The director is responsible for how the commercial comes out. The way you do it, especially as a commercial actor, is exactly the way they want you to do it. It's their product and you have to make other people feel this product is the best.

A lot of times, you have to do it forty times for them. I've done as many as seventy-five takes. It can be tedious and you might not agree with it, but you have to do it. The director saw something you didn't and when he says you have to do it again, you have to do it again. When he says "Be more excited," you have to be more excited. You may think you are the most excited you can ever be . . . you're vibrating in your seat, you have so much excitement. However, if the director says, "Be more excited," be *more* excited. If he says, "Make your eyes bug out of your head," even if you feel your eyes are as wide as you can possibly get them, you have to make them bug out even more. That's what you're being paid for. You're a commercial actor. They hired you because they think you can do what they need you to do.

When you were seven years old, how did you know to take direction from this person?

You would be surprised at how easily kids pick it up. They sense that the director is an authority figure—that they have to do whatever he says. When you are a kid, you just know.

My brother, Christopher, was on the set of *Honey, I Blew Up the Kids*. The twins they were using were only two years old and sometimes they didn't want to use them during lighting and rehearsal periods so they asked if they could use Christopher, who was only five at the time and couldn't stand still for two seconds at home. He gets on the set and he is suddenly this "perfect kid" who takes direction for forty-five minutes to an hour. He would do things for the director that my parents couldn't get him to do. Kids seem to sense that this time is not "play" time. Chris knew that ten feet off the set, he could play and ten feet on the set, he was working. I was the same way. No one ever taught me that.

How do commercial auditions differ from those for film?

At a commercial audition, you go in and see a storyboard above the sign-in sheet. You look at the five words and memorize them. With a film, you get a Federal Express package of six or seven pages of sides (your part of the script), which you have to memorize for the next day (or whenever the audition is held). With commercials, you go in and do it the way the casting director wants you to do it. With film, I find you have a lot more creative leeway to do whatever you want with the character. You make your own character. In a commercial you don't have a character; you very rarely have a name. You are just this kid with a smile on your face who just got a fire engine or something. In a film, you have a name and a character—and you make that character "you."

There is a lot less tension on a film set than there is on a commercial set. It's a lot easier working in an atmosphere where you've been with people for the last month. I feel a lot of pressure doing commercials. They are always racing to get everything done in one day. If there is a problem with a camera on a commercial, all that tension is felt by everyone on the set. Everyone has been hired for one day and it has to be done in that day, which is why you sometimes wind up with a sixteen-hour day. With film, it's not such a tight time frame.

What advice would you give to newcomers to the business?

Stay true to yourself. As an actor, you are manipulated by so many people to do what *they* want you to do. Realize that when you are off the set, you are not that character anymore. You are not going to get pampered. Know where the line is drawn between acting and real life.

One of my mom's big things was to keep a reality around me. You are not always on the set and it's not the biggest thing in the world. You'll audition for things you will get and you'll audition for things you will not get. You are going to work for people over and over again and you'll think they are your best friends, then you go on an audition for them and they don't hire you. It has nothing to do with who you are. They are going to hire whomever they need for that particular job. It doesn't reflect on your personally.

What you have to do is go in and do a good job without taking it too seriously—like it's the most important thing in your whole life. It's not. You are never going to go out and book every job you audition for. You have to know where the line is drawn.

PAT MEEGAN

What was your first exposure to the business?

My son, Robert, was five years old when he first got it into his head that he could act. He was always a quiet child and basically a loner type, so I didn't put a whole lot of stock in what he was saying. By the time he was seven and a half, almost eight, he was hounding me to let him try. I didn't think he would understand the rejection involved, the amount of time and energy, or the time away from home, but I figured I would give it a try and teach him a lesson. I figured he would get real bored with it real fast and that would be a lesson for him, but it backfired. Robert started working immediately. He booked the first four things he auditioned for. We experienced one of those unusual "right place, right time" situations. That is certainly not the norm.

What did you go through as a mother going to auditions?

It's not what people think at all. It's very difficult, very time-consuming. There is a lot of juggling involved and a lot of anxiety. When Robert started, I had another child one year older and I was pregnant. I had to juggle dinner schedules, after-school play dates, extracurricular activities, and house-work.

Because there was no time, I had to juggle someone taking care of my other child. Basically the rule was, if someone else was going to have to raise Robert's siblings, then he couldn't work. It had to be arranged so that there was always a parent present. You cannot forget that the other members of the family have needs too.

Once Robert was offered a commercial which, because of his name, would have been very, very lucrative. That same day, his brother Eric had a championship soccer game, so we turned it down. It was important to Eric that we all be at the soccer game and that was a family success equivalent to Robert booking a commercial.

What do Moms actually do at an audition?

Basically, you have to try to keep the child quietly entertained until he or she is needed. There is a lot of waiting. You lug around their school books. You have to learn the ropes. Sometimes there are catty comments to be ignored. You have to teach your child how to be friendly with the other kids without necessarily listening to everything that comes out of their mouths. You learn to be friendly but not too close and try to teach the child the same thing. It's difficult.

What is it like as a parent on a commercial set?

It can be very boring. It can also be very interesting. If the people on the sets had their way, you wouldn't be there. It's trying to be unobtrusive, looking after your child and never, ever saying something is inappropriate if you feel it is. That's difficult at times. You can feel very intimidated. These are important people doing their jobs but you have to remember, your child comes first. The child should always feel comfortable knowing you're there and *why* you are there. It's up to you to make it fun for your child, yet make it known to him that he is here to do a job, which means no fooling around at certain times.

It's also important to see that your child doesn't get totally exhausted to the point where he begins to hate what he's doing. I feel it's my place to say something if I see my child is getting too exhausted. I have found if you are not being ridiculous, if you are strictly concerned for the safety, comfort, welfare, and education of your child, there may be some moaning and groaning and complaining but you basically get a lot of respect.

You cannot expect to be treated like royalty, but if you are concerned that your child is too hot, tired, and thirsty, or if his schooling is not being done as required on that day, there is nothing wrong with opening your mouth and saying so. It is my job as mom to say something.

What a mother should *not* do is stand in front of the director, voicing her opinion on how the hair or makeup should look. Don't comment on whether or not you like the outfit. You have a right to open your mouth about it being too hot or cold, or if your child is too tired to continue. It's okay to ask, "Can he have a five-minute break?" "Can he have a drink?" Other than that, you have no right to tell anyone how to run a commercial unless something compromises the safety of your child. Be quiet. Your job is basically to keep your child comfortable and occupied between shoots.

How is auditioning for film different from auditioning for commercials?

It's a totally different atmosphere. When your child is doing commercials, you are talking about a lot of auditions. Even when you feel you may have a day off, in the middle of the afternoon your phone will ring. You have to find your child—wherever he is—and get him into the city because they have decided the only time they are going to see him is "right now."

One day, Robert had fourteen auditions between three and six-thirty and we made every one. Three of them were callbacks. With film, you might have anywhere from two to five auditions per week. You could go two weeks without one. It's basically a much easier lifestyle. During the transition, when Robert was going for both, it got a little crazy. You have to prioritize. Do you go on the film or the commercial call? In Robert's case, he wanted to make the switch so we focused on film.

When Robert got the part in *Honey, I Shrunk the Kids* (which was shot for six months in Mexico City), I had my eighteen-month-old with me all the time. My ten-year-old came back and forth with my husband. There was a lot of juggling. I was running two households from a hotel room in Mexico City.

What is your philosophy on handling rejection?

You don't know how your child is going to handle rejection. I think it's difficult for any mother to handle because no matter how open-minded you try to be, this is your child and, of course, to you, this child is the best in the world. I think the kids who don't take it life-and-death serious are normal, natural kids. They don't become jaded, they don't become plastic or act like little robots. The children who do best in this industry are the ones who are really kids at heart. As a parent, you must teach your child that the rejection is not personal.

This is a fun thing you want to do right now. If you get the job, how exciting—how nice. If you don't, that's fine too. There is always another audition if you want to continue to do this. Go into each audition, do your best, and when you walk out the door, forget that one ever existed.

How is it different for a parent on a film set as opposed to a commercial one?

It is different. During the making of a film, Robert's teacher/welfare worker was on the set. On my part, there was a lot of watching to make sure things were safe. There were a lot of special effects and flying.

One thing that's nice is that with a film (as opposed to a commercial) you are working with the same people every day. You kind of become family, tend to fall into a routine, and you can tend to let up on your watchfulness. No matter what though, remember—these kids are a commodity. Robert has made some wonderful friends in this industry but that doesn't mean you can trust everybody you meet. And I will never, ever—I don't care if I've known them for twenty years—hand my son to anyone on a silver platter.

Any advice for parents who have children who want to do this?

Do not fall into the pitfall of believing that this is going to be a glamorous life. There is nothing glamorous whatsoever about this. For a parent, a commercial set is usually about dark little places where they want you to stand in a corner. It's a business. They are trying to sell a product. Your child is not their product. Your child is there to *enhance* their product.

If it's not fun, if your child does not want to do it, keep him home. It can be very lucrative, but the percentage who make that kind of money is very small. There are a lot of expenses involved. The government treats child actors as unmarried single people who pay taxes. There are other pitfalls involved in working in this industry. You really have to want to do it and your child has to be committed to it even more so.

You have to remember that he is a child, part of a family, and a student before a commercial actor. It you can fill all those guidelines, your child will most likely be successful.

ALAN SIMON

Alan Simon is the owner of On Location Education, a company that provides tutors for children in the business while they are on the set. (Alan was previously an actor who supported himself by substitute teaching in the New York City school system.)

The education of children in the entertainment industry is important and definitely not overlooked. On Location Education provides teachers, studio teachers, and educational consultants to work with production companies employing child actors in television, film, theater, national tours, commercials, industrials, and circuses. Children who have alternative life-styles must work their schooling around their production day. On Location Education helps them form an educational plan of action with their home schools.

Legally, at what age does the actor fall under the "child" category?

In the SAG commercial contract, the definition of a minor is fifteen years and younger, which means anyone older technically is not considered a minor and provisions that apply to children under the SAG contract cease to apply. Local and state labor laws may have certain provisions pertaining to the needs of sixteen- to eighteen-year-olds, and those can be found through the local departments of labor.

How do parents find out about specific child labor laws?

A complete set of guidelines is available to all members of either union from the local office (ask for the *SAG–AFTRA Young Performers Handbook*, 3rd edition). Parents should check their local labor laws. No producer is going to tell you. You have to read the code or whatever information you can find for your area.

Are there occasions when you are called to give education on the set?

Absolutely. In California, education is required on the set. There must be a welfare worker present at all times. That person, called a studio teacher, functions in the official capacity of a welfare worker empowered by the state of California to speak for the child's health, education, and welfare. Welfare workers serve many roles. They are there to educate the child and to insure that the physical surroundings are not in any way negative or harmful. They also make sure the wardrobe area is properly situated for boys and girls.

If indeed welfare workers feel a child is being worked by the production company even five minutes over the proper amount of time, they have the right to virtually stop production and call it a day on the child's behalf. In other states the parent will need to have the forethought to negotiate with the producer and request a teacher in advance.

How is education approached on the set?

There are two ways to answer this question. On Location Education or an individual studio teacher can be responsible for finding out the specifics of the curriculum at a child's home school. We contact parents and make sure the kids bring the material they are supposed to cover, be it the text-book, handouts, or whatever. But when there is no teacher provided, then it is up to the parent to get work from the school and, if necessary, hire a teacher to oversee instruction. The ultimate goal is for the child to return to school on par with his classmates.

If a child is booked with only a day or two's notice, does that give you enough time to set up the education requirements?

It's the nature of the beast. These things happen very quickly. Kids who work rather frequently know they have to be prepared to bring their materials with them. Parents who do this frequently are ready for it. Parents who are novices are not. Parents need to have a tutoring support network in place. They should know where to find a teacher while main-taining a positive relationship with their home school. If they are working outside of California, they should never assume a tutor will be provided.

A good agent, at the time of the booking, is always going to tell the parent, "There will be a teacher on the set. Please make sure you bring your books." We are also given the child's phone number, are authorized to contact the family, and will do what we have to do to ensure that the books and materials are there.

What personality traits do you notice in kids who do commercials?

Kids who are successful, who do this regularly, tend to be bright and have a lot of energy. They tend to know how to budget their time. They know what it's like to sit in that green room* and keep themselves occupied.

What is the crucial information parents must have before their children get into the business?

I would say if you want to make this a career, it would be important to cultivate a good relationship with your home school. Make sure the principal knows that your child is doing this and that there are going to be periods of time when, with very little advance notice, your child is going to be called to the set and will be out. Make sure the school staff know that the child's absences are not a reflection on the teacher or the school, that you really want to work with the school, and that you will hold your child responsible for the workload missed. In fact, you will always see to it that the child is tutored on the set, a teacher will be provided, and the work will get done.

You have to look into the issue of excused absences. If your child is going to be out two days here, three days there, all of a sudden that adds up to ten days' absences; before you know it, you have reached the legal limit of absences you can have before your child is considered truant. You need to deal with these issues up front. It is very, very important.

I think most parents are overwhelmed once they get a job on location. I don't think they realize the implications that an acting career has on their kids, on themselves, and their families. For instance, if they get booked and have to travel to another location, usually a father or another parent is left behind, and maybe other siblings as well. Parents have to create a support system in order for this to work. And I think they need to know who to go to in terms of guardianship if that becomes an issue because they both work or are unable to travel. Who are they going to get to travel with their child? What kind of questions should they ask ahead of time? Who on the set will look out for their child's best interest if they are not working in a place where there is a studio teacher empowered to act as the welfare worker?

I think parents don't realize what working their child regu-

---

*A green room is an offstage theatrical waiting room, traditionally painted green.

larly means in terms of wear and tear on the family, as well as on themselves and the child.

SUE SCHACHTER

When is the best time for kids to come to a larger market?

Most children from out of state should not come until summer, so as not to upset the family structure or the child's life. A summer in Los Angeles or New York should be like a vacation. They shouldn't come with the intention of working. The attitude, for instance, should be, "Let's go to New York for the summer and have a great time and perhaps while we're there, we'll get some work," because the ones who come with the intention and the compulsion to work never have a good time and never get enough work.

What do parents need to know about coming to a larger market for the summer?

It's generally an eight-week commitment. The parents will have to find housing. An apartment will be much less expensive than staying in a hotel.

I try to encourage parents to bring the other children—to keep the family together. All too often, because of the money involved and whatever visibility is involved, the mother becomes focused on the one child and forgets the husband and their other children.

My first questions for the mother are, "Do you have family you can stay with in that market? Does your husband have the ability to come up and visit at least once or twice during the stay?" Often the answer is that he cannot because the family is financially stressed, so it becomes difficult because the mother, of course, gets lonely. The children get lonely too, so we try to create more of a vacation atmosphere for them. But, whenever possible, I always encourage them to bring the siblings.

What do you expect from the parents you work with?

I expect parents to be levelheaded and to always remember that their child's welfare is much more important than any check that will come in or any picture on a magazine cover. No one job is going to make or break a child's career.

The child's career is temporary. Very few make the transition—in industry terms, the segue (*"seg*-way")—from the different stages. For instance, you can have a really hot kid at four, five, or six years old. Then their teeth fall out. They come in crooked. They need braces. Or even if their teeth come in straight, now they are interested in sports or ballet or something else and no longer want to focus on the industry.

It's very important to keep the balance of childhood because you want to end up with a healthy adult. It's not unlike Little League or gymnastics or ballet or professional tennis . . . parents can get so absorbed in the child's fame that somewhere along the line, the child loses the childhood. Then the parent loses the child because the child will grow up resenting the parent. I feel the child's welfare is much more important than any money that could possibly be earned because you'll only end up spending it on a good shrink.

There is such a thing as "booking out." What you must do is tell me a week ahead of time if the child has an event coming up in school or social life. Say, "Book Charlie out on Thursday. It's his best friend's birthday," because we both know Charlie is going to be devastated if he can't be at that birthday party.

What do you look for in a child?

I'm looking for a child who's really excited and interested in doing this. There are children who literally say "I want to be an actor/actress" as soon as they can talk. It's not always the parent's idea. There are kids who have those fantasies and those fantasies become reality, but they have to have a great personality, they have to be outgoing, and they have to want to do it.

Do you interview kids and parents before deciding to represent them?

Yes. I always have the parent in the room with me at the interview. When a child is in an interview with a casting director, the parent is never in the room, and rightly so. I like the parent in because I want to see the interaction between parent and child. I want to see how much the child has been schooled to say what he's saying. If the child is very natural and the parent stays totally silent, then this is a child who really wants to do this. When a child keeps looking over at the parent as I'm asking her questions, I know that there's a fear involved here. You can tell a lot by watching the child and parent interact.

"Is there anything in interview situations that really turns you off?

When I ask questions and the parents answer. I wouldn't say it turns me off but it becomes apparent that this child is being controlled. Not that parents shouldn't have control of their children but, for instance, I'll say, "How old are you, Johnny?" and the parent will say, "Oh, he's six." "And when is your birthday?" "Oh, it's May twenty-sixth," says the parent.

Another thing that turns me off is when I ask the child questions and she keeps looking at the parent as she answers me as if to say, "Am I doing okay, Mommy?" "Am I saying the right thing, Mommy?" I mean, it's really kind of sad because that child knows she's being judged and the judgment of the mother depends on how she will do on an interview.

I tell the parents, "When the child goes into the city for an interview, don't school him because if he doesn't get the job, he's going to feel that he disappointed you." He's going into the city. He's going to have a great time. He's going to meet someone and *maybe* he's going to be on TV. If he doesn't get the job, it's for no other reason than because his hair was too dark, he was too tall, he was too short, or they picked someone fat. It had nothing to do with his ability.

When a child comes out of an interview, the parent should never say, "What did he say?" "What did *you* say?" because the child knows he's being judged. Also, when the parent gets home, she shouldn't call her sister or her mother and say, "Oh yeah, she went in but I don't think she did well." Maybe the child is in the next room. She's going to hear you so don't discuss the situation with others. It's over and done with. You go in and "Wasn't that a terrific time?" "We went into the city . . ." And that's the end of it.

If it's the first interview and an agent or manager wants the child, say to yourself, "Hmmm, I must have a pretty good product here. Let's see who else is interested." Shop around. See what other agents and managers have to say.

Talent should audition the person who is going to be handling their lives and never, never, never stay with someone who threatens them if they want to break a contract. How dare any human being put a parent or a child in bondage?

Any contract for a child can be broken. There's a general obligations law in every state that allows a parent to break a contract for any child under the age of sixteen. If you want to leave someone, leave. True, you may owe him commissions for work that was done while you were under his care. However, he holds no right to your future.

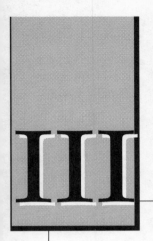

III

WRAPPING
IT
ALL
UP

18 WHAT IT TAKES TO MAKE IT IN COMMERCIALS

Congratulations! You're nearing the end of what we hope has been a wonderful journey through the process of breaking into commercials. To wrap things up, we've summarized tips from agents, managers, coaches, talent consultants, and casting people from all over the country. Their combined wisdom and experience could be instrumental in propelling you toward a successful career in the commericals industry.

We interviewed over seventy-five industry professionals in the course of researching this book, asking what they looked for in an actor, what misconceptions newcomers have about the business, what their "pet peeves" about talent were, and what words of advice they could offer. Below are the results of our findings:

❏ WHAT DO AGENTS AND CASTING PEOPLE LOOK FOR IN AN ACTOR?

- First impressions are important. The personality, the drive, the motivation, the talent, the look—*must* be presented.
- Your personality should be pleasant and outgoing (but not domineering).
- Charisma, determination, energy, and a solid work ethic are requisites for the successful actor.
- Integrity is essential. You *must* present yourself honestly at all times.

- Quality head shots and résumés.
- Good training.
- How you handle yourself at interviews.
- If you are nice and easy to work with.
- If you are easy to direct.
- Availability/flexibility.
- Confidence (but not arrogance).
- Magic in the eyes (expressive, animated, with an obvious love for the industry).
- Eager to work hard.

❏ WHAT ARE COMMON MISCONCEPTIONS NEWCOMERS HAVE ABOUT THE INDUSTRY?

- That this is not work. That it can be done as a hobby.
- That you can be suddenly "discovered"—as the tabloids imply.
- That agents will be able to get you every job.
- That being "pretty" is all it really takes.
- That it doesn't take time, persistence, and a lot of hard work.
- That if you work hard, sooner or later you are going to get what you want.
- Newcomers underestimate how much competition there is in larger markets, as well as:

    (a) How impersonal it is outside a smaller, regional market.

    (b) How tough it is to get a decent agent in a larger market.

- Newcomers also think:

    (a) That they are eligible for every part that comes up.

    (b) That it's going to happen overnight.

❏ PET PEEVES

WHAT ARE THINGS ABOUT TALENT THAT ARE REALLY IRRITATING?

- Being overly fussy (appearing difficult or uncooperative).
- Not being available (especially after indicating you would be).
- Obvious airbrushing or retouching of photographs.
- Not listening.
- Old photographs that don't look like you anymore.
- You think you know it all.
- You talk incessantly.
- Not being prepared for an interview (not having head shots/résumés and/or demo tape out and ready to give to agent).
- Padded résumé that's not realistic or believable.
- A lack of patience.
- Not being realistic about what can be achieved in a given period of time.
- Not following instructions.
- Big egos.
- Prima donna attitude.
- Not showing up on time for an interview, audition, or shoot.
- Not being knowledgeable about the industry and/or not conducting yourself in a professional, businesslike manner.

Remember the following at all times:

- Have a sense of humor.
- Be prepared.
- Take classes.
- It's a business. Treat it as such.
- You are the product.
- Don't expect your agent to get work for you. They get you auditions; *you* get the job.

- Get everything you can out of your regional market before moving on to larger one.
- You can't take no for an answer. Be persistent in your efforts.
- Learn the language of the industry.
- Keep active in workshops and other opportunities to train and network.
- Have your professional tools together.
- Theater is very valuable to your development as an actor.
- Know your strengths and work toward them.
- Be careful of scams.
- Get into productions and showcases.
- Have good head shots—and keep them current.
- Set realistic goals. Be willing to adjust them as necessary.
- Actively market yourself.
- Be as objective about your abilities and limitations as possible.
- Be open to criticism.
- Be persistent, honest, and hardworking.
- Know that it's not a business for everyone.
- Be willing to pay your dues.
- Have some kind of trade you can fall back on.
- Develop a philosophy that will take you through the hard times.
- Be willing to go the extra mile.
- Expect the unexpected.
- If this is something you really, *really* must do, then GO FOR IT!
- Realize that success is built on a concerted effort over an extended period of time.

Whew! That's a lot of wisdom to take in at once. We hope that you've learned a lot about what it takes to make it in the business, and that we have been able to make your transition into it a little bit easier. You know how to prepare a winning promotional package, how to prepare for and give a wonderful commercial audition, and how to follow through after you book the job. By reading this book and acting on the principles herein, you have taken great strides in creating a successful, lucrative career in the exciting world of commercials. Congratulations on completing a journey with us that will enrich your life for years to come.

Here's wishing you a long and prosperous career in the business!

> *ONLY ONE LIFE*
> *THAT SOON IS PAST*
> *ONLY WHAT'S DONE*
> *WITH LOVE WILL LAST . . .*

GLOSSARY

Account executives—Serve as the liaison between the client and the advertising agency.

Action—Director's command to start.

Actors' Equity Association (Equity)—Union governing performers and stage managers in live theater.

AD—Assistant director. In charge of crew; runs set.

Ad lib—Speech or action that has not been scripted or specifically rehearsed.

Agent—Functions as a salesperson with *you* as the product. In exchange for finding you work, the agent is paid a commission (usually ten percent of your earnings).

American Federation of Television and Radio Artists (AFTRA)—Union with jurisdiction over live and taped television shows and commercials, soap operas, disc jockeys, and other radio performers.

Apple box—Wooden box, the size of an apple box, that is used for various purposes on a set. For example, if the camera is too high, the camerman will stand on an apple box.

Art director—The person who visually conceives the spot and makes it come alive through drawings and visuals. The art director is responsible for the entire visual concept of the commercial—the way the commercial will look.

Audition—A tryout or chance to perform for the people who are in a position to give you a job.

Avail (or first refusal)—A handshake agreement between the actor, agent, and casting director in which the actor guarantees that the client will have first option on his time on the specific dates set aside for the commercial shoot.

Barn doors—Metal flaps in front of lighting instruments that control the direction of the light beam.

Blocking the shot—Carefully working out movement and actions of actors and mobile television equipment; done by the director.

Booth—Enclosed, soundproof area with a microphone where the talent record their words. It is separated from the creatives by a glass window.

Cable—Specifically for cable usage.

Callback—Request for an actor to read again for (usually) the director, producer, art director, and writer.

Camera left (or right)—Directions given from the camera's point of view, facing the audience or the camera.

Camera rehearsal—Full rehearsal with cameras and other pieces of production equipment.

Casting director—Person who selects and auditions the actors they feel properly fit the criteria of a character description. The casting director does not work for the actor and does not receive commissions from actors.

Catch lights—Reflections in the eyes caused by the photographer's light(s).

Cattle call—An audition in which hundreds of people may try out for a part on a first-come-first-served basis.

Cheat—To angle the performer or object toward a particular camera; this is not directly noticeable to the audience.

Client—The executive(s) who represent the product that is being advertised.

Close-up (CU)—A shot of the product, actor's face, hands, etc., taken at close range.

Cold reading—An audition at which the talent is asked to act out a script without having adequate time to rehearse.

Conflicts—Being under contract for two conflicting products (such as Tide and Wisk detergents). This is prohibited for union commercials. An advertiser would never want one person on the air advertising both his product and a competitor's.

Coordinator—Assistant to line producer.

Cover letter—A letter of introduction.

Craft service—Food setup all day long on the set.

Creative director—Person responsible for the work of all creatives in the advertising agency.

Creative supervisor—Person who oversees the activities of the art director, writer, and producer.

Creative team (the creatives)—The producer, art director, creative supervisor, creative director, director, account executive, and the client(s).

Cue—Signal to start, pace, or stop any type of production activity or talent action.

Cue card—Card with the script written on it in large letters. It is placed near the camera lens so actors don't have to memorize copy.

Cut—Director's signal to interrupt action.

Dailies—The film of each day's shoot; the film is developed and printed at the end of the day and is usually seen the following day. Also referred to as **rushes**.

Director—The person who directs the spot.

Dissolve—Short double-exposure between the two scenes in which the first scene is replaced slowly by the second scene.

Dolly—Tripod on which the camera is mounted and can move about.

Dry run—Rehearsal without equipment during which the basic actions of the talent are worked out. Also called **blocking rehearsal**.

Dubbing—Replacing one voice or dialogue with another.

ECU—Extreme close-up.

Fade—*Fade up* means coming from black and fading up into the scene. *Fade down* means fading out of a scene into black.

Fitting—Trying on of clothes.

Flap (mouth flap)—In animation, movement of the mouth. If the talking stops and the character's mouth keeps moving, an actor will be called in to add either internally, at the beginning, or at the end of the line so that the mouth flaps match the rhythm of the speech.

Gaffer—Chief electrician.

Gaffer's tape—Electrical tape used to hold things together on a set.

Generic "look"—Neutral, classic, all-American look.

Gofer—Person who does odd jobs (goes for), such as getting coffee, running errands.

Grain—In film, exaggeration of the tiny dots that make up the image, which produces an unacceptable print. This is generally caused by overexposure or overdevelopment of the film (high-speed films are naturally grainy).

Green room—Waiting area (historically painted green).

Grip—Crew member who moves equipment.

Head shot—Your commercial calling card. The trend is to include three quarters of the body in the photograph, with or without borders around the print. Standard head-and-shoulder shots are still most widely accepted in smaller, regional areas.

Hero—The best-looking product on the shoot.

High hat—The lowest platform on which to place a camera, usually about floor level.

Industrials—Promotional films used either to educate employees or to promote companies. They can be produced strictly for in-house use or to be shown at promotional events such as trade shows.

"It's a wrap."—End of shoot.

Line producer—Director's producer.

Lip sync—Synchronization of sound and lip movement.

Load—A technical way to put gum in the mouth for a commercial.

Long shot—A shot seen from far away or framed very loosely.

Looping (loop groups)—Group of people who work together providing additional dialogue for a scene.

Manager—A talent representative who guides the talent's career.

Martini shot—Last shot of the day.

Master shot—A wide shot that shows the scene in its entirety.

Meter reading—Light reading.

Milk her down—Use dulling spray to get rid of unwanted reflections.

MOS—A silent take (from a European director's instructions "mitout sound").

Network—Broadcast all over the country including the three major markets (New York, Chicago, and Los Angeles).

On bells—When shooting sound, a bell rings to indicate there should be quiet on the set.

PA—Production assistant. Does odd jobs.

Pan—Horizontal turning of the camera.

Parent union—The first union you join.

Pilot—The first episode of a potential TV series.

Playback—To replay (on a monitor) scenes that were shot.

Print it—Director likes scene. Scene marked to be printed.

Producer—Person responsible for putting together all the elements that make up the production of a commercial, including budgeting, selecting the director, coordinating all decisions of the people involved, and making sure the production is on schedule, including final editing.

Props—Short for properties. Furniture and other objects used for set decoration.

Residuals—Payments made to the talent every time the spot runs.

Résumé—A one-page summary of your vital statistics, experience, training, and special skills. Used to attract the interest of an agent, manager, or casting director.

Retouching—Work by a photo artist (retoucher) on commercial prints to minimize minor flaws in the image by "touching up" temporary blemishes, stray hairs, and scratches or dust spots (white spots caused by dust enlargement on the negative).

Right to work—In a right-to-work state, companies cannot refuse to hire someone because he does not belong to the union or does not want to join the union.

Room tone—The sound on the shoot in total silence.

Rough cut—The first edit of the filmed scenes.

Run through—Rehearsal.

Screen Actors Guild (SAG)—Union governing actors in film. This includes motion pictures (whether shown on television or in movie theatres) and television commercials.

Script supervisor—Crew member who reads and times script as it is shot.

Seasonal—Shot specifically for a particular holiday or season that must be identified as such in the commercial. For instance, if it is going to run during the Christmas holiday, some Christmas decorations or a Christmas tree would be in the scene. There are no conflicts for seasonal commercials.

Set—Arrangement of scenery and properties.

Slate—To identify verbally and visually before each take. A little blackboard (or white board) upon which essential production information is written (such as title, scene date, and take numbers).

Slugging—Inserting.

Speed—Camera is running properly.

Spot—Placement of a commercial in different spots around the country other than the major markets.

Standard contract—Contract used as written with nothing crossed off the back.

Stand-in—Another person or product used for testing the lighting.

Statistics (stats)—On a resume, your name, union affiliation and agent (if applicable), height, weight, eye and hair color, and a phone number (service, machine, or pager) where you can be reached.

Sticks—Tripod on which the camera can be mounted in a stationary position.

Stylist—Designer or purchaser of wardrobe.

Sweeten—To enrich the background, often with music or sound effects.

Sync sound—Synchronizing sound with picture.

Taft-Hartley—A waiver that allows you to work on as many union jobs as you want within a thirty-day period, after which you become a "must join." This means that you must be prepared to join the union for the next job you get after the thirty-day waiver.

Take—Each time you shoot a scene, it's a "take." A take can also be a surprise reaction by an actor.

Teamster—People hired to drive trucks and to load and unload equipment.

Tear sheets—Samples of a model's published work (print ads, fashion spreads, etc.) torn from the publications to put into her portfolio.

Teleprompter—Electrical device that displays the script in large letters that roll by in front of the camera lens at the speed of the actor's delivery.

Test—A commercial that will run for a limited time in a specific market to be tested for product recognition. The time of usage would be agreed upon at the time of booking the talent.

Trailers—Advertisement of a film previewing selected scenes.

Two-shot—Framing of two people.

Under five—A speaking role of less than five lines.

Voice-over—The actor's voice on the soundtrack. Can also be referred to as a VO or an AVO (announcer voice-over).

APPENDIX

❑ DIRECTORIES/RESOURCES

CALIFORNIA

The Agency Guide (lists talent agents)
Breakdown Services, Ltd.
1120 S. Robertson, 3rd Floor
Los Angeles, CA 90035

Working Actors Guide
Mani Flattery Publications
3620 Fredonia Drive #1
Los Angeles, CA 90068
(213) 850-5597

National Conference of Personal Manager (NCPM)
10231 Riverside Drive, Suite 303
Toluca Lake, CA 91602

Samuel French Book Store
7623 Sunset Boulevard
Los Angeles, CA 90046
(213) 876-0570

CD Directory (lists casting directors)
PO Box 69277
Los Angeles, CA 90069
(310) 276-9166

FLORIDA

FAB (Florida's Actors Book)
3090 Riverbrook Drive
Winter Park, FL 32792-8713
(407) 657-7944 (phone/fax)

Florida Bluesheet (private subscription)
7238 Hiawassee Oak Drive
Orlando, FL 32818
(407) 292-7458

Focus In (newspaper for actors)
PO Box 151242
Altamonte Springs, FL 32715

GEORGIA

Acting in Atlanta and the Southeast
Distributed by In Character (bookstore)
(800) 224-8526

ILLINOIS

Act One Reports
2632 North Lincoln
Chicago, IL 60614

Act One Book Store
2632 North Lincoln
Chicago, IL 60614
(773) 348-6757

NEW YORK

Ross Reports
1515 Broadway, 14th Floor
New York, NY 10036
(212) 764-7300

New York Casting and Survival Guide
Peter Glenn Publications
42 West 38th Street
New York, NY 10018
(212) 869-2020
(800) 223-1254

Back Stage Handbook
BPI Communications
1515 Broadway
New York, NY 10036
(212) 764-7300

Motion Picture, TV & Theater Guide
(referred to as the Little Yellow Book)
Motion Pictures Enterprises
Tarrytown, NY 10591
(212) 245-0969

Drama Book Shop
723 Seventh Avenue, 2nd Floor
New York, NY 10019
(212) 944-0595

National Conference of Personal Managers
964 Second Avenue
New York, NY 10022

NORTH CAROLINA

Reel Carolina
PO Box 1724
Wilmington, NC 28402
(910) 392-5445

On Location North Carolina
Official State and Video Directory
Film Commission
North Carolina Film Office
301 N. Wilmington Street
Raleigh, NC 27601
(919) 733-9900

❏ **PRINTERS**

ABC Pictures
1867 E. Florida Street
Springfield, MO 65803-4583
(417) 869-9433

Dan Demetriad
119 W. 57th Street, Suite 200
New York, NY 10019
(212) 245-1720

❏ EDUCATION HOTLINE

Breaking Into Commercials
Education Center
(For workshop and other educational inquiries.)
(800) 239-3548

❏ SAG BRANCH OFFICES

UNITED STATES

ARIZONA
1616 East Indian School Road, Suite 330
Phoenix, AZ 85016
(602) 265-2712

BOSTON
11 Beacon Street, Suite 515
Boston, MA 02108
(617) 742-2688

CHICAGO
75 E. Wacker Drive, 14th Floor
Chicago, IL 60601
(312) 372-8081

CLEVELAND (AFTRA) (Caretaker)
1030 Euclid Avenue, Suite 429
Cleveland, OH 44115
(216) 579-9305

COLORADO, NEVADA, NEW MEXICO, & UTAH
950 South Cherry Street, Suite 502
Denver, CO 80222
(303) 757-6226

DALLAS–FORT WORTH
Suite 302, LB 604
6060 N. Central Expressway
Dallas, TX 75206
(214) 363-8300

DETROIT
28690 Southfield Road, Suite 290 A&B
Lathrup Village, MI 48076
(810) 559-9540

FLORIDA
7300 North Kendall Drive, Suite 640
Miami, FL 33156

GEORGIA
455 E. Paces Ferry Road N.E., Suite 334
Atlanta, GA 30305
(404) 239-0131

HAWAII
949 Kapiolani Boulevard, Suite 105
Honolulu, HI 96814
(808) 538-6122

HOUSTON
2650 Fountainview, Suite 326
Houston, TX 77057
(713) 972-1806

LOS ANGELES
5757 Wilshire Boulevard
Los Angeles, CA 90036
(213) 549-6777

MINNEAPOLIS (AFTRA) (Caretaker)
708 North First Street, Suite 343 A
Minneapolis, MN 55401
(612) 371-9120

NASHVILLE
PO Box 121087
Nashville, TN 37212
(615) 327-2958

NEW YORK
1515 Broadway, 44th Floor
New York, NY 10036
(212) 944-1030
fax: (212) 944-6774

PHILADELPHIA
230 South Broad Street, 10th Floor
Philadelphia, PA 19102
(215) 545-3150

SAN DIEGO
7827 Convoy Court, Suite 400
San Diego, CA 92111
(619) 278-7695

CANADA

ACTURA (Association of Canadian TV & Radio Artists)
2230 Yonge Street
Toronto, Canada M4S 2B5
Fax: (416) 489-1435

SAN FRANCISCO
235 Pine Street, 11th Floor
San Francisco, CA 94104
(415) 391-7510

SEATTLE (AFTRA) (Caretaker)
601 Valley Street, Suite 200
Seattle, WA 98109
(206) 282-2506

ST. LOUIS (AFTRA) (Caretaker)
906 Olive Street, Suite 1006
St. Louis, MO 63101
(314) 231-8410

WASHINGTON, D.C.–BALTIMORE
5480 Wisconsin Avenue, Suite 201
Chevy Chase, MD 20815
(301) 657-2560

INDEX

Academy Directory, The, 89
Account executives, 122, 231
Acting
  and animation voice-overs, 167
  as craft, xii–xiii
  and models, 176
  training in, 44–48
Acting coach, 45–46, 47
"Action," 96, 231
Active visuals, 120
Actor(s)
  chemistry between, 131, 132
  and contract, 135
  and shoot, 135–36
  what is expected from, 133–34
Actor's directories
  nonunion, 89*n*
  union, 89
Actor's Equity Association (Equity),
    80, 81, 231
Adler, Charlie, 167, 168
Ad lib, 231
ADR (additional dialogue
    replacement), 156
Ads seeking talent, 52
Advertising agency, 122, 124, 125,
    130
Age, 29
Agency book fees, 50
Agents, 37, 69–79
  actor dropped by, 79
  and auditions, 88
  and booking time, 84
  and children, 192, 204, 216
  contract with, 78
  and cover letter, 35, 84
  defined, 69–70, 77, 231
  dropped by actor, 78–79
  finding good, 73
  and head shot/résumé, 84
  interview with, 74–77, 85
  keeping in touch with, 77–78
  in larger markets, 150
  licensing and franchising, 72, 73
  vs. manager, 86
  networking with, 59
  and nonunion actors, 85–86
  phony, 55–57
  questions to ask, 75
  registering with several, 73
  and résumé, 28
  signing with, 83
  in smaller markets, 148–49
  up-front fees, 50, 52, 55, 56–57
  and voice-overs, 161
  what is looked for by, 83–84,
    225–26
American Federation of Television
    and Radio Artists (AFTRA), 80,
    81, 231
  franchised agencies, 56, 72
Anger, 101, 114*n*
Animation voice-overs, 167–70
Annual books showcasing talent, 50
Answering machines, 40–41
Answering services, 42
Apicella, Karen, 184, 190, 197, 199
Apple box, 231
Appointment records, 43
Art director, 121, 125, 130, 134, 231
Assistant director (AD), 135, 231
Atlanta, 88, 148, 151, 155
Attitudes
  defining, in script, 116–20
  positive, and audition, 99–100,
    102–3, 109–10, 120
  and voice-overs, 165

Audition News, 12
Audition record-keeping, 43
Audition room, 96, 97
  entering, 102
  leaving, 120
  taking mark, 105
Auditions, xv, 88–120, *97–98*
  and agent, 78–79
  and analyzing script, 114–20
  and body language, 104–5
  and camera, 107–8
  and career development, 32
  and casting director, 70
  children's, 195–96, 204–5, 209–10,
    212–13
  and competitive edge, 99–101
  defined, 232
  described, 96–99
  early calls, 85
  entering room, 102–3
  expanding space, 103–4
  in Europe, 177
  finding out about, 88
  and "framing," 108–9
  getting job, 99
  how actor is selected for, 88–89
  information to get about, 92
  memorizing copy, 107
  and nudity or harassment, 51
  rehearsing, 109
  SAG/AFTRA report, *94*
  selection process after, 121–27
  slating your name, 109–10
  technique for, 102–20
  and truth in eyes, 111
  and visualizing, 111–13
  what to wear, 93
  what to do when called for, 89–92
  what to expect at, 93–95, 100–1
Audition tape, 124–26
"Avail," 128–29, 232

Back Stage, 12, 88, 161
*Back Stage Producers and
  Production Guide,* 161
Back Stage West, 12, 88
Bad slate, 110
Barn doors, 232
Baskow, Jaki, 80
Beats
  and attitude changes, 117–20

  dividing script into, 115–16
  and voice-overs, 170
Beepers, 42
Berry, Halle, 173–74
Better Business Bureau, 54, 56, 73
Bialik, Mayim, 201–2
Bicoastal actors, 148
Biel, Jesica, 173
Black, wearing, 93
"Blocking the shot," 232
Blue Book, The, 161
Body language, 104–5, 108–9
Bonet, Lisa, 202
Bonney, Mark, 77
Booking, information to get at, 132
Booking out, 83, 219
Booth, 158*n*, 232
"Bought-out," 138
Bouldin, Gregory, 73, 147
"Breakdowns," 70
Brochures, 12
Bucille, Ashley, 173
Business license, 54, 56, 73
Button line, 114, 120
Buy-out fees, 140

Cable, 129, 232
  and holding fees, 142
  and residual fees, 143
Callback, *98,* 128–32, 232
  and booking, 132
  and client, 126
  information to get, 128–30
  and talent selection, 124–26
  what creatives look for, 131–32
  what to wear, 129
  who will be at, 130
Call screening, 41
Camera
  rehearsal, 232
  relating to, 107–8
  and slating name, 110
Career, xiv
  developing, 84, 87
  and goals, 61–62
  and manager, 70
  and training, 32, 46–47
Carmen, 180–81
Casella, Max, 202, 203–6
Casting directors
  and auditions, 89, 95, 96, *98*

and cover letter, 35
defined, 70–71, 232
and head shots, 88
getting list of, 37
networking with, 59
and talent selection, 121, 122
Catalogs, 12, 173
Catch lights, 14n, 232
"Cattle calls," 88, 232
Cellular phones, 42–43
Chamber of Commerce, 54
Character
    breakdown, 89
    look or type, 7–8
Cheat, 233
Chicago, 29, 35, 73, 88, 143, 148,
    149, 155, 158
Child labor laws, 215
Children, 184–221
    and agents, 192, 218–21
    and auditions, 195–96
    and education, 214–18
    and head shots, 186–89
    interviews with, 202–14
    and larger markets, 197–98
    and manager, 193
    and money, 200–1
    and parents, 199–200, 212–14
    and résumés, 190–92, 191
    safeguards for, 196–97
    and scams on parents, 55–56
    and shoot time, 136
    and training, 194
    types that do well, 184–86
    what it takes to make it, 201–2
    and unions, 81
Cirrincione, Vincent, 173
Classes
    and career, 46–48
    and résumé, 32
    types, 45–46
Client, 122, 124, 126, 134, 165, 233
Close-up shots, 137, 233
Clothing
    and agent interview, 76
    and auditions, 92, 93
    and callback, 129
    changes, your rights and, 197
    and children's headshot, 187–89
    and heat shot, 9–11, 15–17, 19
    wardrobe fees, 141

Clout, 87
Cold reading, 233
    classes, 44, 45
Commercial composites, 11, 12
Commercial print work, defined, 12
Commercials
    and agent, 69
    and children, 184–221
    earnings from, 1, 86, 138–45
    entering field, 1–2
    experience, and résumé, 29–30
    history of, 126–27
    importance of, in career, 85, 87
    key players in industry, 69–71,
        123
    misconceptions about, 226
    number of roles in, 1
    and pet peeves about talent, 227
    and print models, 171–83
    shooting, 133–37
    studying actors in, 8–9
    training for, 44–48
    types defined, 7–8
    what it takes to make it, 225–29
    See also Auditions; Callbacks;
        Head shot, commercial
Commercial space
    and body language, 104–5
    expanding, 103–4
Commercial technique, 7, 99
    classes, 44–45
Commissions and fees
    and agents and managers, 74
    and casting director, 71
    and nonunion agent, 78
    up front, and scams, 50, 57
    See also Payments
Communications equipment, 40–43
Community theater, 29, 32
Commuting, 148–49
Conflicts with competitive products,
    82
    and agents, 70
    and auditioning, 92
    defined, 130, 233
    and holding fee, 142
    and radio, 144
    and reinstatement, 142
    and session fee, 139
Consecutive employment fee, 141
Contact sheet, 21, 25

Contract
  agent or manager, 75, 78
  head shot photographer, 19–20
Contract, commercial
  for child, 220–21
  maximum period covered by, 142
  and shoot, 135
  standard, 129–30, 238
  type of, 129–30
Coogan Law, 200
Coordinator, 233
Copyright, and head shots, 19–20
Corporate videos, 12
Cost-of-living adjustments (COLAs), 81
Cover letter, 35, 36, 48, 84, 233
Craft service, 233
Creative director, 122, 233
Creative supervisor, 121, 233
Creative team
  and callback, 131–32
  defined, 121–22, 123, 233
  and shoot, 134–35
  and talent selection, 122–24
  and voice-overs, 165, 166–67
Creativity
  and audition, 101
  and training, 47
Crew, 134, 136
Cue, 233
Cue card
  defined, 96, 98, 233
  how to work with, 106–7
"Cut," 96, 234

Dailies, 234
Daily planner/appointment book, 43
Dallas, 88, 155
Danielli, Traci, 76–77
Dauk, Jinsey, 9, 15
Dealer use residuals, 145
Demo commercial residuals, 144
Demo tape, 84
  TV commercial, 84, 175n
  voice-overs, 158, 159–61
Director, 59
  and callback, 130
  and children, 209
  defined, 71, 122, 234
  and shoot, 134, 137
  and talent selection, 122, 124–25
Dissolve, 234

Dolly, 234
"Donut," 158
Double-time, 140
Drama-Logue, 12, 88
Dry run, 234
Dubbed tape, 124
Dubbing, 156, 234

Ebb, Fred, xii
ECU, 234
Enlargements, 25
Equity Membership Candidate
  Program (EMC), 81
Equity. See Actor's Equity
  Association
"Ethnic" type, 8
Europe, 177, 178
Exclusivity, 141–42, 144
Exercises
  body language, 105
  cue card, 106–7
  expanding commercial space, 103–4
  sense memory, 112
  slating technique, 110
  truth in eyes, 111
  two-person audition, 109
  visualizing and reacting, 111–12
Expense tracking, 43
Experience
  in résumé, 29–30
  in secondary markets, 151–52
Extra performer
  buyout fee, 140
  sessions fee, 139
Eyes
  slating your name, 110
  truth in, 111

Fade, 234
Farrell, Chris, 55, 72
Film, 149
  credits, and résumé, 29
  crossover from modeling to, 173–74
  union, 80
  and voice-overs, 156
Fionte, John, 44–45
First impressions, 225
First refusal, 128, 129, 232
Fittings/wardrobe fee, 141, 234
Flap, 234

Flexibility, 101, 133
Florida, 148, 150–51, 155
Fogelman, Laura, 75–76
Food commercials, 92, 195–96
Ford, Eileen, 182–83
Foreign markets, 176–77
Framing, 103–4, 108
Franchised agencies, 72
Freelancing actor, 73, 83
Frustration
    and analyzing script, 115, 117,
        118–19
    and audition, 101, 114n
    how to deal with, xiv–xv
Fryer, J. D., 150

Gaffer's tape, 234
Garrin, Steve, 157, 161, 162
"Generic" look, 234
Glasses, 16
Goals, 60–66
    journal, 43, 60–61, 64
    -planning sheet, 66
Gofer, 234
Goldman, Barbara, 163–66
Good slate, 110
Grain, 15n, 235
Green room, 235
Grip, 235
Grooming, 17

Hairstyling, 9, 17, 25
Haley, Suzanne, 148
Hand model, 140
"Handsome" look or type, 8
Hartigree, Kathy, 76, 79
Hat, 16
Head-and-shoulder shots, 12n
Head shot, 7–26, 175
    and agent, 76, 84
    and auditions, 93, 95
    attaching résumé, 33–34
    for children, 186–89, 188
    commercial, vs. theatrical, and
        composite, 9–12
    contact sheets, 21
    copyright and reprinting, 19–20
    cost of, 25
    day of shoot, 19–21
    defined, 9–11, 10, 235
    finding photographer for, 12–15
    hair and makeup for, 17–18
    and larger markets, 48
    lighting, 14
    mailings, 35–37
    makings of good, 7–9
    name and format, 23
    picture postcards of, 23–24, 24
    preparing for shoot, 15–16
    printing, 14, 15, 23, 25
    retouching, 21–23, 25
    time frame, 25–26
    wardrobe checklist for, 16–17
Health insurance, 81
Hero, 235
High hat, 235
Holding fee, 139, 141–42
Humor, in script, 114, 120

Improvisation classes, 44, 45
Indulging in beat, 112
Industrial films, 11–12, 235
Ingber, Carol, 82, 83
International Model and Talent
        Association, 173
Interview with agent, 74–77, 85
"In-your-face" reads, 162
"It's a wrap," 235

Jacobs, Judith, 46, 148
J-card, 160
Jewelry, 16, 93
Johnson, Patrick, 182–83
Jourdan, Tom, 151–52
Journal, 43, 61

Kallis, Patty, 41, 46, 88
Kander, John, xii
Kruschke, Karmen, 17

LA 411, 161
Laird, Heather, 147, 150
Lewis, Emmanuel, 206
Line producer, 235
Lip sync, 235
Load, 235
Long shot, 235
"Look" or type, 74
    and agent interview, 76
    list of major, 7–8
    and talent selection, 124, 125–26
Looping, 156, 235

Los Angeles, 29, 35, 73, 74, 83, 88, 129*n*, 143, 145, 147, 158, 161, 167, 168, 198
  when to move to, 149, 150, 151–52
McNally, Terrence, xii
MacPherson, Elle, 178–80
Madison Avenue Handbook, 161
Magazine ads, 12
Mailings, 35–37
Major markets, 2
  and auditions, 88
  moving to, 149–52
  and networking, 48
  and résumé mailings, 35–37
  and training, 47–48
"Major production house," 53–54
"Majors"
  and radio residuals, 145
  and TV residuals, 143
Makeup, 9, 17–18
  cost of, for head shot, 25
  and shoot, 134
Managers, 59, 235
  vs. agent, 86
  and children, 193
  defined, 70
  finding good, 87
  interview with, 74–77
  as mentor, 60
  models moving to commercials, 173–74
  pros and cons of, 74
  up-front fees, 50, 52
Marketing, xiii
  and picture postcards, 24
  as print model, vs. commercials, 175
Markets
  and children, 197–98, 218
  and commuting to, 148–49
  defined, 129*n*
  misconception about larger, 226
  and moving, 149–52
  opportunities by state, *153*
  See also Major markets; Smaller markets
Marquee Talent Agency, 77
Martini shot, 235
Master shot, 137, 236
Maximum period of use, 142, 144
Meegan, Christopher, 209

Meegan, Eric, 211
Meegan, Pat, 202, 210–14
Meegan, Robert, 202, 206–10
Men, makeup and jewelry, 16–18, 93
Mentors, 59–60
Message retrieval system, 41
Meter reading, 236
Miami/Orlando, 88
Milk her down, 236
Models, print, 171–83
  vs. commercials, 174–75, 180–83
  crossover to commercials, 175–76
  and foreign markets, 176–77, 178
  interviews, 178–83
  and payment, 177–78
  and training, 176
Modeling agencies, and scams, 56
Modeling and talent conventions, 172–73
Model's Mart, 55
"Model" type, 8
Moneys per cycle, 130
MOS, 236
Mullins, Barbara, 133–37
Multi-listed actor, 73

National Conference of Personal Managers, 75, 193
"National network," 129
Negotiation, 142
Networking, 58–60
  and audition, 95
  and journal, 43
  and moving to big city, 48
Networks
  radio, 144–45
  TV, 143, 236
New York, 29, 35, 56, 73, 74, 83, 88, 89, 129*n*, 143, 147, 155, 158, 161, 198
  when to move to, 149
New York Production Guide, 161
Night premium, 140
Nonunion agents, 73, 78
Nonunion commercials, 80
  payment for, 138
  in right-to-work state, 82
Nudity, 51, 197
National commercials, 146

Off-camera fees, 139, 144
Omana, Nick, 158, 159, 166

On bells, 236
On-camera fees, 139, 143, 144
On Location Education, 214, 216
Onorato, Al, 82
"Open calls," 88
Opportunities chart, 153
"Out clause," 78
Outdoor shoot, 129n
Over exposure, 154
Overtime fees, 140–41

Pageants, 187, 188, 190
Pan, 236
"P & G" look, 8
Parents, 210–14, 216–20
Parent union, 81n, 236
Patrick Swayze Productions, 54
Payment (fees)
    and animation voice-overs, 170
    buyout, 140
    and children, 200–1
    confirming, 130
    consecutive employment, 141
    fittings/wardrobe, 141
    holding/exclusivity, 141–42
    and income tracking, 43
    maximum period of use/
        exclusivity, 144
    and models, 177–78
    overtime, 140–41
    potential, from single
        commercial, 86, 138
    radio, 144–45
    residuals, radio, 144–45
    residuals, TV, 143–44
    session, radio, 144
    session, TV, 139–40
    travel time, 141
    and TV, 138–45
    and union scale, 80–81
Pension coverage, 81
Personality, 225
    and agent interview, 76
    and analyzing script, 114, 115,
        117–20
    and commercial space, 104
    and head shots, 14, 17
    and slating name, 109
    and technique classes, 44
Philadelphia, 148
Phone calls
    equipment, 40–43

notes, 89
number on résumé, 28, 29
Photographer
    head shot, 12–15, 19, 25
    scams by, 53, 57
    and sexual harassment, 51
Picture postcards, 23–24
    and agent, 77–8
    cost of, 25
Pilot, 148n, 236
Pittsburgh, 148
Playback, 236
Player's Guide, The, 89
Plays, 73
Polaroid, audition, 95
Powell, Michael, 77, 149
"Pretty" type, 8
"Pretzel," 158
Printer
    head shot, 19–20, 23, 25
    résumé, 33–34
"Print it," 236
Priorities, 62–63
Producer, 59, 71, 121, 124, 125, 130,
        134, 135, 236
    ad agency, 130, 135
Product, 114–15, 135
Production assistant (PA), 236
Production company, 130
Props, 236
Publicity, 20
Put-down, in script, 119

"Quirky/pretty and funny" type, 8

Radio
    payments, 144–45
    union, 80
    voice-overs, 156, 163, 164
Reacting, 111–13
"Real read," 162
Record-keeping, 43
"Regional," 129
Regional or secondary markets, 2,
        146–52
    and audition calls, 88
    casting and production in, 37
    and children, 198
    and commuting to larger markets,
        148–49
    and moving to larger market,
        149–51

Regional or secondary markets
(cont.)
and nonunion agents, 73
pros and cons of, 146–48
and résumé, 29, 31, 32, 35–37,
151–52
and voice-overs, 161, 163
Rehearsing
and audition, 109
and voice-overs, 170
Reinstatement fees, 142
Rejection, xiv–xv
and children, 210, 213
Residuals, radio
dealer use, 145
network, 144–45
wild spot, 145
Residuals, TV, 143–44
cable, 143
defined, 143, 236
and models, 172
network use, 143
union vs. nonunion, 138
wild spot, 143
Residuals, voice-over, 154
Résumé, 28–39, 175
and agent, 76, 84
attaching, to head shot, 33–34
building, 147
for children, 190–92, 191
cover letter, 35, 36
defined, 28, 237
and larger markets, 48
layout and printing, 33–34
listing experience in, 29–30, 32
mailings, 35–37, 73
quantity to print, 34
sample, 30, 31
to-do list, 38–39
updating, 33, 34–35
what to include, 28–29
Retouching, 14, 21–23
cost of, 22, 25
Reuse fees, 139
Righini, Alberto, 177
Right-to-work states, 82, 237
Roland, Steve, 166–67
"Roll camera," 96
Room tone, 237
Ross Reports, 37, 161
Rough cut, 237
Run through, 237

SAG/AFTRA commercial audition
report, 94. See also Screen
Actors Guild
Saunders, Tim, 181–82
Savage, Judy, 185, 194, 199, 201–2
Scale payments, 130, 139
Scams, 49–57
avoiding, 50–52
common, 52–54
investigating, 54–55
Scene study classes, 44, 45
Schachter, Sue, 202, 218–21
Schaffmaster, Jane, 76
School, and children, 206–7, 214–18
Screen Actors Guild (SAG), 1
and children, 215
defined, 1n, 80, 237
-franchised agents, 37, 50, 72, 73,
75
joining, 80–81
and moving to larger market, 150
and voice-overs, 170
Script
analyzing, 114–20, 115
audition, 95, 97
memorizing, 107
Script supervisor, 134, 237
"Seasonal," 129, 237
Segments, 137
Selection process, 121–27
Sell line, 115, 119
Sense memory exercises, 112, 113
Session fee
radio, 144
TV, 139–40
Session runner, 96
Set, 237
Sexual harassment, 51
Shoot
date of, 126, 128–29
length of time for, 136
process, 133–37
Showcases, 73
Shurin, Sandy, 47–48
Signed town, 73
Signing, with agent, 83
Sign-in sheet, 95, 97, 195
Simon, Alan, 202, 214–18
Size card, 95
Slate, 237
Slating your name, 109–10

"Slightly off-beat/slightly quirky" type, 8
Slugging, 237
Soap operas, 80
"Special provisions," 139
Special skills, 32, 190
Speed, 238
Spielberg, Steven, 167
"Spot," 129, 238
  run type, and payment, 138–39
Stand-in, 238
Statistics or stats, 28n, 238
Steven, Jack, 147
Sticks, 238
Stoll, Katie, 139
Storyboard, 89, *90–91,* 95, 97
Studio teacher, 215, 216
Stylist, 25, 238
"Suburban" type, 8
Success
  and follow through, 63
  and individual, xv–xvi
  and time frame, 152
  strategies for, 64–66
Sweeten, 238
Sync sound, 238

Taft-Hartley, 85n, 238
Takes
  and children, 208–9
  defined, 238
  number of, 137
  and voice-overs, 166
"Take your mark," 96, 105
"Talent payment" people, 139
Talent scouts, 52, 53–54
Tanner, Kay, 147
Taxes, 43, 214
Teamster, 238
Tears (tear sheets), 53n, 175n, 238
Technical advisor, 135
Teeth, 9
Teleprompter, 239
Television
  and models, 173, 175–76
  and payments, 139–44
  and union, 80
  and voice-overs, 155, 164–65
  See also Commercials
Test, 239
Thank-you notes, 43, 59

Theater credits, 29, 147, 149
  union, 80
  and voice-overs, 163
Theatrical headshot, *10,* 11–12
Three-quarters body shots, 12, *13*
Time and a half, 140
Tobias, Maurice, 160, 163
Trade publications, 12, 88
Trailers, 239
Training, 44–48
  for children, 194
  cold-reading, 45
  commercial technique, 44–45
  cost of, 46
  finding coach, 45–46
  importance of, 46–48
  improvisation, 45
  for models, 176
  and résumé, 32
  scene/monologue, 45
  voice-overs, 158–59, 163
Travel, 134
  days, 128
  log, 43
  payment, 141
Tutors, 214–18
Two-shot, 239
Two-way recording, 41
Types. *See* Look or type

Under Five, 81n, 239
Union-produced directories, 89
Unions, 80–82
  and agency franchise, 56, 72
  agent and actors not in, 85–86
  defined, 80
  in Europe, 178
  joining, xiii, 54, 80–82
  and networking, 48
  and payment, 138–39
  and résumé, 28
  and scams, 53–54
  and shoot time, 136
Unprofessional conduct, 79, 85
Up front payments, 50, 52–54, 56–57
"Urban/city" type, 8
Use fees, 142

Vando, David, 55–56
Variety, 161
Vazquez, Suzette, 175–76
Versace, Vincent, 9, 14, 15

Visualizing, 111–13, 120
Voice mail, 42
Voice-overs, 153–70
    and animation or cartoons,
        167–70
    booking job, 162
    defined, 154–55, 239
    demo tape for, 159–61
    film, 156
    getting started in, 158–61
    marketing yourself, 161–62
    radio, 156, 164
    and regional markets, 163
    session described, 163–66
    television, 155, 164–65
    tips on taping, 166–67
    training for, 158–59
    trends in, 162
    what it takes to succeed, 157

Waivered into union, 85n
Wardrobe fees, 141
Washington, D.C. Market, 148
Weather days, 128–29
Weekend and holiday pay,
    140–41
Welfare workers, 215–16
West, Joel, 173
White, wearing, 16–17, 93
Wild spots
    radio residuals, 145
    TV residuals, 143
Williams, Robin, 157
Wilmington, N.C., 148
Wood, Elijah, 173
Work for hire, 19
Writer, 121, 124, 125, 130, 134
Wyman, Lori, 131, 138, 150